From Fjord to Frontier

GENERATIONS

A History of Canada's Peoples

From Fjord to Frontier

A History
of the Norwegians in Canada

Gulbrand Loken

Published by McClelland and Stewart Ltd. in association
with the Multiculturalism Directorate,
Department of the Secretary of State
and the Canadian Government Publishing Centre,
Supply and Services Canada.

Copyright © Minister of Supply and Services Canada 1980

Government Catalogue No. CI44-6/1980E

The Canadian Publishers
McClelland and Stewart Limited
25 Hollinger Road
Toronto, Ontario
M4B 3G2

CANADIAN CATALOGUING IN PUBLICATION DATA

Loken, Gulbrand, 1917-
  From fjord to frontier

(Generations, a history of Canada's peoples)
Bibliography: p.
Includes index.

ISBN 0-7710-5330-4 bd.   ISBN 0-7710-5331-2 pa.

1. Norwegians in Canada.   2. Norwegians in
Canada – History.   3. Norwegian Canadians.*
4. Norwegian Canadians – History.*   I. Title.
II. Series.

FC106.N6L65   971'. 0043982   C80-094163-2
F1035.N6L65

Printed and bound in Canada

To
an unselfish mother and father
who prevailed in the new land
to the great benefit
of those who came after

Contents

Editors' Introduction

Canadians, like many other people, have recently been changing their attitude towards the ethnic dimension in society. Instead of thinking of the many distinctive heritages and identities to be found among them as constituting a problem, though one that time would solve, they have begun to recognize the ethnic diversity of their country as a rich resource. They have begun to take pride in the fact that people have come and are coming here from all parts of the world, bringing with them varied outlooks, knowledge, skills and traditions, to the great benefit of all.

It is for this reason that Book IV of the *Report of the Royal Commission on Bilingualism and Biculturalism* dealt with the cultural contributions of the ethnic groups other than the British, the French and the Native Peoples to Canada, and that the federal government in its response to Book IV announced that the Citizenship Branch of the Department of the Secretary of State would commission "histories specifically directed to the background, contributions and problems of various cultural groups in Canada." This series presents the histories that have resulted from that mandate. Although commissioned by the Government, they are not intended as definitive or official, but rather as the efforts of scholars to bring together much of what is known about the ethnic groups studied, to indicate what remains to be learned, and thus to stimulate further research concerning the ethnic dimension in Canadian society. The histories are to be objective, analytical, and readable, and directed towards the general reading public, as well as students at the senior high school and the college and university levels, and teachers in the elementary schools.

Most Canadians belong to an ethnic group, since to do so is simply to have "a sense of identity rooted in a common origin . . . whether this common origin is real or imaginary."[1] The Native Peoples, the British and French (referred to as charter groups because they were the first Europeans to take possession of the land), the groups such as the Germans and Dutch who have been established in Canada for over a hundred years and those who began to arrive only yesterday all have traditions and values that they cherish and that now are part of the cultural riches that Canadians share. The groups vary widely in numbers, geographical location and distribution and degree of social and economic power. The stories of their struggles, failures and triumphs will be told in this series.

As the Royal Commission on Bilingualism and Biculturalism pointed out, this sense of ethnic origin or identity "is much keener in certain individuals than in others."[2] In contemporary Canadian society, with the increasing number of intermarriages across ethnic lines, and hence the growing diversity of peoples ancestors, many are coming to identify themselves as simple Canadian, without reference to their ancestral origins. In focusing on the ethnic dimension of Canadian society, past and present, the series does not assume that everyone should be categorized into one particular group, or that ethnicity is always the most important dimension of people's lives. It is, however, one dimension that needs examination if we are to understand fully the contours and nature of Canadian society and identity.

Professional Canadian historians have in the past emphasized political and economic history, and since the country's economic and political institutions have been controlled largely by people of British and French origin, the role of those of other origins in the development of Canada has been neglected. Also, Canadian historians in the past have been almost exclusively of British and French origin, and have lacked the interest and the linguistic skills necessary to explore the history of other ethnic groups. Indeed, there has rarely ever been an examination of the part played by specifically British – or, better, specifically English, Irish, Scottish and Welsh – traditions and values in Canadian development, because of the lack of recognition of pluralism in the society. The part played by French traditions and values, and particular varieties of French traditions and values, has for a number of reasons been more carefully scrutinized.

This series is an indication of growing interest in Canadian social history, which includes immigration and ethnic history. This may particularly be a reflection of an increasing number of scholars whose origins and ethnic identities are other than British or French. Because such trends are recent, many of the authors of the histories in this series have not had a large body of published writing to work from. It is true that some histories have already been written of particular groups other than the British and French; but these have often been characterized by filio pietism, a narrow perspective and a dearth of scholarly analysis.

Despite the scarcity of secondary sources, the authors have been asked to be as comprehensive as possible, and to give balanced coverage to a number of themes: historical background, settlement patterns, ethnic identity and assimilation, ethnic associations, population trends, religion, values, occupations and social class, the family, the ethnic press, language patterns, political behaviour, education, inter-ethnic relations, the arts and recreation. They have also been asked to give a sense of the way the group differs in various parts of the country. Finally, they have been asked to give, as much as possible, an insider's view of what the immigrant and ethnic experiences were like at different periods of time, but yet at the same time to be as objective as possible, and not simply to present the group as it sees itself, or as it would like to be seen.

The authors have thus been faced with a herculean task. To the extent that they have succeeded, they provide us with new glimpses into many aspects of Canadian society of the past and the present. To the extent that they have fallen short of their goal, they challenge other historians, sociologists and social anthropologists to continue the work begun here.

Jean Burnet
Howard Palmer

[1] *Report of the Royal Commission on Bilingualism and Biculturalism.*
[2] Ibid. Paragraph 8.

Introduction

This is the story of people who sought to escape poverty in Norway by seeking better opportunities in the New World. In the nineteenth century, the United States received nearly all the immigrants from Norway. However, as the frontier receded in the United States, Canada eventually became "the land of another chance." Under the progressive policies of Sir Wilfrid Laurier and his aggressive Minister of the Interior, Clifford Sifton, Norwegians were attracted to Canada. The first to come were largely an overflow from the United States, people with some resources already schooled in "sod-busting" and other related frontier skills. After 1900 many others came to Canada directly from Norway with both groups settling mainly in the West.

As a minority group, Norwegians have been most visible in the four western provinces of Canada. There are two interrelated reasons for this. First, the majority of the Norwegian immigrants, particularly in the early decades of the twentieth century, settled in these regions of Canada lured by the offer of free homesteads. Second, it is in the West that Norwegians were able to establish and maintain distinctive ethnic institutions. Therefore, the history of the Norwegians in Canada is most closely interwoven with the story of western settlements.

The facts of history often speak for themselves. Therefore, it has been an aim of this study to quote individuals who were close to the actual events related herein. Such people can by their own words provide both reality and vitality for that era. For this, the reader can form his own conclusions with a minimum of interpretation by the author.

Largely, the interpretation has been provided by the framework or outline in which this history is developed. By maintaining a perspective of related and important developments in the Canadian setting, the particular story of a minority group in the vastness of Canada can be better understood. Because history is the sequence of events over time, it has been deemed important to develop the account chronologically within an interpretative framework. However, particular attention has been given

1

to beginnings and to those decades that mark turning points in the history of the Norwegians in Canada.

Many Norwegian people in this land, but especially those in Norway and the United States, have little understanding of the Canadian milieu. As Canadians it has long been true that we learn more about other peoples than we do about ourselves. Therefore, the inclusion of both perspective and purview has been deemed to fulfill a useful purpose. It has also been deemed important to select major or typical events to set forth the general story of the Norwegians in Canada. History is considered to be the flow of events with initial causes leading to developments over time. Always there is an interplay of societal forces within the total social milieu. Moreover, the Norwegians in Canada did not exist as an island removed but participated freely in the mainstream of Canadian life.

The first four chapters develop major aspects of the history of the Norwegians in chronological order. By providing historical perspectives for each era, the part played by Norwegians can be placed in the context of the Canadian milieu. The last three chapters examine the major evidences of ethnic solidarity among the Norwegians over the years, the impact of the new land upon the group and their unique associations, and the prospect for their continued identity and contribution to Canada.

The Norwegians are not isolationists, but yet there is that uniqueness which identifies them as a distinct people. While their national history is often politically intertwined with the other Scandinavian countries of Iceland, Denmark and Sweden, Norway has always been a separate entity for an identifiable people with a special history and a diverse heritage. This uniqueness has carried over into the New World and today is a part of the sparkle of the Canadian mosaic. Many Norwegians continue to exhibit their unique traditions, culture and spiritual life in the battle with those forces which would melt Canadian life into dull uniformity and conformity. Here Norwegians can be both independent and tenacious, as evidenced in their struggle to maintain identity in their institutions.

The spiritual life of Norwegian immigrants was anchored in the teachings and practices of the Lutheran Church. It was this particular Christian faith that provided stability and solace in the new land. Of course, there were those who severed their roots after they emigrated. However, this history will concentrate on the majority who remained identifiable in their attachment to their Norwegian religious heritage. Among Norwegian pioneers, the Lutheran Church and its institutions became the primary and prominent organizations of their ethnic identity also in Canada.

The Norwegian element is still identifiable in Canada but without divided national loyalty. Perhaps some still live between memory and reality. Much has been preserved from a proud heritage and a rich Nor-

2

wegian history which continues to be translated into the uniqueness which is Canada.

The author is indebted to many people for materials and help. Thanks is accorded to P.B. Stolee, J.B. Stolee, Magda Hendrickson, C.A. Ronning, J.H. Rostad, K. Bergsagel, G. Moi, E.F. Marken, G.O. Evenson, A. Anstensen, officials of the Royal Norwegian Embassy at Ottawa and finally to the Norwegian-American Historical Association for providing free access to and use of their archives and publications.

It is not practical to mention all who supplied histories and early photographs of local communities, churches and families and those who gave of their time to be interviewed and taped. There is a new appreciation of librarians, archivists and educators who helped in the search for vital materials often not available on the Norwegians.

The University of Calgary granted a six-month sabbatical late in 1976 to complete this history project which was commenced in the fall of 1972. The faithful work of Gladys Whyte and Corrie Marles as typists and the support of colleagues is acknowledged.

Finally, the project could not have been accomplished without help, direction and support from the Secretary of State and everyone connected with the Canadian Ethnic Studies project for which the Federal Government is commended. In particular appreciation is expressed to Dr. Howard Palmer of The University of Calgary and Dr. Jean Burnet of Glendon College at York University for editorial assistance and constructive suggestions during the writing of the history.

G. Loken

ONE

Early Transient Migration

Norwegians are descendants of the ancient West Vikings who came to the New World shortly before the year 1000 A.D. The Nordic sagas tell of travel back and forth to this continent for the next 12 years. These first contacts came to naught even though the Vikings made several attempts at early exploration and settlement in Canada. Evidently, they met their match in the bands of fierce Indians who drove them back to their ships and the shelter of southern Greenland.

Over eight centuries later, Norwegians again began leaving their homeland in sailing ships for America. For more than a century thereafter, this flow of immigrants was very large for a country as sparsely populated as Norway. For the most part, they first docked at Quebec City, but Canada could not hold them. The few who were persuaded to settle in Upper or Lower Canada sooner or later left to join the others in the United States. In fact, of all the Norwegians who came to Canadian shores from 1000 to 1885, it can be said in general that they came but chose not to stay.

HISTORICAL PERSPECTIVE

After Charlemagne's empire began crumbling following his death in 814, and thereafter until the middle of the eleventh century, most of the known world fell under the sword of ruthless Viking raiders coming from Nordic lands. The prolific Vikings reached out for more land and new means to support their increasing numbers. So they took to their ships – the finest in the world – and forged the Viking Age.

In 787 the North Sea rovers made their first recorded attack along the English Channel. In years thereafter, Danish Vikings sailed up the Seine and plundered Paris, and later pillaged Spain and North Africa. Swedish Vikings dominated the Baltic regions and the vast territories of Russia. Norwegian Vikings also invaded the British Isles and Ireland, and went south far into the Mediterranean.

But the Vikings from Norway had one route of conquest almost to themselves: *Vestervegen*, "the westward way," across the North Sea. Norse settlers reached Iceland some time around the year 870. In 982 Erick the Red explored Greenland, 200 miles farther west, and colonization soon followed. Bjarni Herjulfsson sighted the New World in 986, but it was Eric's son, Leif the Lucky, who landed at a place called Vinland (probably Newfoundland) just before the year 1000. Also, according to the ancient sagas, the Norse mounted at least one major effort to colonize Vinland. However, the Vikings could not maintain the settlement against the persistent attacks of the natives whom they called *skraelings*. The New World would wait almost five centuries for fresh exploration and permanent settlers from European lands.

The year 1347 marks the last recorded Norse voyage to Markland (probably Labrador). In the fourteenth century the Black Death completely paralyzed much of western and northern Europe, and Norway lost about half of its population. Some of her western communities were almost completely wiped out, to the extent that in one province only one woman was left.

The Viking world had shrunk and the thriving settlements in Greenland were decaying. As Norse seamanship declined, few captains were willing or able to cross the stormy Atlantic. First the Greenlanders and then the Icelanders were left completely to their own resources. For Greenland, the isolation proved fatal, for around 1350 the Norse remnant there was either dead or had departed. Scientists excavating a Norse site in Greenland now suggest that the colony was wiped out by the Black Death. In any event the colony vanished mysteriously around 1350 A.D.[1] Alone among the colonies, Iceland survived as a relic of the eleventh century.

Politically, Norway was united with Denmark from 1380 to 1814 but the geographical features of Norway prevented any total control of the country by the Danes. Because Denmark had supported Napoleon in his wars and Sweden had sided with England, the Danish king was forced to cede Norway to Sweden by the Treaty of Kiel in 1814. The infuriated Norwegians were in no mood to recognize this type of bargaining. On April 19, 1814, 112 delegates from all over Norway assembled at Eidsvoll, determined to draft a national constitution and to declare themselves a separate and independent kingdom. This historic group drafted, approved, and adopted a new democratic constitution. It bears the date of May 17, 1814, which ever since has been the festival day of national liberty for Norway. Of course, Sweden opposed the independence move by Norway, and after some military skirmishes and considerable negotiation, Norway and Sweden agreed to have a common Swedish king. However, Norway retained its new constitution and existed for all practical purposes as an independent kingdom. This dynastic union was terminated in 1905. Freedom and independence have always been treasured by the Norwegians but it was the fire of nationalism and the spirit of independence that created a separate political entity really distinct from both Sweden and Denmark.

THE LAND THEY LEFT

Norway rises from the sea "furrowed and weatherworn." So writes Bjornson in that stirring poem now the national anthem of Norway, "Ja, vi elsker dette landet" (Yes, we love this country).

A flight from Oslo to northern Norway on a clear day provides a bird's eye view of an exceedingly rugged land. Indeed, the terrain below appears hostile to human occupancy – great expanses of barren rock, ice fields, dense forests, mountain lakes, swamps, chasm-like valleys, and numerous lengthy indentations of the sea reaching inland from the coast – the world famous fjords. It has been estimated that roughly 74% of the land area is covered by barren mountains, mountain lakes and icy glaciers; that 23% is forested; and about three per cent is arable land – cultivated meadows, natural meadows and grain fields. Many view the land of Norway as a stony series of valleys bordered and isolated by hills or mountains of varying height and ruggedness, and with only a thin layer of soil in some favoured places.

The total area of Norway is 125,064 square miles, or about half the area of the Province of Alberta. Fertile land has always been a scarce resource in Norway – so scarce in fact that it was a struggle to support the population adequately, especially prior to the growth of industry in the twentieth century.

Norway is the northernmost country in the world. Hammerfest at 70°39'48" North latitude is the northernmost town in the world. The Arctic Circle crosses the middle of this long and narrow land which stretches over a distance of 1089 miles. The midnight sun is visible at the North Cape from May 15 to July 31, but in the winter this part of Norway is shrouded in darkness for many long months.

The coast of Norway is shaped like the edge of a lumberman's jagged saw due to the intricate penetrations of bays and fjords. Glaciers and rivers have cut deep valleys in the mountains which are long and sloping towards the east and south, but short and steep towards the west. The numerous fjords are continuations of these valleys into the sea. The fjords are usually narrow and penetrate far inland, the greatest being the Sogne fjord which is 114 miles long. The shorelines are dotted by some 150,000 rocky islands so that in all the coastline exceeds 12,000 miles or half the distance around the world's equatorial belt. The fjords and harbours are open the year around as far as the Arctic Ocean. It is the open sea that has made it possible for people to settle along the naked coast.

The rugged topography of this northern land has posed severe problems for its people because of inland isolation, land transportation, food production and separated communities. As is characteristic of mountain people, Norwegians have been rugged individualists fiercely resisting any encroachments upon their personal freedom. The Norwegian peasant has never known the bondage of serfdom. His lot at times has been miserable enough, but he has never ceased to be a free man.

THE VIKINGS FROM NORWAY

The wild Atlantic waves that batter Norway's rugged shoreline and its numerous coastal islands did not isolate the Norsemen. From the security of numerous deep and mysterious inlets of the sea, they could venture forth into rougher waters. So fretted is the coast with indentations and archipelagos that the sea was their highway to adventure and exploration. Contrary to popular opinion, the fjords are not icebound but are warmed by the Gulf Stream. At sea level, temperatures tend to be moderate, although inland the high forested slopes can be bitterly cold in winter. At higher levels, barrenness gives way to icefields whose glaciers under summer sun melt into torrents of water that crash over the face of the mountains in tumultuous splendour.

The rivers, the fjords, the islands, and the ever-challenging sea forged a race of skilled shipbuilders, navigators and seafaring wanderers. Very early the Norsemen developed longships which were both speedy and easy to land. As they went island hopping, they first rowed forth from their farms near the sheltered fjords but depended upon square sails on lofty masts to speed them on their way over the open sea. As they watched the steady westward flights of birds over the sea, they knew there was land beyond. In their hearts they desired to follow the birds to new islands. One adventure led to another. Occasionally, stormy gales blew the Vikings off course only to bring them to new wonders and strange lands.

What research has now established, an examination of a map also makes credible. A pair of compasses on a map demonstrates that Bergen is nearer to the Shetland Islands than it is to Denmark and closer to Aberdeen than it is to London. In fact, when the routes of the Vikings are examined it becomes apparent that rarely did they have to cross more than 400 miles of open sea at one time as they sailed from one island to another. Over time their navigation skills developed, their ships were improved and their confidence surged.

The Shetlands, Orkneys and the Western Isles of Scotland, which were Norwegian territory for centuries, served as half-way houses. The Vikings came to regard England, Scotland and Ireland as rich countries from which they could wrest adventure, treasures and romance. Strange new wealth could be bought and plundered even from churches and monasteries. As a lusty heathen lot they had no scruples in taking women as captives. "Free us, O Lord, from the outrages of the Norsemen; they ravage our land and kill women and children and even those who are

7

old," people prayed in churches throughout Europe. In those days many read the ancient prophets and thought they understood Jeremiah when he wrote: "Out of the north an evil shall break forth upon all the inhabitants."[2]

To picture the Vikings simply as sailing pirates is to do them injustice, for they were also merchants and colonizers. They explored, traded, raided, conquered and settled all the way from the British Isles to Canadian shores. Their exploits are recorded in their sagas – works of considerable literary quality.

The ancient sagas record that Iceland, Greenland and the mainland of America were first discovered by daring sailors who were driven off their course by stormy gales. For years, many people were not convinced that there was any truth in these sagas; rather they regarded them as myths. In more recent times, the spade has been more convincing than the pen in these matters. World renowned archeologists have unearthed evidence to corroborate important aspects of the sagas and to verify the exploits of the Vikings. Consequently, the emotional controversy about who first discovered America is just about over. The evidence is compelling in favour of the Vikings.

Recent research and exciting discoveries at L'Anse aux Meadows, on the extreme northern tip of Newfoundland, have established that the Vikings occupied this area as far back as 1000 A.D. In 1970, the *National Geographic* reported:

Eric the Red's Saga and The Greenlanders' Saga record the ill-starred Norse attempt to colonize America. Leif came first to a forbidding mass of mountains and glaciers which he named Helluland, meaning Flatstone Land. Then he sailed south and went ashore on a sandy beach with woodlands beyond, which he called Markland, or Forestland.

Farther south still, he and his crew came upon a land "so choice, it seemed to them that none of the cattle would require fodder for the winter." They found "salmon there in river and lake . . . bigger than they had ever seen before," and grapes as well. Leif built a house and wintered there. He called his discovery Vinland. Virtually all scholars now agree that Helluland was Baffin Island and Markland was Labrador. Vinland has not been positively located, although some identify it with the Island of Newfoundland.

Another son of Eric, Thorvald, explored the new continent even farther. At a certain headland, he and his party came upon "three skin boats . . . and three men under each" – Indians or Eskimos! They killed eight of these Skraelings, but one escaped. Other Skraelings then attacked the Norsemen; an arrow dispatched the luckless Thorvald.

The Norse mounted at least one major effort to colonize Vinland. Early in the eleventh century, according to The Greenlander's Saga,

Thorfinn Karlsefni fitted out three ships, loaded them with 65 people and ample livestock, and sailed to Leif's old winter quarters in North America. His colony prospered for two years – during which time Karlsefni's wife gave birth to a boy named Snorri – the first white child born in America.

Then trouble developed again with the Skraelings, culminating in a pitched battle. At the end of the second winter, Karlsefni gave up the struggle and sailed back to Greenland.

Historians speculated for centuries about these saga accounts until Norwegian scholar Helge Ingstad vindicated them completely in 1962, when he discovered a Viking settlement at L'Anse aux Meadows near the northern tip of Newfoundland. Carbon-14 testing dates it at approximately A.D. 1000.[3]

Helge Ingstad and his wife, Anne Stine, an archeologist, spent eight years excavating at L'Anse aux Meadows. At his suggestion, the Government of Newfoundland built huge barn-like structures to protect the most important excavations unearthed by Ingstad and his crew. Their findings are corroborated by both American and Canadian archeologists. The site became a Canadian National Park in 1972 and excavations are continuing. Under the Federal Historical Sites Service, the Viking site at L'Anse aux Meadows has become the scene of major restoration of a Norse settlement in Canada. Peter Bennett, assistant director of this federal service, has stated that this is "one of the most important sites in the whole of North America." These "Vinland" ruins prove that the Vikings founded the New World and attempted settlement. Ingstad reports as follows:

On our last day I walk around all the excavations. They speak to me, intimately now, about a brave and simple people. I look at the smithy with the broken anvil, the great hall with the hearth and ember pit, and all the other mementos of these people of the past.

L'Anse aux Meadows is rippling gold in the sunset. Northward, Belle Isle looms like a fairy castle. Farther off, day dims along the Labrador shore, where the Vinland voyagers came coasting south almost 1,000 years ago.

I easily visualize the scene. I can see the smoke rising from the smithy and hear the rhythmic sound of hammering. Groups sit around fires in the houses, talking about the new and amazing land they have come to.

Think of the courage of those Norsemen, setting out to sea in open boats, wives on some voyages, compasses on none; driven by lust for adventure, and by the need to find good new land where families could settle and live.

Thus it was that young sailors stood once under a square sail gazing wonderingly across the water where a strange coastline rose from the sea – the New World.[4]

A *National Geographic* foreign staff writer has recorded his impressions of the excavations in Newfoundland:

Ten Newfoundland families inhabit the tiny hamlet of L'Anse aux Meadows, hard by the Viking site. Curiously, they live not unlike the old Norsemen. They keep cattle and sheep, and the pasture does indeed last through the winter. With the seasons, they take trout in the streams and seals in the bay. In the autumn they hunt for ducks and, whenever the opportunity arises, they trap a few lobsters. And, as one man told me, they like their way of life "wonderful well."

With Mr. Ingstad I walked through the excavated relics of the Viking settlement – past the smithy with its scattering of thousand-year-old charcoal, past the trenches streaked with the dark-brown, time-compressed layers of turf that had formed the walls of the longhouses. Green moss creeps inexorably across the earthen floors, engulfing the cooking and storage pits and even the great central hearths. A sizable group – certainly no smaller than Karlsefni's – had occupied this site.

"Why did the colony fail?" Mr. Ingstad echoed my question. "Probably because the Vikings' weapons were no better than those of the Skraelings, and the Skraelings far outnumbered the Norse. Columbus succeeded, I think, largely because he had firearms."[5]

A British scholar, George Painter, who was one of a team of international experts brought together in 1957 to study the Vinland map, says that he is convinced of its authenticity as the earliest known map of the New World. After seven years of painstaking research, the team declared the map genuine in 1965.[6]

Thus the first known Europeans to attempt a settlement on Canadian soil were Norsemen, and this occurred some 500 years before Columbus sailed into Caribbean waters. In fact, it is now known that before Columbus ventured forth he visited Iceland about 1477 to confer with Norsemen, perhaps to validate the reports of a new land across the Atlantic.

Today, the trail of Viking relics grows richer. The discovery of three burial ships in or around the Oslo Fjord in Norway has provided the greatest discoveries among dozens of ship findings. In 1893 a replica of the Gokstad ship discovered in 1880 was built and satisfactorily crossed the Atlantic. It was properly named the *Viking*, and a Norwegian sea captain, Magnus Andersen, sailed her across the stormy Atlantic in 28 days.

The modern Canadian who now jets his way to Norway in a matter of hours usually visits the world famous Viking museum in Oslo. There the unexpected splendour of the Viking Age comes alive. He accepts the revealing discoveries of an heroic race of Norsemen who plundered and colonized far corners of Europe and North America a thousand years ago. He is convinced that they first found his Canada, but wonders why they did not stay. More answers may yet be found on the fog-bound coasts of Canada's eastern shores.

The Viking era was one of major discoveries and of interrupted colonization taking place in a period of warm climatic conditions favourable to both sailing towards northern islands and settlement on the shores beyond the Greenland sea. This period has assumed new importance in recent years. Archeological discoveries and painstaking research have established the importance and validity of the ancient Scandinavian sagas. Farley Mowat puts the era in interesting perspective in the final paragraph of his book *Westviking*:

> The Norse westward ventures during the decade at the turn of the millennium cannot be written off as isolated and unimportant incidents out of the mainstream of North American history. It was the voyagers of those times who traced the track over the pathless western ocean – the track which became a great sea highway over which other men of Europe later sailed to seize and occupy a continent.[7]

KENSINGTON RUNE STONE

For several years a storm of controversy has raged over the "Kensington Rune Stone," which was found on a farm near Kensington, Minnesota, in 1898. It is generally believed, but has so far not been definitely proven, that the Stone was set up by a group of Norwegians and Swedes under the leadership of one Paul Knutson. In 1355, he had been commissioned by the King of Norway and Sweden, Magnus Erickson, to seek out and win back to Christianity the refugees from "Western Settlement," one of two settlements on Greenland founded by the Norseman Erik Thorwaldson towards the end of the ninth century. The news of the disaster was brought to the king by a delegation from the "Eastern Settlement"; they reported that "Western Settlement" had been attacked and destroyed by Eskimos and they urged the king to send an expedition to look for the survivors who had fled to a vast island to the west.

The expedition sailed from Bergen, Norway, in 1355, and nine years later it returned. So far it is recorded history; the rest of the story has yet to be proven. It says that Paul Knutson, after a futile search in Markland, eventually found the mouth of the Nelson River. Realizing that this was not an island but a vast new continent he gave up hope of finding the refugees but decided to explore the New World. As ships could not ascend the Nelson, he left his ship and 10 men and embarked in small boats with 29 men – eight Goths (Swedes) and 22 Norsemen – to explore the river. With the help of sails and oars the party sped along, up the Nelson, through Lake Winnipeg and up the Red River as far as the Buffalo River. There they got lost among small rivers and lakes and only after many hardships did they finally find their way to the Mississippi.

11

While the outcome of the adventure was still uncertain, they decided for all eventualities to leave a record of what had happened to them thus far; they cleaned a large stone on an island and their priest engraved in runic characters a brief account of their adventures.[8] The inscription tells of a party of Swedish and Norwegian Vikings who set out from their settlements in *Vinland* in an exploration westward. It is dated 1362, or 130 years before Columbus discovered America. Some scholars have regarded the stone as a forgery, while others have defended it as genuine. It is in the possession of the Alexandria, Minnesota, Chamber of Commerce. A replica has appeared on exhibit in the National Museum in Washington, D.C.

THE MUNK EXPEDITION

In 1619 King Christian IV, who ruled over both Denmark and Norway, sent an expedition in search of the North West Passage to Asia. Jens Munk, an experienced navigator born in 1579 at Bardu, Arendal, Norway, was placed in command of two ships and 66 men. Although they sailed from Copenhagen on May 9, 1619, a stop was made at Karmsund in Norway where several members of the crew bade farewell to loved ones in their homes. Then, sailing past the Shetland Islands, the Faroes and Cape Farewell, they crossed to Davis Strait and entered Frobisher Bay. Thence they sailed through Hudson's Strait, exploring and taking possession of the country in the name of King Christian. The harbour of Churchill was discovered September 7, 1619, and here the expedition wintered. Pastor Rasmus Jensen of Aarhus, Denmark, who accompanied the expedition, conducted regular religious services here until his death in January, 1620. Thus he was the first Lutheran pastor to Canada.

Because of severe illness during a long, harsh winter, all died except Jens Munk and two of his crew, who were able to reach Norway on September 25, 1620, returning both ships. Munk's complete diary of this tragic expedition is now in the Royal Library at Copenhagen and has also been published as *Navagatio Septentrionalis*. The governments of Norway, Denmark and Canada have erected a monument at Churchill in commemoration of this ill-fated journey.

THE CANADIAN CORRIDOR

The first shipload of Norwegians to come to America sailed from Stavenger on July 4, 1825. Motivation for this sailing had come from Kleng Pedersen (Cleng Peerson) who had left Norway in 1821 and returned briefly in 1824 with a report of economic opportunities in the new land. This small vessel of some 45 tons was a rebuilt sloop renamed *Restauration* and it carried a load of rod iron as well as 52 passengers plus the baby Larson born on the way. Many of these "sloopers" were

Quakers seeking relief from an intolerant state church. The long trip across the ocean required 97 days. The date of their arrival at New York, October 9, 1825, is considered an historic landmark for Norwegians. The 53 passengers and the crew inaugurated a migration that in the next 100 years brought about 800,000 Norwegians to the United States of America and Canada. The magnitude of this migration can best be understood when it is known that the official population of Norway in 1801 was 883,000. No other European land except Ireland has contributed so large a percentage of its people to the new lands in North America.

In the decade following 1825 there is no record of ships leaving Norway for North America. However, in 1836 the *Norden* and *Den Norske Klippe* sailed with 167 passengers aboard, and two more vessels sailed in 1837. Official Norwegian reports indicated that only 1,200 emigrants left in the years 1836 to 1840, but 5,000 left during the next half decade and 12,000 in the following years.[9] In short, from 1836 to the middle of the nineteenth century, Norwegian migration to North America was modest but growing. The great waves of Norwegian migration to the United States were yet to come.

American government records of the Norwegian emigration do not agree with Norway's official reports. This discrepancy can be explained by the fact that no records were kept of entries to the United States by the Canadian route during the nineteenth century. From 1850 on, Canada played a major role in the emigration of Norwegians to the United States. Norwegian statistics report that of 49,600 emigrants in the period from 1854 to 1865, all but 2,800 came to America via the Quebec route.

In 1849 England repealed her monopolistic navigation laws. After this date Norwegian ships engaged in unrestricted freighting with various British colonies. Very early they realized the potential that the growing passenger traffic had for their shipping business. Thus, after 1850 more and more Norwegians on their way to the United States of America came via the St. Lawrence waterway, landing for the greater part at the port of Quebec. Not only were the Canadian ports much closer to the Norwegian and English ports of embarkation, but the St. Lawrence waterway offered a sheltered passageway of beauty in contrast to the endless ocean. Then the ships could return from Canada with cargoes of cheap Canadian lumber designated for the European market. Ship owners could make money both ways, and passenger fares could be reduced. However, this operation reveals much concerning the type of passenger accommodation of these ships that could transport people one way and products of the forest on the return voyage.

Based on official emigration reports, Table 1 represents the Norwegian emigrants who disembarked at Quebec[10] and New York[11] during the decade from 1850 to 1859. However, the records are definite that nearly all of those who first came to Canada later emigrated to the United States of America. They moved on from Quebec both by rail and by steamer for another thousand or more miles for a steerage fare of slightly less

13

TABLE 1

Norwegians Disembarking at Quebec and New York in the 1850s

Year	Quebec Arrivals	New York Arrivals
1850	250	3,150
1851	225	2,112
1852	2,317	1,889
1853	5,056	377
1854	5,663	81
1855	1,290	203
1856	2,830	438
1857	6,416	62
1858	2,656	3
1859	1,757	36
Decade Total	28,460	8,351

than $9.00. Steamers from Quebec brought them to Toronto, then the immigrants often travelled by rail for 93 miles to Collingwood on Lake Huron, from where steamers transported them across Lake Michigan to Chicago, Milwaukee and Green Bay.[12]

In the nineteenth century Canada was the corridor or passageway to the United States for over a half million Norwegians. The records of these migration patterns are stored in the National Archives at Ottawa. The early Canadian Sessional Papers contain various reports filed by the Chief Emigration Agent at Quebec which reveal much of the pathos and the hardships of these long voyages by sailing ship. For example, Report No. 12, covering the period from August 26 to September 19 in the 1855 shipping season, states:

> The emigrants arrived during the period embraced in this Return have landed in good health, with the exception of those by the ship 'Crown' from Liverpool. Ten deaths occurred on the passage, and eighteen sick were sent to hospital at Grosse Isle.[13]

In 1855, eight vessels left Norway for Quebec, averaging 45 days on the journey. In all there were 1,275 passengers and one birth en route, but one adult and seven children died on the way and one passenger was quarantined as soon as he arrived. Finally, 1,265 passengers cleared the port at Quebec. A typical report covering such new arrivals reads: "The Norwegian emigrants have all proceeded direct to Green Bay and Milwaukee in Wisconsin."[14]

The Report for 1856 states that 14 sailing vessels from Norway, averaging 54 days on the journey, started out with 2,821 souls. There were four births, 13 deaths and 6 placed in quarantine upon arrival; thus 2,806 were landed. The Report provides these insights into the problems faced by the emigration agent at Quebec:

> A party of 50 paupers were sent out by the "Orion" from Stavanger (Norway); they were all desirous of proceeding to the Western States but being without means the above number were sent to Buffalo and Lake Huron Railway for employment, and where laborers are much needed, but will doubtless proceed after their friends as soon as they acquire sufficient means. . . . The Norwegians per "Gifion" all proceeded to the State of Wisconsin, where they have friends. A party of 60, who stated they were without means and unable to proceed were offered a free passage to Ottawa City with a promise of employment during the winter, if they would proceed to that locality; they, however declined the offer, and as afterward informed, with the assistance of their fellow passengers, succeeded in obtaining sufficient money to enable them to reach Chicago.[15]

The Emigration Reports[16] for the 1857 season indicate that 213 sailing ships averaging 44 days across the ocean brought 19,997 people from European lands and 18 steamships requiring only 12 days brought another 789. Deaths en route were 206 and 32 were quarantined upon arrival. The greatest mortality occurred among the Norwegians, with 100 deaths reported among 6,507 immigrants, or 1.53 per cent.

The government records for these early years report ships lost by fire, lost by storm and completely missing, and ships running aground on dangerous reefs and rocks. It is apparent that many emigrants never reached Quebec in the first place. There are also tragic reports of train derailments and of a train plunging into the river because of a rail bridge remaining open for ships to pass up the river. Reports of these tragedies circulating in Europe must have caused many prospective emigrants to change their minds or at least to have serious misgivings about coming to Canada.

The Emigration Report for 1859 states that 16 ships from Norway brought 1,756 persons to Quebec, and provides the following commentary:

> A large portion of the people who immigrate from North Germany and Norway is composed of farmers, as distinguished from labourers, than is the case in the emigration from the British Isles; and they more generally seek for land for immediate settlement than the English or Irish families. . . . It is highly desirable that means should be found for communicating with the immigrants from the Continent of Europe, generally who pass by way of Quebec, in order that they might be put in possession of the means of judging

15

how far they promote their own interests by engaging through passages to the distant West.[17]

In December, 1859, Christopher O. Closter, a Canadian emigration agent at Quebec who was of Norwegian background,[18] reported thus to his superior, Chief Emigration Agent A.C. Buchanan:

In my report of last year I took the liberty to call your attention, by showing an Abstract Statement from Official Returns of the number of Emigrants arrived at this Port from Norway, during a period of nine years, and by adding this year's arrivals it will show, during a period of ten years, a grand total of 28,460 persons, whom it is estimated have brought with them nearly a million dollars, and with but few exceptions, say 400 persons, all have proceeded to the Western States.

I also showed in the same Report that great evils existed, and pointed out the main cause why the Norwegian farmers had not before adopted this country as their future home. It will, therefore, not be necessary now to refer to the same again.

May it not be sufficient, under the present circumstances, on the whole, to glance at the general features of the Norwegian Emigration on the one hand, and at the natural advantages this country offers to the industrious farmers on the other hand, and from thence proceed to the consideration of its importance; and whether the existing policy to secure the Settlement of Norwegians could not in some way be amended to meet the requirements by such means as would be warrantable and consistent with the general interests and prosperity of the country, and to engage more actively in promoting, not only the continuation of Norwegian Emigration to pass through the country, but also to induce them to settle within our territory on such conditions as would not fail to be a lasting benefit both to the Emigrants themselves and the country at large.

We cannot ignore the fact of the settlement of the Great West (U.S.) by American enterprise; for no sooner is one Territory organized than another is taken possession of and provision made for the reception of European Emigrants. We must, therefore, necessarily provide against the many influential efforts that are made and will be made by the Western States, to retain in future the tide of Norwegian Emigration; and the twenty or thirty thousand Norwegians, with their millions of money, who have landed at this Port and proceeded West (besides the large number who have landed at the Ports of Boston and New York,) will be sufficient to warrant them in their efforts to continue to secure the Norwegians to become the Settlers of the West.[19]

The 1850s concluded without any major settlement of Norwegians in Canada. In fact, Canada had helped many of them to travel on to the

United States. Dozens were helped in their time of illness and quarantine on the unoccupied Grosse Isle, thirty-three miles downstream from Quebec. Concern was growing among Canadian authorities to have and to hold these people for Canada, but so far it was "American fever" that drove thousands to cross the line to the United States.

COLONIES THAT FAILED

So concerned did Canada become over the extensive departure of emigrants to the United States that the government appointed a Special Committee on Emigration composed of 11 men. They were asked to determine the extent and causes of this steady Norwegian departure from Canada and to propose some means to stop the movement across the line. The opening paragraphs in their report to the government were descriptive of the prevailing situation:

> When an ancient people become, by a redundant increase of their numbers, as compared with the extent of territory which they inhabit, confined and ill at ease in their native land, the emigration of a portion becomes a blessing to all, and not only to the country which the emigrants leave behind, but also to that new land, to which they bend their steps, and to the species in general.
>
> But when a people still in the early youth of their national existence, weak in numbers, though distinguished for sobriety and hardihood, inhabiting a vast territory of an extent and fertility sufficient for the residence and abundant support of fifty times their number, abandon their homes, emigration is an evil, a public calamity to be deplored, and, if possible, averted. An exodus like this, without legitimate cause, must of necessity be the consequence of a radical social defect, which it is the business of society to detect, and, if possible, to cure, by the application of timely remedies.[20]

The report makes it plain that the lack of roads and bridges posed almost insurmountable obstacles for the early settlers in Canada, great land companies had taken advantage of the emigrants, profitable employment during long winters was lacking, and there was inadequate organization to help the new settlers. Not only does the Report propose that problems in the above areas must be resolved, but it recommends the granting of 100 acres of free land with the settler to receive title "as soon as he shall have opened a road along the front of his farm, cleared six acres of land . . . erected an habitable house, and another building for the reception of his crop."

On many subjects, the report is outspoken. For example:

> Provision should be made, by law, for the protection of the poor settler against the grasping ambition and the covetousness of the

great land owners. Your Committee cannot but express their regret that the Bill passed by Your Honorable House in the present session, providing for the protection of both parties, in their respective rights of the latter as proprietors, of the former as *de facto* possessors and *bona fide* occupiers, has not received the sanction of another branch of the Legislature. It is by no means their intention to make any remarks which may be construed as a censure of any, but they are bound to declare that a law which justifies one man in enriching himself at the expense of another is bad in principle, unjust and vexatious in operation, and behind the times in policy[21]

Canada had a strong competitor in the United States where the emigrant "acquries land at a cheap rate (particularly in Illinois), on easy terms, and with an indisputable title." In Canada, the trusting settler often discovered to his dismay "the right which is accorded to the lessee of timber limits, to strip the land belonging to the settler, when he is in possession and improving it." The Committee on Emigration also reported that, "money is now worth from 12 to 15 per cent. The reason of this is, that the greater part of this capital has already left the country; the channel through which it has left us being the import trade."

In spite of such severe problems confronting the European settler in Canada, a small settlement of Norwegians was begun in the Gaspe Peninsula of Lower Canada as early as June, 1854. In all there were 14 families and 60 people who arrived at Quebec on the *Flora* from Christiania. Their aim was to settle near Sherbrooke where two Norwegians had settled in 1853. Four of these families purchased farms; the rest found employment on the railroad. In his report for 1856, the General Emigrant Agent for Canada, A.C. Buchanan, reported:

> This is the first party of Norwegians of any consequence who have established themselves in Canada, and their attraction thereto is attributed to the favourable reports which they had received from two of their countrymen, who settled in that district in 1853. Should they prove successful, and of which I have little doubt, we may look for a further addition to their numbers, during the ensuing season.[22]

Johan Schroder, who travelled in the United States and Canada in 1863, reported that a group of Norwegian immigrants, led by an agent, settled in Bury in the Eastern Townships in 1856.[23] One of the first settlers in this area was Captain John Svenson who died in 1878.[24] A land company sold them the land at prices ranging from $2.50 to $5.00 an acre. The Norwegians cleared some of the wooded lands and built houses, but a number of them abandoned their property after a year or two. It was too difficult to make a living if they had to pay the land company for the land in addition to trying to provide food, clothing and shelter.

In 1857 Christopher Closter petitioned the Canadian government to set aside land for the establishment of Norwegian colonies. In response, the commissioner of crown lands suggested Ottawa County, the Gaspe district and St. Maurice as most suitable for Norwegians. By September, 1857, Closter returned to Norway to work at attracting large numbers of his countrymen to Canada.

Eventually, some Norwegians must have gone to Ottawa County because in 1861 the government furnished $500 for the relief of Norwegians at Ottawa. The emigration agent there, in his report for 1862, reported that the number of Norwegian immigrants to the Ottawa district had decreased to 43; apparently a larger number had settled the year before. "The Norwegians are a very valuable class of settlers," he said, "being from their industrious and frugal habits . . . peculiarly well adapted for our backwood settlements." In 1863, the Ottawa agent reported that the Norwegians were leaving the area. In January, 1864, the agent wrote to Buchanan:

> The Norway element last year was entirely excluded from the Ottawa. This is to be regretted; for had that population continued to flow into this section of Canada, they would have formed an important part of its settlers; it does appear unfortunate that the Norwegians did not give a fair opportunity to test the capabilities of the Ottawa, as a settlement point for the redundant population of their country.[25]

On December 7, 1958, Closter submitted his first annual report to A.C. Buchanan.[26] From this we conclude that some 90 persons had been persuaded by the British-American Land Company to settle in the Eastern Townships of Quebec in 1857, but that 30 had been persuaded to leave for the United States in the spring of 1858. Closter had advised in his first report as follows:

> It will therefore in future be no inducement to recommend them to go there unless the Government would feel interested to set apart a tract of land in some part of the Eastern Townships for the purpose of offering the Norwegian emigrants some additional inducements with the natural facility of the country, comparatively with that offered them by the Western States in other respects.[27]

By 1859 Closter reported that there were some 25 families with 126 persons in all on the Gaspe Peninsula. The settlers had purchased more than 3,000 acres from the land company at $3.00 per acre. Later, when Closter visited the new settlements, he found that many desired to move to the United States where conditions were more favourable. The new settlers were unhappy that they could not secure land along the shores of the St. Lawrence and thus combine farming and fishing. They were unable to secure outside employment and thus there were financial troubles. The Norwegians at Gaspe were suffering both distress and disillusionment.

19

Nevertheless, the Report for the year 1860 by Buchanan, Chief Agent for the Emigration Department at Quebec, stated:

The Norwegian emigrants, as in previous years, have nearly all proceeded to the Western States. The large settlements of these people in Illinois and Wisconsin naturally tend to draw their countrymen around them: every vessel which arrives here has always a majority of her passengers who are coming out to join their friends, and who exercise an important influence upon the others. These, just arrived in a strange country, and unacquainted with our language, naturally prefer to accompany their countrymen to encountering difficulties of which they have no proper knowledge, and which parties, from interested motives, are more inclined to exaggerate than otherwise.

Of the 1,781 Norwegians who arrived at this port during the past season, about 60 have remained in the Province. Nine families, numbering 50 souls, have proceeded to settle in the District of Gaspe. They were accompanied by Mr. Closter, who rendered them every assistance in selecting their lands, which they have taken up in the Township of Malbay . . . The selection of Gaspe, as a nucleus around which to draw Norwegian immigrants, has many advantages. Its situation is such that vessels from Europe may land their passengers without being subjected to more than a few hours detention; and, when landed, the emigrant is within a few miles of the Government lands, should he be disposed to settle on a farm of his own; or of the large fishing establishments, where steady employment, with wages according to capability, is offered to all inclined to work; and an emigrant family at Gaspe can locate themselves on a lot of land for less money than they would have to pay at Quebec for their inland transport to the Western States.[28]

But the Gaspe colonists were already beginning to depart for the United States.[29] The winter of 1861-62 was extremely severe. The company who sold them land at prices from $2.50 to $5.00 an acre had not provided the Norwegians with tracts along the coast.

Dramatic insight into this early colony in Canada has been provided by N.C. Brun (1846-1919), who arrived in 1861 as a teenager with his parents and several other relatives. The place he came to was on the Gaspe Peninsula in the southern part of St. Lawrence Bay, about 50 miles south of the island of Anticosti. His impressions of his first year in Canada were published in a Norwegian article which has been translated and included in the Appendix.[30]

In 1862, a Norwegian Lutheran pastor was engaged by the Illinois Central Railroad to work at Quebec during the emigration season. This company had received a grant of two and one-half million acres of land to aid in construction of their state railway. With the Civil War on, there were many from Europe who feared to emigrate to the United States. To maintain the flow of Scandinavians to the United States, Jacobson was supplied with 5,000 circulars that were printed in Norwegian on one side and Swedish on the other.[31]

Pastor Jacobson plunged into the work among his fellow countrymen at Quebec, devoting as much of his time to relief work as to directing emigration. Indeed, so valuable did his relief work become that the Canadian government made him a grant of money to show its gratitude, not aware that he was at the same time acting as an emigration agent of the Illinois Central.

Jacobson's daughter has left this record of her father's work at Quebec:

> Father went first to the quarantine station at Quebec, where many Norwegian immigrants had been detained because of an epidemic of "ship fever." He ministered to these unfortunate people, but many of them died, and their sorrowing relatives had to continue on the journey without them. In later years Father would occasionally meet some of the survivors. They were always happy to see him, the first Norwegian minister they had met on the American continent.
>
> He made two visits to the colony at Gaspe, which had been founded in 1861. The tragic plight of this group has been described in the Norwegian magazine *Symra*, by H.R. Holand in 1909, and by Pastor N.C. Brun in 1911. Incidentally, Pastor Brun, after leaving Gaspe with his parents, was among those who met Father in Quebec and heard their first Norwegian sermon after leaving Norway. . . .
>
> Father loved to pick up souvenirs, and on his return from Quebec in the fall of 1862 he brought a pair of cannon balls from the Plains of Abraham, the famous battlefield near Quebec. These cannon balls accompanied us to Wisconsin in 1868, where Father went to serve a parish. Later they were returned to the home farm in Iowa where they have lain ever since, arousing curiosity and delight for the boys and young men who have tried their strength at lifting and throwing them. Together with the old map, the yellowed document and the black-bordered letters, they serve as a reminder of Father's summer in Quebec and on the Gaspe so many years ago.[32]

The failure of the Gaspe settlement for Norwegian immigrants to Canada led to considerable further soul-searching by the Canadian government. The story of the colony has been characterized as the saddest chapter in Norwegian-American history.[33]

According to a Canadian official, three hundred Norwegian families had been living in Gaspe. By the fall of 1862, all except 10 had left the colony.[34] Canadian officials tended to blame the failure on the type of Norwegian settlers. Eden wrote to Buchanan that the "last Norwegian emigrants were little better than paupers and not over fond of work . . . of rambling disposition, very similar to English Gypsies." He also mentioned that they lacked a church or minister "but was also inclined to believe that some secret agency made them discontented with Gaspe and turned their attention to the United States."[35]

The Chief Immigration Agent continued to show confidence in the Norwegians and reported these people to be "a fine, hardy race . . . considered by the United States to be the best class of emigrants they get." He went on to report that "preliminary steps are now about being taken, which may perhaps enable me, during the ensuring season, to offer the Norwegian immigrant strong inducements to stay in Canada."[36]

In 1864, they endeavoured to place a Canadian emigration agent at New York to accommodate those settlers "as had made up their minds to settle in Canada; owing to the state of affairs in the neighboring Republic [Civil War], [but] we were informed the application, to our very great disappointment, could not be complied with." In his 1864 report, Chapais could not veil his disillusionment:

> Having had to deal with colonization in Lower Canada, the observations I propose making will apply to that province only.
>
> I do not wish to be understood as desirous of depreciating our wild lands, still less of discouraging settlers, or of driving immigrants from our shores, far from that; but I desire to place the question of colonization in its true light, and to examine it from a strictly practical point of view. . . .
>
> In the times in which we live, everything is reduced to theory, and very often, almost always indeed, there is a vast gulf between the theory and the practical reality.
>
> Financial theories have resulted in stupendous ruin, agricultural theories have been productive of wide spread delusion, and theories respecting colonization have entailed, even amongst ourselves, the most cruel disappointments. Now no result can be more prejudicial than this, for disappointment often leads to discouragement, and with the settler courage and perseverance are the most essential qualities.[37]

In the meantime the policy of helping immigrants to reach their destination came under scrutiny. In 1864, Jorgensen, the Foreign Immigration Officer, reported to Chief Agent Buchanan as follows:

> A system was adopted this year, requiring poor immigrants who wished to obtain free passages to their destinations, in the Western States, where their friends resided, to leave their luggage as security for the repayment of the assistance given, amounting to $544.50, for 18 families; but I regret to say that, of the Norwegians, not one pledge has as yet been redeemed, and of the Germans, only one amounting to $35.00. This system has been in operation at New York for some time, and has there worked very successfully, but I fear that the value of luggage belonging to the poor Norwegians arriving here, is so small that they care very little about redeeming it.

The amount of assistance granted to the Norwegians and Swedes is very large, but although the system is both expensive to the Government, and detrimental to the settlement of the country, still it cannot be averted, unless work can immediately be procured for the poor on their arrival. The expense of lodging and feeding these people for an indefinite period would be far greater than to pay their transport through the country. . . .

If the persons assisted would settle in Canada, this expenditure would be very judicious, but I have reason to believe that, although it would appear from the Returns as if a considerable number had remained here, the greatest portion of the Norwegians, who received free passages to places within the Province, have ere this found their way to the Western States. Some of the immigrants who were landed at Grosse Isle, remained there sick a very long time, and it was found on their arrival that they were destitute of means, and not being in a position yet to earn their livelihood, they were furnished with free passages direct to their destinations in the West.[38]

On April 25, 1868, J.C. Tache, Deputy Minister of Agriculture, wrote as follows to the Canadian Emigration Agent abroad:

I am instructed to inform you that the policy adopted by the Canadian Government is to the effect that no more passage money or land transport is to be given immigrants on their reaching our shore.[39]

The failure of the Gaspe project registered very adversely in Norway. Norwegian newspapers, notably *Morgenbladet* and *Drammens Blad*, warned Norwegians against doing business with private land companies but recommended dealing only and directly with the Canadian government. Other articles ridiculed the very idea of Canadian colonization. Official Canadian efforts to settle Norwegians had largely failed in this early period.

The great westward movement into the western provinces was still far in the future. In the meantime, the Norwegians continued to pour through Quebec, using the Canadian corridor as the best way to reach into the heartland of the United States. It was a great disappointment to Canadian authorities that so many failed to stay after first coming to Canada.

IN RETROSPECT: 1000-1885

The bold and extensive voyages across the Atlantic which the Vikings undertook were an adventurous epoch in Norwegian history and in Canadian history. During the fourteenth century a decline set in and Norwegian enterprise seemed to stagnate for a long period.

The period of national decline was not entirely without its spirit of bold adventure. Twenty years before Columbus, an expedition set sail in

23

1472 under the leadership of two Norwegian admirals, Pining and Pothorst, from a harbor in North Norway with the object of discovering land west of Greenland. This expedition reached Labrador and thus rediscovered America. Another voyage from this period was the journey by Hans Egedes to Greenland in 1721. During the 15 years he spent there, he acted as priest and colonizer, carrying out several extensive voyages of discovery that proved to be of fundamental importance to later generations.[40] In later years, these polar expeditions were dramatically repeated and extended by the famous explorers Fridtjof Nansen, Otto Sverdrup, Roald Amundsen and Henry Larsen.

By the middle of the nineteenth century the old land of the Vikings began to reach out to the new world again. By the thousands, Norwegians came to the American continent. Canada largely lost this century to the United States because of its colonial land system and the attendant lack of development and opportunity as compared with the United States. In the nineteenth century the emigrants from Norway had many glimpses of Canada from steamers of the St. Lawrence waterway and the Great Lakes or from railway cars that paralleled the waterways. Census records for Canada's early years fail to isolate the Norwegians as a distinct national identity. The 1871 Census reports 1,623 Scandinavians in Canada and 5,223 for 1881. However, these figures include Norwegians, Danes, Swedes and Icelanders. Of these, there were many Icelanders. A major volcanic eruption in Iceland in March, 1875, brought about a major migration of Icelanders to Canada. As many as 1,400 are estimated to have settled on Lake Winnipeg in 1876. They also came to Canada via Quebec.[41] Outside of the Icelanders, most of the other Scandinavians eventually migrated to the United States.

NOTES

1. Dr. Peter Schledermann, Professor of Archeology at the University of Calgary, was the sole Canadian who worked at a site near Godthaab, Greenland, in 1976.
2. Jeremiah 1:14.
3. Howard La Fay, "The Vikings" (Washington: National Geographic, 1970), p. 530.
4. Helge Ingstad, "Vinland Ruins Prove Vikings Found the New World" (Washington: National Geographic, November, 1964), p. 734.
5. La Fay, *op. cit.*, pp. 533-34.
6. *The Calgary Herald*, Jan. 28, 1974.
7. Farley Mowat, *Westviking* (Toronto: McClelland and Stewart, 1965), p. 304.
8. Documentation Section, Canadian Citizenship Branch, Ottawa.
9. *Utvandringsstatiskk* (Oslo: Sentralbyra), series 7, No. 25.

24

10. Canada, *Sessional Papers*, XVII, No. 3, Appendix 19, and XVIII No. 3, Appendix 18.
11. *Ibid.*, XVIII No. 3, Appendix 18.
12. *Ibid.*, XIV No. 5, Appendix 44.
13. *Ibid.*, XIV No. 5, Appendix 44.
14. *Ibid.*
15. *Ibid.*, XV No. 8, Appendix 47.
16. *Ibid.*, XVI No. 6, Appendix 41. Return No. 1 from May 22 to June 2 states: "The Norwegians, 1,173 in number, have all gone to Illinois and Wisconsin." Return No. 2 from the 2nd to the 13th of June: "The Norwegians arrived numbered 1,733, all of whom have proceeded to the Western States – (12½% of the Norwegians required assistance to proceed)." Return No. 4 from the 20th to the 30th of June reports: "The large steamer *Montreal* plying between Quebec and Montreal, and on this occasion having on board as nearly as can be ascertained 350 passengers, took fire soon after leaving this City, and was totally consumed . . . of the Norwegians one only, a child is among the saved." The final report for the shipping season of 1857 is Report No. 10 for the period August 31 to September 19: "The 383 Norwegians have all proceeded to the Western States. These people are generally poor, more so than any previously arrived this season, and upwards of 80 persons had to be forwarded from here. They consisted of helpless families proceeding to join their relations in Wisconsin."
17. *Ibid.*, XVII No. 3, Appendix 19.
18. *Public Archives of Canada*, Department of Agriculture, Report of Executive Council, May 21, 1857.
19. *Ibid.*
20. *Ibid.*, XV, Appendix 47.
21. *Ibid.*
22. *Ibid.*, XIII No. 13, Appendix.
23. Johan Schroder, *Skandinaverne i de Forende Stater og Canada*, p. 53.
24. Harold Engen, *A History of the Evangelical Lutheran Church of Canada* (Saskatoon, 1955), p. 5.
25. Report to Buchanan for 1864 quoted in Norwegian-American Historical Society archives at St. Olaf, Northfield, Minnesota.
26. Canada, *Sessional Papers*, XVII No. 3, Appendix 19. All of Closter's Annual Reports are very lengthy and revealing.
27. *Ibid.*
28. *Ibid.*, XIX No. 3, Sessional Paper No. 14.
29. An account of this colony has also been written by T.C. Blegen, *Norwegian Migration to America*.
30. N.C. Brun, "Foste Aars Oplevelser" in *Symra*, Vol. VII, No. 2, 1911, pp. 111-119. (Translated by K. Bergsagel.) The author of this article went on to college and seminary training in the United States. In the later years of his life he was a frequent visitor to Canada, for his son Stephen immigrated to Saskatchewan in 1907, eventually settling west of Strong-

field where he and his wife Laura became leaders in the Green Valley Lutheran congregation. It was the suggestion of the elder Brun to a church conference in Saskatchewan in the spring of 1909 that Norwegian Lutherans in Saskatchewan should have a church high school that led to the establishment of Outlook College. When the school opened in January, 1916, his daughter-in-law was one of the first teachers. She was a leader for several decades in the Women's Missionary Federation of the former Norwegian Lutheran Church of Canada. She spent her last years at the Lutheran Sunset Home in Saskatoon where she died in 1978.

31. Paul W. Gates, "The Campaign of the Illinois Central Railroad for Norwegian and Swedish Immigrants" in *Norwegian-American Studies and Records* (Northfield, Minnesota: Norwegian-American Historical Association 1931), pp. 53-88.

32. Clare Jacobson, "Days That Are Gone" in *Reform* (Eau Claire, Wisconsin *Reform* (Norwegian newspaper), Dec. 19, 1929). (Translated by Charlotte Jacobson)

33. Hjalmar R. Holand, "Gaspe: Et trist blad i vor nybyggersaga" in *Symra*, 5:2-8 (1909). (A sad page in the saga of our new settlers.)

34. Canada, *Sessional Papers*, XXI, No. 3, Appendix 3.

35. *Ibid.*, Appendix 4. See also another report on the failure of this colony in the 1862 Report of the Minister of Agriculture.

36. *Ibid.*, XXIV No. 2, Appendix 6.

37. *Ibid.*

38. *Ibid.*

39. Dominion of Canada, *Sessional Papers*, I No. 7, Appendix 33.

40. See Thor Heyerdahl *et al, Great Norwegian Expeditions* (Oslo: Dreyers Forlag), p. 11.

41. See Walter J. Lindal, *The Icelanders in Canada* (1967).

TWO

The Push and Pull of Migration

The exodus from Norway can best be understood within the context of the great folk migrations from Europe to America in the nineteenth and early twentieth centuries – migrations so vast as to constitute a major phenomenon in world history. However, there were particular and special causes for the extensive migration from the land of Norway. Explanations are required for the failure of Canada to attract and hold Norwegian immigrants until toward the close of the nineteenth century as contrasted with the early success of the United States. At the end of the nineteenth century there was a dramatic reversal in that Canada began to attract Norwegians who had passed through Canada on their way to the United States where they first lived and struggled for several years on the American frontier.

PERSPECTIVES ON MIGRATION

It has been estimated that over 30 million people crossed the Atlantic from Europe to find homes in the New World. The majority of them migrated to the United States and played major roles in the rapid building of that country into a great nation. For the newcomers, there were vast interior farming regions that proved to be most attractive. Others were drawn by the growing labour market created by a rapidly expanding industrial system in the United States.

The Scandinavians were among those who participated in these folk migrations. Although the Norwegians were the earliest of this group to migrate in considerable numbers, the Swedes and Danes followed their example, and by the middle of the nineteenth century the migrations of all three were well under way. In all, about two million Scandinavians emigrated to America. The total overseas immigration from Norway was 880,000 persons, and most of these settled in America in the Middle West and the Northwest, following accustomed occupations on innumerable farms and in villages and cities serving those farms.

Economic factors were the impelling prod for this massive exodus from Europe. In the early nineteenth century crop failures and economic crises came in quick succession in Europe and created unemployment and misery. In spite of the Industrial Revolution, the increase in the labour force could not be absorbed. While the population of Europe increased by 214 million in the nineteenth century, simultaneously 55 million Europeans emigrated overseas. Of these, 38 million came to the United States of America, but only about 700,000 to Canada. This gigantic emigration started slowly, but eventually gained momentum like a flooding river because more and more streams were pouring into it. Emigration became the safety valve for bringing into better relationship the high natural increase of European populations in the nineteenth century and the limited capacity of most European states to support that population.

The new immigrant who succeeded in gaining a firm foothold in the new country became the best salesman to encourage others to follow him. Therefore the stream of immigrants grew. Variations in the numbers who left depended largely upon the prevailing economic conditions in the homeland from decade to decade.

In summary, the causes of the great folk migrations of the nineteenth and twentieth centuries can be classified into two broad categories: adverse conditions in Europe, and attractions of North America. Adversity included such factors as economic distress, overpopulation, religious or political oppression, class distinctions that created an underprivileged class in respect to education and other opportunities to get ahead. In the main, attraction to the New World was anchored in the prospect of free land and job opportunities. Unfortunately, the promotion agents often painted the new prospects in unduly attractive colours. Adversity pushes people to leave; attraction pulls people to come. Thus migration possesses dimensions of both push and pull.

GENERAL SOCIAL MILIEU IN NORWAY

Beginning in the sixteenth century there were religious, educational and political movements that activated Norwegians to look outward. In addition, there were demographic changes in the population which created social problems for the people in Norway.

By 1536, the Lutheran reformation was introduced with its emphasis on the Bible, a living faith and universal education. Soon the Lutheran faith was accepted generally across the land. As in Germany, it led to the promotion of universal education. The 1539 church ordinance for Norway stated:

> The children must everywhere be so instructed that the children of the peasants as well as others must obtain knowledge of that which not alone peasants, but even the nobles and kings, have hitherto not known.[1]

According to the Danish and Norwegian law of two centuries later (Frederick VI, 1739), every parish had to erect a schoolhouse and name a teacher. These early beginnings eventually led to a high degree of literacy among all the Norwegians, including the many emigrants who left for America in the nineteenth century. The Lutheran faith also played an important role in the cultural heritage and the historic individuality of the Norwegian people. In their homes, the stolid Norwegians clung to their Bibles, the catechism, their hymn books and devotional books. This strong undercurrent of pietism became the base of a sweeping religious revival under the leadership of Norway's famous lay preacher, Hans Nielsen Hauge, whose preaching career began in 1796 and continued until 1804. After much harassment by the leadership of the State Church, which had become rationalistic and increasingly dictatorial, Hauge was imprisoned under a remote Conventicle Act of 1741 which declared itinerant lay preaching illegal. He was released from prison in 1814, and although in poor health, he continued his religious crusade and wrote a great number of books. The almost incredible number of 250,000 copies of his writings were distributed.[2] When he died in 1824, his influence had spread over all of Norway and many who had previously opposed him were won over to his teachings. By 1842, and over the heads of many of the clergy, Norway abolished its Conventicle Act.

A tremendous surge of Christian revitalization pulsated through Norway in the nineteenth century, a movement which came to have social and political repercussions. The emergence of a strong folk high school movement promoted enlightenment and adult education.[3] The emphasis on participatory democracy was infused into the Norwegian citizen. The typical emigrant from Norway brought this vital heritage with him to America – a heritage of Christian vitality and personal piety, ideals of freedom and personal dignity, universal education, and concepts of stable political democracy. It was a heritage of generations of humble, thrifty folk, accustomed to hard work and respecters of property. This produced honest, aggressive, independent citizens anchored in egalitarian principles.

Prior to 1750 the total population of Norway tended to hold around the 600,000 mark. Even though birth rates were high, the deaths at times exceeded the births. After 1750, the birth rate continued at high levels while the death rate slowly declined. In 1750, the total population was 625,000 persons. By 1825, it had increased to 1,051,318 and by 1890 this was doubled to 2,000,917. Such growth was accomplished in spite of very considerable emigration which began early in the nineteenth century and later developed into mass emigration as Norwegian farmers were lured away by the reported magnificence of wide-stretching lands in North America.[4]

As the nineteenth century progressed, it became increasingly possible for the people in Norway to compare economic, political and social conditions in their home district with those described in various guidebooks

TABLE 2

Norwegian Immigration
to North America, 1850-1910

Decade	Immigrants
1850-1859	37,870
1860-1869	85,015
1870-1879	79,928
1880-1889	195,015
1890-1899	93,830
1900-1910	189,353
Total	681,011

Sources: *Utvandringsstatistikk* (Oslo: Sentralbyra), Series 7, No. 25

from across the ocean. A stream of "American letters" conveyed a message of new hope for those oppressed at home. Then, many emigrants returned for visits and convinced a great number that emigration was infinitely preferable to remaining in Norway. To the contrary, there were strong warnings and admonitions from government officials and the clergy who did their utmost to discourage leaving the homeland.

To the hard-working farmer struggling to keep above poverty on a small plot of land in Norway, the vision of 160 acres of free land was the final compelling argument. The "America fever" swept like a fire throughout the country, from one district to the next, penetrating even the most remote mountain valley. In some districts almost the entire population left. Thousands upon thousands found their way to the ships, taking most of their meagre belongings with them. They must see for themselves if the new land was indeed a land of hope and glory.

So great was the migration from Norway in the nineteenth century that Norway was second only to Ireland in the proportion of its population that emigrated. The climax was reached in the years 1880 to 1885: in these years, per 1,000 of population, Irish emigration was 15.8, Norwegian 11.1, English 5.7, and German 3.8.[5]

By 1850, about 15,000 Norwegians had come to America. In the decades that followed, the exodus to the United States rapidly increased, with some decade fluctuations, as shown in Table 2 based on official Norwegian statistics.

When a new family arrived from Norway, they would stop for a time in one of the established communities. Further moves were governed by the advice of earlier settlers, the influence of land companies and railroads, land surveys and reports of new areas, but especially reports sent back by land scouts. Eventually a new frontier became a settled community and it in turn became the springboard for settlements farther west.

It was not until late in the nineteenth, but especially in the early twentieth century, that the tide reached Western Canada. Norwegians first settled very extensively in Wisconsin and Illinois. Every 10 to 15 years, the settlements continued to spread another 100 miles or so to the northwest to penetrate Iowa, Minnesota, the Dakotas, and eventually the great plains of Western Canada.

SPECIFIC CAUSES OF MIGRATION FROM NORWAY

Religious intolerance by the State Church in Norway appears to have provided the initial impulse for emigration. The sailing of the first emigrant boat for America was initiated by Quakers and was under the leadership of Quakers.

The fact that there was a small group of Quaker dissenters in Norway is in itself a strange combination of factors anchored in historical events. During the Napoleonic Wars, England, by the supremacy of her navies, imposed a continental blockade upon Europe. This worked extreme hardships on Norway. Many private Norwegian ships attempted to run the British blockade to secure food and supplies. Here, the Norwegians were not so much fighting for Napoleon as for their own lives. In the struggle, the British captured many Norwegian ships and imprisoned the sailors in ships anchored on the Thames River. Here the prisoners of war were brought food and clothing, comfort and hope by the English Quakers. Several were converted to the teachings of the Quakers.

When Napoleon was defeated in 1815, a group of returning prisoners established the first Quaker assembly in Stavanger, Norway. The State Church proved to be exceedingly intolerant and brought persecution upon these dissenters. In common with their Quaker brethren in England, many began planning the escape to America to find religious freedom.[6]

In 1821, Cleng Peerson was sent to America as their advance agent. He returned to Norway in 1824 and urged the Quakers to emigrate. On July 4, 1825, the first boatload of 52 persons sailed for New York with Skipper Helland at the helm. Thus Cleng Peerson became not only the father of Norwegian migration to America but a pathfinder of Norwegian settlements in the American West. In fact, he founded the first permanent colony of Norwegians in America in the Fox River area in Illinois in 1835.[7]

By the middle of the nineteenth century, there were frequent crop failures and mounting poverty in Norway. As yet, the industrial revolution had not urbanized or diversified Norway. However, her ships reached out all over the world. Many sons of Norway signed up for service in the merchant marine and sailed to various ports of call. For many,

31

this provided windows on new opportunities. Some sailors jumped ship to become inland adventurers. These were the first to bring news to the isolated valleys of Norway of a vast hinterland of virgin land in what they called "America." These scattered reports were so exciting to a depressed people that this was the beginning of "American fever." For the Norwegians, the oceans and seas were no real obstacles, as they had been sailing out of their fjords to new frontiers for centuries. Fjords, seas and oceans again became their highways to adventure and new horizons.

There were special factors that pushed the Norwegians out again. Despite the fact that only a small percentage of the total land area of Norway is suited to agriculture, in the nineteenth century over half of the inhabitants gained their livelihood by farming. Mining and industry occupied most of the others, and the rest were engaged in trade, navigation, fishing, and professional work. The agricultural population, from which until recently the bulk of the emigrants have come, was composed of several classes: the *bonder* or freeholders, who in turn were divided into small and large landholders; the *husmand* or cotters; the renters; the labourers; and the servants.

The first group, the *bonder*, constituted a class not unlike the yeomanry of England – a politically self-conscious and economically powerful class that during the nineteenth century opposed domination by the official class and the state clergy with increasing success and formed the backbone of the Norwegian nationalistic and democratic movements. The *bondestand* dates back to early Norse history, and the reassertion of its rights in the nineteenth century against the *embedsstand* or official class provides a political background of discontent that contributed to the emigration of many *bonder* to America. Added to the political dissatisfaction was a strong reaction against the formalism and barrenness of the State Church, manifesting itself most notably in the pietistic movement inaugurated by Hans Nilsen Hauge in the early nineteenth century, and in the growth of minor dissenting sects, such as the Quakers. But above all, the fact that economic opportunities were restricted and hedged about by regulations caused the *bonder* to look longingly toward the "land of freedom" across the sea in America. The younger sons, who were prevented not only from acquiring part of the home farm or *gaard* by the *odel* system, which required the descent of the family land to the eldest male heir, but also from obtaining lands elsewhere because there simply was not land, also looked to America for opportunity.

The *husmand* or cotters were free men who had never been serfs, as had members of their class in other parts of Europe. Practically speaking, however, it was virtually socially impossible for a *husmand* to rise above his station, and it was only the exceptional individual who was able to achieve economic independence. In return for the use of a few acres and a hut, the *husmand* rendered services a certain number of days a week for the *bonde*. To them, the free and cheap lands of America seemed almost too good to be true. Thousands sold their meager possessions or were financed by benevolent *bonder* and sailed for the new Canaan. The renters, labourers, and servants obviously could hope for little in a rigidly stratified society. Parallel circumstances among the professional classes caused many to emigrate and establish themselves in the cities and villages of America as preachers, teachers, physicians, and tradesmen, serving the settlements of Norwegians wherever they were located.[8]

In an early analysis of migration factors, Ham points out that Norway was overcrowded and therefore unable to furnish sustenance and employment to all of her people. He asserts that in those years 85% of the immigrants to America were from rural districts and that material considerations played the most important role in pushing the emigrants to America. Dr. Ham summarized the influences that promoted the emigration to the United States in the nineteenth century:

> First, the prospect of material betterment and the love of a freer and more independent life; second, letters from relatives and friends who had emigrated to the United States and visits of these again to their native country; third, the advertising of agents of emigration; fourth, religious persecution at home; fifth, church proselyting; sixth, political oppression; seventh, military service; and eighth, the desire for adventure. Fugitives from justice . . . have been few, and paupers and criminals in the Scandinavian countries are not sent out of the country; they are taken care of by the government.[9]

Most of these causes are self-explanatory. However, it should be noted that military service was compulsory in Norway and many young men faced with the choice of harsh military service or leaving Norway chose to emigrate to America.

In 1865, A. Jorgensen corroborated many of these factors from the Canadian point of view. As a Norwegian immigration officer in Quebec City he had special opportunities to come to his own conclusions:

> The real acting cause of emigration during the present period seems in Norway to be economical pressure. If an emigrant is asked why he leaves the country, the answer is nearly always that he finds great difficulty in obtaining a livelihood at home, and that in America they are not so much exposed to failure of crops. Complaints are seldom heard about the pressure of high and unreasonable taxation and more seldom still of the conduct of the authorities. But the complaints are most frequent of want of work and small wages particularly during the winter, and these complaints are no doubt made with good reason, as there are parts of Norway where an ordinary labourer, during the winter, cannot earn more than 3 to 4 pence a day besides his board. It is often said by the better class of farmers that they would like to remain at home, but that it is on account of their children that they undertake the voyage, as they have heard

33

that it is comparatively easy in America to obtain an independent position, even for those who have but little means to commence with.[10]

A later study by Blegen quotes numerous sources and then lists these special reasons for the extensive migration from Norway:

1. The gloomy prospects in Norway for the future of the rising generation, coupled with the hope of independence and happiness in America.
2. The fact that for the "producing and working class," Norway is too circumscribed; that there is not room enough; and that the time is not distant when "a slavish dependence" will become general.
3. General dissatisfaction with the administration of Norwegian law, especially with reference to relations between debtors and creditors, where the regulations in force work the ruin of the former.
4. A general feeling that the state does too little to promote agriculture and the welfare of the common people, though it devotes large sums of money to other purposes.
5. Dissatisfaction with Norwegian officialdom and the clergy, which form a caste that looks upon an ordinary citizen as an inferior.
6. Failure in Norway to realize the freedom and equality that the Constitution of 1814 promised.
7. The pressure upon the *bondestand* of poor-relief burdens.
8. The pressure upon the same class of burdens connected with the Norwegian road system.
9. Uncertainty of crops and sterility of the soil.
10. Idealization of America.[11]

A somewhat different perspective is provided by Boe when he wrote:

In contrast to the smiling social democracy it is today, Norway in the last century was an overpopulated land of sharp class distinctions. The government, an insular monarchy, allowed only a privileged few any political expression. The clergy were aloof to the blunt realities of poverty and injustice. Nature had yielded her blessings in scant measure, but nothing was done to help or encourage the tens of thousands struggling to survive on little scraps of barren soil. Neighbor had quarreled with neighbor for every square foot of those steep, stony, stumpy upland meadows and the plots staked out were too small to support a family. Indebtedness was inevitable, the grip of creditor on debtor strangulating. Stills on the farms were legal and too many of the luckless could find their only consolation in drink.

In the early decades of the nineteenth century reports began drift-ing in from across the Atlantic that painted the New World in the colors of the Promised Land. A trickle of migrations from Norway to America started in the 1830s. Most of these emigrants set out for the frontiers of Illinois and Wisconsin, where land was available. Their letters home and the eyewitness accounts of visiting mis-sionaries fanned the flames of discontent back in the Old Country and provoked new waves of emigration.[12]

In all of the analyses of factors promoting the great folk migration from Norway, there is substantial agreement. Basically, early, middle and late nineteenth century migrations were all focused on the hope of better conditions in the new land.

The attractions of the United States were strong and positive but especially so after the passage of the Homestead Act of 1862, whose generous land policy was an incentive for potential emigrants. All of these migration factors are of consequence to Canada, for after 1885 many who first went to the United States would be the very pioneers who later came to Western Canada.

The analyses as set forth by the investigators quoted above were also largely confirmed for Canada in a series of interviews conducted by the author. To the question of why the pioneers had left Norway in the first instance, the predominant answers related to the lack of economic op-portunity in Norway and the promise of better opportunities in the New World.

Here, Ole Loken's explanation was typical of many.[13] When his father died in 1900, the farm became the property of Anton, the oldest son. The small farm at the base of a mountain was like "a gravel pit unable to pro-duce good crops." It could no longer support the family of seven children, ranging from age 12 to 28, and widowed mother. He could not get work with satisfactory pay. Therefore, he borrowed $35.00 from an uncle and left for Minneapolis in 1902 where he was told there was plenty of work and money to be made.

Peter Notland had a rather special reason for leaving Norway.[14] At the age of fourteen, his Norwegian independence was ruffled by the heavy taxes imposed upon his catches of herring. Therefore, early in 1903 he left for Willmar, Minnesota, to work for an uncle on his farm there.

Another early fisherman saw no future in catching the North Sea her-ring. Brynkjolf J. Stolee has left this record:

. . . had to decide what to do in the future. There were the following possibilities: I could be a hired man on one of the farms at a hun-dred crowns a year ($25), I could go to sea as a merchant seaman or I could go to America. My mother didn't like to have me go to sea and would rather have me immigrate to America. The winter of 1883 my uncle Halvor came home to visit, and so it was arranged that I should go with him to America. I borrowed money at the bank (about $60) for a ticket to Trail County, North Dakota. . . . I worked there that first summer for my uncles and so was able to pay my debt to the bank.[15]

The impact of this vast exodus of people caused much soul searching in Norway. One of the foremost writers on this subject, Ingrid Semmingsen, concluded:

In spite of differences in places and periods, one must attempt to find a general background – factors which were effective during the whole century. Among these reasons I believe one of the most important to have been the great increase in population. . . . It is obvious that the great increase in population – the damned-up reserves in the rural communities – created the materials for both internal migration and emigration. . . . One must not overlook the new attitude of young people – they wanted to get away. . . . The old agrarian society was breaking up. A new period had begun, when people did not live and work where they were born. . . . The mass movement of population began in earnest with the great nineteenth century transformation in Norwegian economic and social life. The times, local traditions, and economic conditions in the various parts of the country determined how many of the emigrants were to remain in the country and how many were to emigrate. . . . The great stretches of land in America were of special significance for the Norwegian emigrants. But American wages, and, later on, the ties of kinship and the tickets that were sent home to Norway were also important. Steamship lines, American railroad companies, and land speculators had their agents all over the country. But the most effective agents were after all the letters which came from America throughout the whole century. They told of economic progress in a country where democracy and social equality ruled, and the same letters stimulated those who remained in Norway to demand greater democratic rights for themselves.[16]

A supplementary Norwegian point of view is afforded by the following incident. When Chester Ronning was Canadian Ambassador to Norway, he visited his mother's ancestral home, the Rorheim farm. On this farm the soil is fertile and in the lower valleys there are masses of delicious wild plums. As Ronning bit into one of the plums and looked out to sea, past beautiful islands, he asked a descendant of his great-grandfather, "How could my grandparents leave this lovely place with such fine fruit and scenery?" He replied, "Your grandparents with a large family could not live on wild fruit and scenery."[17]

From 1905 to 1925, the Norwegian government has reported some statistics on the reasons for the exodus from the homeland. These are summarized in percentages as follows: lack of access to profitable occupations 79%; hired or seeking hire abroad three per cent; to join families 17%, and other motives one per cent.[18]

EARLY REPULSION FROM CANADA

As early as 1873 Canada was advertised in almost every newspaper in the Scandinavian countries. Pamphlets and circulars, in the languages of these countries, were printed and distributed. In 1873 Will MacDougall was sent as a special emigration agent to the Scandinavian countries.[19] He was given wide discretionary powers, and was instructed to copy the methods followed by the agents of the United States in soliciting emigrants. He wooed the Norwegians with indifferent success, for the hardships and failures of the colonists that had attempted to settle in the Eastern Townships of Quebec had received wide and adverse publicity in Norway, Sweden, and Denmark, and opposition to Canadian emigration was intensely unfavourable. "In fact we cannot do open work in Norway and Sweden," was the opinion of Canadian agents in those countries.

Also, it was unfortunate for Canada that absurd and fallacious ideas concerning Canada had been circulated among the Norwegian public. William MacDougall found it necessary to expose the damaging effects of the inefficiency and the dishonesty of some Canadian agents in their dealings with the press and transportation officials in the Scandinavian countries. "Canada," he said, "had to clear her name of complicity with those rascally agents before confidence could be restored."[20]

An example of the glowing advertising carried out is provided by the following excerpt from an early pamphlet widely circulated in Europe:

Free Homes

Lands Awaiting for the Settler to go in and Occupy them
Fertile Homesteads Free to All in the Canadian North-West

In Manitoba and the North-Western Territories of Canada there are over eighty millions of the finest wheat raising land upon the face of the globe, and these lands are to be had by any man for the asking.

There you can obtain free, without cost, a homestead of one hundred and sixty acres of the most fertile land known. It is a vast prairie of rich, deep, dark loam upon which the yield of grain is marvellous. Free homesteads are there offered to every man who will go in and settle. There are no forests to cut down, but the clear, open prairie awaits the plow to turn the sod and reveal the rich and productive earth. You can secure a free homestead of 160 acres and a pre-emption right of 160 acres more, which you can buy at the Government's low prices at once or at any time within three years after making application. Your sons, if they are eighteen years of

37

age or over, can each secure a like amount of land. The sole condition attached to this liberal offer is that the settler shall reside upon and cultivate his land for the short period of three years. At the end of three years the settler can take a second homestead upon the same conditions. This is an offer which is not made by any other country in the world.[21]

Thereafter, the pamphlet extolled the great opportunity available in the West and presents a very rosy picture of the rapid progress of Manitoba. The pamphlet also fights back against the dominant choice of emigrants to go to the United States:

It is an unfortunate fact that much misapprehension exists regarding the homestead and colonization and the railway policies of the Government of Canada and yet it is not strange, when we consider the falsehoods which have been concocted regarding those laws and the climate and soil of the Canadian North-West by railway companies who have lands in the United States of which they wish to dispose. These companies and their immigration agents in the United Kingdom and Europe have not hesitated to misrepresent in the most unblushing manner everything connected with the Canadian North-West, conscious that the facts would show that their country as a home for the emigrant is not to be compared in any respect with that under the protection of the British flag in Manitoba and the Canadian North-West Territories. On no one point has there been more misrepresentation than with respect to the land regulations. Yet those of the United States are not to be compared with the Canadian laws in regard to liberality. Look at the following comparisons:

CANADA

The head of a family or any male person not less than 18 years of age is entitled to a homestead entry.

Such entry may be for any quantity not exceeding 160 acres in any lands open therefor, the even-numbered sections on about eighty millions of the most fertile lands being free for selection.

Until the 1st January, 1885, the settler will have the right of pre-emption of an adjoining tract of the same extent as his homestead, which he can purchase at the end of three years at Government prices.

He obtains a patent at the end of three years' residence and cultivation.

He may have a second homestead entry.

He may commute by purchase after one year's residence.

THE UNITED STATES

Any male person not less than 23 years is entitled to a homestead entry.

Such entry may be for any quantity not exceeding eighty acres in the first or $2.50 class, or one hundred and sixty acres in the second or $1.25 class of lands open therefor.

The homestead settler has not the right of pre-emption.

He obtains a patent at the end of five years' residence and cultivation.

He cannot have a second homestead entry.

He may commute by purchase after one year's residence, but it is recommended that this privilege be modified and restricted.

Thus it will be seen that in Canada your son can make his homestead entry *three years before* he could in the States, and have his deed *five years sooner*. This is practically a saving of five years in a man's lifetime. In Canada a second homestead is granted – in the States, none. In Canada a pre-emption is attached to the homestead, but not so in the United States; and so on a comparison of the land laws of the two countries will show the Government of Canada to be much more liberal and fair to the settler.[22]

The pamphlet provided testimonies from visitors who endorse "the land of promise" and declared that it is indeed "favorable in the extreme."

Pamphlets of this type were translated into many European languages, including Norwegian. For example, on October 31, 1900, the Superintendent of Immigration under the Department of the Interior reported that out of a total of 1,050,000 pamplets prepared in the previous year, 20,000 copies had been printed in Norwegian.[23] In Norway such materials were distributed in bulk by special emigration agents of the Dominion Government, by agents of the aggressive steamship companies, notably the Allan Steamship Company, agents of the CPR and land companies. However, not all Norwegians were readily convinced as the following demonstrates:

The Canadian government offered to pay the fare and other travelling expenses to any province in Western Canada. . . . I and a good many others who were planning on immigrating thought it was a real good offer. But even 64 years ago they knew how to circulate false propaganda. We were told, especially by elderly people, that if we accepted the offer we would sell ourselves and never be free again. So, I and many others, decided to go to the United States and pay our own expenses.[24]

Meanwhile, the Government of Canada continued to vacillate between various policies respecting its vast reserves of lands. For example, in the

39

year 1881, the Cabinet changed its mind thrice by orders in council on March 24, July 29 and September 7.[25] The first authorized the sale of all undisposed lands at the price of $2 per acre; the second postponed all sales, and the third permitted squatters to purchase at $3 per acre any lands actually occupied. But definite action was postponed, and for years there issued from Ottawa a bewildering series of orders and counter-orders, petitions and counter-petitions for and against disposing of blocks of land to ethnic groups to the special consternation of the early Mennonites.

The government had passed *The Homestead Act* in 1872 whereby an adult could pay a fee of $10 for a quarter section and thereafter meet a five-year residence requirement to qualify for the title. However, lacking the benefit of any railroads in the West, there was no immediate rush for homesteads in Canada. The first man to homestead in the West was John Sanderson who set up his log home near Portage la Prairie in July, 1872.

In 1881, the Dominion Government granted the CPR an initial payment of 25 million dollars and 25 million acres in the West. This vast assignment of land required changes in the homestead regulations. All the odd-numbered sections in a township consisting of 36 sections were given tax-free to the CPR. Section 8 and three-quarters of section 26 were reserved for the Hudson's Bay Company. Two sections were set aside as "school lands" which could be sold to help pay for the construction of a school. In a typical township only 16¼ sections were now available for home-steading. The fee of $10 was still charged, the residence requirement was reduced to three years and the age for filing was reduced from 21 to 18. The above pattern contributed to early pioneer isolation, effectively blocked ethnic consolidation and brought about heavy taxes on the scattered homesteaders when they established area services such as roads and schools. The railway lands were tax exempt from the beginning.

In the tradition of colonial governments, the Dominion government continued to be a bastion of vested interests. Apparently, the West was envisioned as a fiefdom of a new landed gentry. Then to protect interests in Eastern Canada, the Canadian government raised the tariff on farm machinery from 25% to 33% in 1883. Thus farm machinery prices in Canada became very high in comparison to prices in the United States. To friends of the party in power was given the privilege of forming colonization companies which could obtain tracts of land beyond 24 miles from the CPR mainline or its branch lines while reserving the available even-numbered sections for homesteaders. Such lands could be purchased at $2.00 or more per acre, but most of the land companies made no cash investment whatever. They had the privilege of paying later. In fact, most of them were speculators who hoped to gain handsome profits for their land companies. At the end of 1883, there were at least 26 companies holding about three million acres of land.[26]

In the early decades of Confederation, famous prime ministers, now glamorized, were far from scrupulous in matters of patronage and exploitation for political gain. Scandal after scandal clouded political futures, but the voting public usually had a short memory. Eastern Canadian financial tycoons and friends of Sir John A. Macdonald formed giant ranching conglomerates that were given leases of vast acres of southern Alberta at one cent per acre. These ranchers supplied cattle to feed the crews who built the CPR. They also specialized in raising polo ponies for the English aristocrats who were prominent among the shareholders. Their culled and worthless cattle were sold to the Department of Indian Affairs to feed the starving Blackfoot on the nearby reserves.[27]

The largest of these ranches, the North-West Cattle Company, was under the control of Sir Hugh Allan, a Montreal merchant and president of the Allan Line of ocean steamships. Originally, in 1873, the contract for building the CPR had been awarded to the private company headed by Sir Hugh Allan but then the opposition discovered that he had made large contributions to help elect the Conservatives in the recent general election. Thus came the Pacific Scandal which led to the defeat of Macdonald and delayed the commencement of building the CPR by eight long years.

The policies pursued by Canada for most of the nineteenth century drove most of the Norwegians to established settlements in the United States. Meanwhile, the land speculators and privileged elite in Canada largely failed in their schemes. Macdonald put the whole matter in gentle perspective when he wrote:

> In a free society, human beings cannot be driven like sheep in a preconceived direction, nor can a sparsely-settled, comparatively undeveloped country, with huge stretches of unoccupied land and poor means of transportation, either attract or hold a sufficient number of suitable settlers. This axiom was particularly true of Canada . . . in the years immediately following Confederation, and in fact up to the end of the century, progress was slow, spasmodic, uncertain.[28]

CANADA'S TURN

In the first decade of the present century, 44% of the homestead entries made in Western Canada were by immigrants from the United States. This dramatic turn of events in Canada's favour must be explained.

The early Norwegians had prospered in the western United States. By the 1890s their numbers had multiplied and the good land was almost entirely occupied. Around the turn of the century there had been two decades of agricultural depression, much severe drought and generally deplorable economic conditions, especially for labourers and renters. Farms had been mortgaged in order to expand but credit in the western United States was inadequate and interest rates were high. In 1900 farm labourers constituted about one-third of the population in the farming

41

areas and they were very poorly paid. Tenants, who operated about half of the farms for those who had been able to establish large holdings, faced many severe problems such as high rentals, increasing costs of production and the prospect of remaining renters for the rest of their lives.

Into this experience of adversity, where so many were shackled by debts and doubts about the future, came the rich promises of Canadian land agents sponsored by the CPR and various land companies, and the vigorous advertising campaign of the Dominion government.

An early example of the new pull by Canada in attracting Norwegian pioneers to leave Minnesota has been recorded by Steen and Hendrickson:

> It was in 1892 that Nels Jevning and Martin Finseth, two neighbors farming near Crookston, Minnesota, first dreamed of going to Canada. A Canadian immigration agent had recently opened an office in Crookston. The literature distributed gave glowing accounts of the productivity of the Canadian soil. Displays of grasses and grains, and even letters from settlers already there, seemed to establish the fact that here indeed was a vast area of exceedingly productive soil awaiting development. Railways had begun to penetrate the wilderness. Free homesteads in all of this immense territory were offered to any prospective settlers.
>
> The Jevning, Finseth and Anderson families, who had been living in the Red River Valley since they arrived there from Norway in 1876, were intrigued by the prospects of free land. Business reverses, sickness and lack of land for their sons and daughters were among the reasons which caused them and many of their neighbors to be more or less dissatisfied with this district around Crookston where they had been among the first settlers. . . .
>
> Martin Finseth started negotiating with the Canadian Government agent and finally obtained the promise that several representative farmers of the district would be given free transportation if they wished to inspect the country he represented. The result of these negotiations was that in the spring of 1893 Nels Jevning, Martin Finseth, Andrew Malmberg, and John Wallerbeck went to inspect the Canadian Northwest. Their objectives was the parkland country along the recently built Calgary-Edmonton railway line in what later became the province of Alberta. . . . The soil and vigorous growth of plant life convinced them that here indeed was a country with a great future.[29]

However, not all those who came to see were convinced as reported by Anderson:

> One man expressed himself this way, "This is a miserable land. There is no milk, neither is there decent drinking water to be found. I am almost dried up!"

When it came right down to facts, there were so many things to consider. The difficulties seemed many and difficult. Here we were more than fifty miles from the nearest trading centre, and no one knew if it would ever be any closer. The outlook of the future seemed so dark that many lost heart and did not take out homesteads. There were those who prophesied that we who stayed would need help to get out in a few years. This, of course, was not encouraging. But several of us, so to speak, had burned our bridges behind us and had come prepared to stay.[30]

It was under the Liberal leader Sir Wilfrid Laurier, who came to power in 1896, and his aggressive Minister of the Interior, Clifford Sifton, that new policies were enunciated. Both men had great faith in Canada provided that it could be peopled with settlers. They put a stop to the perpetual Canadian folly of giving away the best land to political favourites, privileged speculators and aggressive railway companies. They forced the latter to colonize the lands under their control or forfeit their privileges. It was decided to spend large sums in both Europe and the United States to promote immigration. Not only did these progressive policies pull in people from the United States but also from every country in Europe.

It was indeed fortunate for Western Canada that Sifton, a man of rare intelligence and drive, was placed in the position where he had full charge of both land policy and immigration policy. Not only did he overhaul the homestead regulations but he streamlined procedures in his own department and determined to fill the West with immigrants from any country whence he could draw them. From 1897 and on, Canada's immigration drive was in high gear. Agencies were set up in the upper Midwest states whereby special promotion could be set in motion to attract Nordic people to Canada. Many of these were farmers of considerable means and years of experience on the frontier.

To the Norwegians in the Middle West, mired in rural depression, agricultural crises, mounting debts, few new opportunities for expansion and growing families, the Prairie Provinces offered the opportunity of a second chance. To a people schooled in farming on the American frontier the Prairie Provinces just across the border exerted a dramatic appeal and a means of breaking out of the economic trap that currently held them. The timing was excellent.

Bicha records that 560,389 settlers arriving from the United States between 1901 and 1914 gave Saskatchewan and Alberta as their destination.[31] Many of these eventually returned but many early Norwegians who came to Canada from the United States made Canada their permanent home. The 1921 Dominion Census reported 68,856 persons under the ethnic grouping of Norwegian. Of these 22,186 (32.3%) were born in the United States, 23,102 (33.6%) in Norway and 23,568 (34.2%) in Canada.[32]

Another example of the effectiveness of the Canadian campaign to attract Norwegians from the United States to the Northwest Territories has been provided by Matthew S. Anderson:

> I was also, at this time, somewhat concerned with my own personal circumstances. I seemed not to be progressing the way I had hoped for in the New World. Consequently, when I called for my mail at the Crookston (Minnesota) post office one Sunday, I examined with new interest some large posters on the wall describing how one could get free land in Canada.
>
> The posters carried beautiful pictures of what they called "A northwest paradise". One showed a lovely lake with fish jumping out of the water.
>
> As I was looking at the posters, a man approached me and asked if I would be interested in taking up a Canadian homestead. When I replied in my somewhat broken English he began to speak in Norwegian. He was a Norwegian and was employed as a sub-agent for a land company in Canada. He invited me to come and see him to discuss a possible move. A friend, Matthew Munson, my brother Peter and I went to see him that very afternoon.
>
> When we told our acquaintances that we were considering the advantages and disadvantages of moving to Canada, they told us it would be a very risky move. It was a very lawless country, they said. We were to find out that they did not know what they were talking about.
>
> Paying their advice no heed, we bought tickets for a place called Regina, Northwest Territories, Canada. Some days later, we were impressed when the train pulled into Regina to see many scarlet-coated mounted policemen lined up on the platform to give immigrants the impression, we were told, that there was law and order in Canada. We soon found out this was not a token demonstration, it was a fact. . . . The following day we filed on homesteads located in the same section near a place called Bulyea, which we were told lay 45 miles north of Regina.[33]

In thousands of cases, the "American fever" had now subsided and many now caught "Canada fever" while down in the United States. For example, the Bardo pioneers had first left Norway in 1875 to homestead in Crookston, Minnesota. By 1894, many of them became pioneers again by moving to the District of Alberta in the Northwest Territories of Canada. Later this same group provided the impetus for another settlement in the Peace River Country in 1912. In fact, many of the Norwegians from the States would be instrumental in developing more than one settlement in Canada. They were experienced and capable settlers, usually of some means. Canada was very fortunate to secure these particular Norwegians.

IN RETROSPECT: 1850-1929

The tradition of "Family Compacts" in early Canada delayed the rapid settlement and development of this vast Dominion. The various privileged elitist cliques served themselves and their favoured friends.

The hard-working pioneer could not pay their land prices coupled with high interest rates and make a living for his family. In some areas, upon buying the land he soon discovered that he could not cut any timber, for these rights had been given to some district lord. Vast reserves of land were completely tied up. Their owners made no improvements but held their land solely for speculation.

For many long years the Norwegians poured through Canada by the thousands to possess the lands of Wisconsin, Iowa, Minnesota, the Dakotas and parts of Montana. It was a peaceful Viking conquest that remains. Today it is estimated that there are more people of Norwegian lineage living in the United States than the four million people living in all of Norway.[34]

One cannot but speculate if Eastern Canada would be different had the vast Eastern Townships of Quebec and counties about Ottawa been able to hold and then multiply the Norwegian settlements there in a manner similar to what happened in several important states below the line. But those who came to Canada from 1850 to 1885 proved to be mostly transients.

As the nineteenth century progressed, it became increasingly possible for the people in Norway to compare economic, political and social conditions in their home district with those described in various guidebooks from across the ocean. A stream of "America letters" conveyed a message of new hope for those oppressed at home. Then, many emigrants returned for visits and convinced a great number that emigration was infinitely preferable to remaining in Norway. To the contrary, there were strong warnings and admonitions from government officials and the clergy who did their utmost to discourage leaving the homeland.

To the hard-working farmer struggling to keep above poverty on a small plot of land in Norway, the vision of 160 acres of free land was the final compelling argument. The "American fever" swept like a fire throughout the country, from one district to the next, penetrating even the most remote mountain valley. In some districts almost the entire population left. Thousands upon thousands found their way to the ships taking most of their meagre belongings with them. They must see for themselves if the new land was indeed a land of hope and glory.

As shown in Table 16 in the Appendix, 11,446 Norwegians came directly to Canada in the decade from 1900-1909. The decade from 1910-1919 was partially interrupted by World War I but still another 9,343 Norwegians came. From 1920-1929 the number reached 19,575. This flow was almost stopped by the Depression of the 1930s and World

War II which followed. Thus by far the largest number of Norwegians to find permanent homes in the West had come to Canada by 1929. This was true of those who came directly from Norway and the much greater number who came to Canada via the United States. See Table 17 in the Appendix.

NOTES

1. Nicholas Hans, *Comparative Education* (London: Routledge and Kegan Paul, 1950), p. 92.
2. P. Ljostveit, *Innermission Church History* (Minneapolis: Hauge Lutheran Innermission Federation, 1948), p. 393.
3. G. Loken, *A Study of the Government of the Folk High Schools of Norway* (Edmonton: The University of Alberta, unpublished doctoral dissertation, 1968), pp. 121-122.
4. *Statistisk Arbok* 1966 (Oslo: Sentralbyra 1966), p. 5.
5. H. Kobt, "Utvandringen fra Norge" in *Nye Innhogg og Utsyn* (Oslo, 1964), pp. 187ff.
6. O.M. Norlie, *History of the Norwegian People in America* (Minneapolis: Augsburg, 1925), pp. 112-121.
7. By 1836 there were about 200 Norwegian settlers at Fox River according to Norlie. In 1841 the first Lutheran house of worship in America was built in this settlement. In 1843 a lay preacher, Elling Eielsen, was ordained – the first Norwegian Lutheran pastor in America.
8. Theodore C. Blegen, *Norwegian Migration to America 1825-1860* (Northfield, Minnesota, 1931), pp. 10-11.
9. G.T. Flom, *A History of Norwegian Immigration to the United States* (Iowa City, 1909), p. 88.
10. A. Jorgensen, *The Emigration from Europe During the Present Century* (Quebec: C. Darveau, 1865), p. 8. This rare document is in the National Archives.
11. T.C. Blegen, *Norwegian Migration to America 1825-1860* (New York: Arno Press, 1969), p. 167.
12. Eugene Boe, "Pioneers to Eternity: Norwegians on the Prairie" in *The Immigrant Experience* (Pelican), p. 51.
13. Conversation of author with his father, August, 1967.
14. Taped interview with Peter Notland, Morrin, Alberta, March, 1973.
15. Brynhjolf J. Stolee, *Some Memories from My Youth* from Jacob B. Stolee (Camrose, 1973).
16. Ingrid Gaustad Semmingsen, "Norwegian Emigration to America During the Nineteenth Century" in *Norwegian-American Studies and Records* (Northfield, Minnesota: Norwegian-American Historical Association, 1940), pp. 69-81.
17. Chester Ronning, *A Memoir of China in Revolution* (New York: Random House, 1974), p. 5.

18. Arne Hassing, "Norway's Organized Response to Emigration" in *Norwegian-American Studies* (Northfield, Minnesota: The Norwegian-American Historical Association, 1972), p. 58.
19. Norman Macdonald, *Canada: Immigration and Colonization 1841-1903*, pp. 205-206.
20. *Ibid.*, p. 144.
21. Thomas Spence, *Useful and Practical Hints for the Settler in Canadian Prairie Lands* (Winnipeg, 1881), p. 1.
22. *Ibid.*, p. 4.
23. Canada, *Sessional Papers*, XXV (10), No. 25.
24. Matthew S. Anderson, *Bold Experiment* (Regina, 1961), p. 19.
25. Macdonald, *op. cit.*, p. 204.
26. J.W. Grant MacEwan, *West to the Sea* (Toronto: McGraw-Hill, 1968), p. 101.
27. Heather Robertson, *Grass Roots* (Toronto: James Lewis & Samuel, 1973), pp. 55-56.
28. Macdonald, *op. cit.*, p. 92.
29. Ragna Steen and Magda Hendrickson, *Pioneer Days in Bardo, Alberta* (Tofield, Alberta: The Historical Society of Beaver Lake Hills, 1944), pp. 15-17.
30. P.B. Anderson, translated documents in Norwegian from the family files of Magda Hendrickson, Camrose.
31. Karel D. Bicha, *The American Farmer and the Canadian West, 1896-1914* (Kansas, 1968), pp. 140-141.
32. Census of Canada, 1921.
33. Anderson, *op. cit.*, p. 19.
34. *Facts About Norway* (Oslo: C.S. Forlag, 1966), p. 6.

THREE

New Furrows in the Canadian West

Western Canada is usually considered to be that vast region lying between the Canadian Shield on the east and the Rocky Mountains on the west. First and foremost, it is an area of great plains – an expanse of treeless prairie, bright sunshine and persistent winds. Often this area is referred to as "big sky country." But it also includes regions of parkland north and east of the plains in which bluffs of poplars and patches of prairie are intermixed. Much of the land seems endlessly flat but, as the pioneers discovered, it is often intersected by dry water courses called coulees and deeply grooved with numerous rivers, tributaries and smaller streams originating in the Rocky Mountains. These drain across the steppes of the West all the way to Hudson Bay.

It was this land of grass, bluff, buffalo and Indian that became the home of thousands of Norwegians who overflowed from the abundance of people that first populated the midwestern American states. When they had established a beachhead here, they attracted thousands more directly from Norway. The era from 1885 to 1929 is the time of the major establishment of Norwegian settlements both in Western Canada and in the Province of British Columbia. This chapter focuses attention on the beginnings of several typical settlements.

PERSPECTIVES ON EARLY WESTERN HISTORY

The Hudson's Bay Company was founded under royal charter in 1670 when Charles II capriciously assigned vast territories to a company of gentlemen adventurers. From this beginning, and on occasions thereafter, Western Canada was territory to be given away to political or corporate favourites by those in power.

In the next two centuries, the major activity in that empire known as Rupert's Land was directed by traders who exploited the harvest of furs garnered by the Indians. At that time the fashions of the elite of Europe created a strong market for good furs.

The first white man to visit the Canadian plains was a young fur trader, Henry Kelsey. From the Indians who brought their furs to York Factory on Hudson Bay, he heard exciting stories of a great inland country, and became determined to see this for himself. In 1691 he travelled by canoe with the Indians through the heavy forest regions to the treeless prairies which he has described in his journal, "Inland Country of Good Report."[1] By the end of the eighteenth century, other fur traders and adventurers journeyed by canoe, horse or foot into the great Northwest and extended their trading posts from Fort Rouge to Fort Edmonton. Except for the fur traders and early missionaries who roamed through the territories on their long travels, the Indians lived their nomadic lives largely undisturbed and much as they had for centuries.

In 1869 the Hudson's Bay Company surrendered to the Dominion government its right to govern the vast lands but still retained its charter and trading rights. The price arrived at was 300,000 pounds sterling and seven million acres of land in the "fertile belt" of Canada. In this way by 1870 the total monopoly of a great fur trading company was broken. In that year a small area was designated as the Province of Manitoba. From 1870 to 1876 the vast territories of the West were under the control of the Lieutenant-Governor of Manitoba assisted by a North West Council chosen by the Dominion government. By 1882 the four provisional districts of Assiniboia, Saskatchewan, Alberta and Athabasca were established, each with limited rights of self-government but all under the tutelage of the Department of the Interior. In 1905 these districts were aligned to form the provinces of Alberta and Saskatchewan.

The era of the fur trader and the explorer was coming to an end; that of the rancher, the speculator, the politician and the farmer was now to begin. The West was destined for greater things than to remain the hunting ground of nomadic Indian tribes and the private preserve of a favoured fur trading company.

ISOLATED NORWEGIAN SETTLERS

It has been observed that a new country passes through three major stages of development: a period of exploration, then one of speculation, and finally one of construction. The Norwegians possess a venturesome readiness to explore new frontiers, often on an individual basis. There are a few recorded instances of these isolated individuals who ventured forth on their own to probe the unknown country.

One of the most interesting of the early Norwegian personalities was Willard Ferdinand Wentzel, who spent most of his active life in the service of the North West Company in Athabasca and Mackenzie regions during the boisterous days of the fur trade. He was chosen to accompany Sir John Franklin on his overland expeditions in 1819-1820 to explore the polar coast line east from the Coppermine River as far as possible.[2] Wentzel could speak the Chipewyan language of the local Indian tribe

49

and enjoyed their complete confidence as manager of the trading post. His duties during the year he was with the expedition were, according to Captain Franklin, "the management of the Indians, the superintendence of the Canadian voyagers, the obtaining and the general distribution of the provision, and the issue of the other stores. These services he was well qualified to perform, having been accustomed to execute similar duties, during a residence of upwards of twenty years in this country. We also deemed Mr. Wentzel to be a great acquisition to our party, as a check on the interpreters."[3]

Holand has reported the following about this early fur trader:

This man whom circumstances for a time had appointed doorkeeper to the Canadian arctic was a Norwegian. . . . The date of his birth and his birthplace are unknown, but he must have been in his twenties in 1799 when he first appeared on the outermost Canadian frontier. Twenty-seven years he spent in that desolate region; and he retired, apparently in good vigor, in 1826.[4]

In spite of the desolate and isolated post which he occupied, Wentzel maintained contact with others through the annual supply group that made the 2,000 mile canoe journey from Hudson Bay to Great Slave Lake to deliver goods and news and to take back furs and letters. In Masson's *Les Bourgeois* are printed 15 of Wentzel's letters written between 1807 and 1824.[5] In one letter dated April 30, 1811, he briefly describes a period of starvation which he and the Indians experienced. Most of his letters deal with questions and conditions of public interest, written in excellent style and with lucid explanations.

At one time Wentzel planned to write a history of the Northwest. To get reliable information, he addressed letters of inquiry to a number of factors and clerks. The summary written by Wentzel is a monograph of some 10,000 words, describing the country, its waterways, mountains, minerals, fauna, flora and climate. It also describes the Indians' mode of life, their customs, religion, character, government, habitations, hunting, food and warfare. Finally, it contains a vocabulary of 300 common Indian words. The treatise is dated March 27, 1807.[6]

Captain Franklin recorded a favourable account of the work of Wentzel in the performance of his assigned duties. During the long winter he entertained the expedition force with his excellent skill on the violin, also leading the crew in boisterous singing of *voyageur* songs and telling strange Indian tales from his large repertoire. On the way back to the Coppermine, supplies of food gave out and most of the Indians starved to death.[7]

As was common with Europeans in the wilderness, Wentzel married an Indian woman by whom he had two children, a boy and a girl. His son Alexander became a carpenter and built the church at St. Norbert in 1853. Holand has recorded this final tribute to Wentzel: "He was an advance scout of civilization at the very ends of the earth, but he filled his arduous post with patience, bravery and efficiency."[8]

Most Canadians have read about the first Red River settlers brought to the forks of the Red River in the years 1812-1815 by Lord Selkirk. Few are aware that there were Norwegians here. This settlement was supplied by the ships of the Hudson's Bay Company which arrived annually at York Factory on Hudson Bay, from where supplies were brought for more than 700 miles by rivers, portages and lakes to the Red River. As an aid both to the HBC and the new settlement, Lord Selkirk decided to build winter roads connecting York Factory to the interior. For this he needed men who could endure the rigours of northern winters and who had experience as a woodsmen, fishermen and farmers but who above all were strong, resourceful and reliable. Consequently, some 15 Norwegians were recruited under the leadership of a man named Holte.[9] There is some evidence that these men may have been conscripted from Norwegian ships captured during England's blockade of the Continent directed against Napoleon. This little band sailed from Yarmouth on June 10, 1814, in the Hudson's Bay Company ship the *Prince of Wales* and arrived at York Factory on September 3, 1814. Some of the Norwegians were sent to Moose Factory at Moose River on James Bay, while the rest accompanied Holte to the place where the Jack River emptied into the northern end of Lake Winnipeg. Here they spent the winter clearing the way for roads and building a station which to this day is called Norway House. It is one of the oldest trading posts and Indian missions in the West and is still an active HBC centre.

The Selkirk papers record that Holte, Peter Dahl, Peter Isaacson and Nils Muller came to the Red River settlement in the fall of 1815. Governor Semple described them as "the finest fellows in the world," and Colin Robertson, a Scotsman in the service of Lord Selkirk, spoke of them as "industrious, well disposed men, and well calculated for the new country, being in general good axmen."[10]

On June 19, 1816, the Seven Oaks massacre took place. The constant feud between the Hudson's Bay Company and the North West Company as rivals in the fur trade broke into open battle. Governor Semple and 20 men of the settlement were killed by Métis who had been incited to this foul deed by offers of great rewards by officers of the North West Company. According to the Selkirk papers, the first man killed in the massacre was the Norwegian Holte. He was buried in an unmarked grave somewhere at the forks of the Red River.

No other Norwegian is mentioned in connection with the Seven Oaks episode, and none of Holte's band have been traced except Peter Dahl and Peter Isaacson, who remained at the Red River. Fragments of their later life may be gleaned from census reports of the Red River Colony.

Isaacson was the older man. The Census of 1831 records that he was 51 years of age, possessed two oxen, two cows and one pig. He owned no land, apparently never married, and lived most of the time with Peter Dahl. When Professor Hind came to the Red River in 1857 he wrote, "I had a long conversation with the single Norwegian who now remains at Red River; he is a very old man between 90 and 100 years; he came to Rupert's Land more than 40 years ago. . . ." This description fits Peter Isaacson better than it does Peter Dahl who was younger by about 10 years.[11]

Peter Dahl secured land in the Red River colony in 1817 and it is recorded in the HBC land register that he owned lots 186 and 606. The census report of 1831 states his age as forty-two, "born in Norway, Protestant." He then had three sons and two daughters under 16 years of age, and he possessed "1 house, 1 barn, 1 mare, 5 bulls, 7 cows, 5 calves, 2 pigs, 1 plough, 1 cart, 1 boat, 1 canoe, and 7 acres of cultivated land." All subsequent reports reveal steady economic progress for the Dahl family. Throughout these early years, Peter Dahl had more land under cultivation and owned more livestock than most of the farmers in the colony. Obviously, he more than held his own in competition with the canny Scots who were the majority among these early settlers.

It is probable that Peter Dahl's wife was Scottish for they named their first son Alexander. Peter Dahl appears to be the only one of Lord Selkirk's venturesome Norwegians to become a land-owning farmer in the historic Red River settlement – the first of many of that nationality to live in the Red River Valley.[12]

The above accounts are indicative of several isolated Norwegians who were scattered so far and wide in the new land that they could establish no meaningful contact with their own ethnic group. These early immigrant workers did not establish any enduring colonies or settlements but they paved the way for later developments. Many died on the frontier at an untimely age; others found their way to the United States; and some returned to Norway to report on the great land that was so large and challenging that it was almost unbelievable to those who knew only Norway. Then there were those who were quickly absorbed into the Canadian scene and soon ceased to be identifiable as Norwegians.

OPENING OF THE WEST

The first land trail from the United States began at Fort Benton and snaked 200 miles northward into Canada pushing east to Fort MacLeod, later north to the junction of the Bow and Elbow rivers, and eventually as far north as the territory of the future Red Deer and Edmonton districts.

Fort Benton, situated at the head of navigation on the Missouri River in Montana, was very closely involved with the early history of Western Canada. Though this town had a small core of respectable businessmen and settlers, on the whole it was a hotbed of unrestrained fortune hunters, desperadoes, gunslingers and ruthless free traders who recognized no international boundaries. These were the men who built a chain of whiskey trading forts along the infamous Whoop-up Trail connecting Calgary and Fort MacLeod with Fort Benton.

In 1870, the lieutenant-governor of the North West Territories dispatched a military officer to investigate conditions in the West. He returned with the grim news that the entire northwest was "without law, order or security for life and property." William F. Butler also reported to Ottawa that he felt "convinced that if proper means are taken, the suppression of the liquor traffic of the West can easily be accomplished."[13]

The unscrupulous American whiskey traders from the Missouri Valley had abruptly changed the complexion of life on the plains. An era of lawlessness and bloodshed was beginning that could have rivalled the chaotic and violent development of the American West. The law of the gun had begun to take root. Tales of massacre and robbery drifted all the way back to Ottawa where Sir John A. Macdonald as Canada's first Prime Minister was struggling with the problems of his young Dominion. For example, he learned that in the spring of 1873, a group of American traders on their way back to Fort Benton with the winter's take of pelts, lost their horses to a party of Indians and had to finish their journey by foot to Fort Benton. Here they rounded up new horses and set off after the horse thieves. They tracked a large party of Assiniboine Indians to the Cypress Hills where they mercilessly massacred some 22 Indians.[14]

Thus on May 23, 1873, the Parliament of Canada approved *An Act Respecting the Administration of Justice and for the Establishment of a Police Force in the North-West Territories*. The major expressed reason for organizing the North West Mounted Police was to stop the commercial activities of those American traders who dignified their operations by the name of "whiskey trading with the Indians." But the American frontiersman was also a threat to colonization of the West under the British flag.

The establishment of the red-coated cavalcade of the West was another turning point in Canadian history. George McClellan, an ex-RCMP commissioner speaking at Camrose to celebrate the force's centennial in a talk entitled "Roads of Glory" said:

> What do we celebrate in marking this Centennial? We celebrate the settlement of the greatest, vastest country ever settled peacefully. No other country so big has ever been settled with so little savagery, so little plunder, so little lawlessness. It was the police who made it possible for the farmers and settlers to move into this country bringing their wives and children with them.[15]

Settlement of the West was made possible by a combination of several other important developments. The recognized pattern of American Indian warfare was to exterminate the natives and to "kill every buffalo you can for every buffalo dead is an Indian gone."[16] In the Canadian

53

West the buffalo was also killed off in a thoughtless and vicious slaughter partly for pemmican, but also for tongues which gourmets considered to be great delicacies, and for hides selling up to five dollars apiece. By 1880, the thundering herds were gone; their bleached bones now dotted the prairie everywhere and Indian tribes faced starvation. A Calgary editor of the day wrote: "The hold which the whites have during the past half-dozen years managed to secure over at least some of the Indians has been due to the dependence to which the extinction of the buffalo has reduced the latter."[17]

From 1871 to 1877, seven important treaties had been made with the Indians. Under the *Dominion Lands Act of 1872*, the Dominion Government set in motion a vast survey never equalled before or since. Within 12 years over 67 million acres of western Canada had been surveyed. In many ways these surveyors were unsung heroes and special pioneers of the frontier. Also, in 1872, it became possible to secure a homestead for a registration fee of $10. Further, the quelling of the second Riel Rebellion in 1885 lessened the fear of moving West.

Above all it was the building of the Canadian Pacific Railway, approved in 1871 but pushing west from Winnipeg in 1881, that opened a practical way for the settlers to come from many places and other lands. What canoe routes and cart trails had not been able to accomplish, the new railroad quickly achieved, ushering in a great era of western colonization.

When the CPR was completed in 1885, it opened up the world's greatest wheat lands and ushered in the greatest immigration period in Canadian history. For the creation of the CPR was followed by an orgy of railroad building which soon crisscrossed the West with main lines, branch lines and spur lines. Each new line opened up additional territory to settlers even though much of the land in some areas was unprofitable for grain farming and should never have been opened up.

In 1886, *The Calgary Herald* carried an editorial entitled "Retrospect" in which it commented on a speech by an outstanding leader about the opening of the West:

> The Rev. John McDougall in a very interesting speech declared that it was not until the arrival of the N.W.M.P. in '74 that law and justice became possible and life and property safe.
>
> The transfer [of land from HBC to the Dominion], the police [North West Mounted Police], the railroads are the three epochs in the history of the North West. The first makes the change from an irresponsible to a responsible government, the second the introduction of law and order, and the third the arrival of civilization. Each of these changes has had an almost magical effect.[18]

In the Canadian West, unlike the American West, religion, law and government preceded the influx of settlers by many years. The negotiated treaties with the natives prevented the vicious Indian wars and the attacks on settlers so much a part of the American frontier.

THE FIRST COLONY: EAU CLAIRE AT CALGARY

The first more or less permanent settler on the site of the future Calgary was Fred Kanouse, described as a gunslinger, whiskey trader and deputy sheriff from Montana. He had a cabin up the Elbow within the present city limits and traded with the Indians during the winters of 1870-1871 and 1871-1872.

Kanouse was only one of dozens of American whiskey traders who came into what is now southern Alberta between 1870 and 1874. The trade was profitable since a buffalo robe could be bought for a pound of tobacco or four yards of cotton cloth or half a gallon of whiskey. During one winter the whiskey trade of Kanouse has been estimated at $12,000 – a considerable sum in those days.

The potent "fire water" caused much destruction and death among the Indians. As many as 70 Blood Indians died in 1870 from fights, freezing to death while drunk and from the toxic effects of the crude whiskey. Early in 1872 a band of drunken Indians held Kanouse and his companions at bay in his trading post. After withstanding the seige, he got the message and returned to live at Fort Benton, Montana.[19]

Exploitation of the Indian tribes continued unabated until the North West Mounted Police sent 50 men into the Calgary area in the fall of 1875. Thereafter, law and order increasingly prevailed. However, in 1875 Fort Calgary was really only an isolated NWMP outpost in Indian country.

In 1877, by the signing of Blackfoot Treaty No. 7, the Blackfoot confederacy came to terms with the police and the white government. By 1881, Calgary consisted of the police fort, the I.G. Baker store, the HBC store, the commanding officer's residence, a small church and some scattered tents. The population numbered 75 persons. Fort Calgary could be reached from the south by ox teams plying the Whoop-Up Trail. The Red River Cart was the favoured means of transportation between Winnipeg and Fort Edmonton and then south to Calgary along the Edmonton trail.

The coming of the railroad to Calgary in August, 1883, really opened the area to both homesteaders and entrepreneurs. If there was to be an influx of settlers, a building boom would ensue. This would require piles of lumber on the bald prairie. Thus the first industries in Calgary were involved with the manufacturing of lumber.

In the early 1880s, before the railroad reached Calgary, an Ottawa lawyer named Kutusoff MacFee learned about the valuable timber stands west of Calgary. He realized also that the new railway would bring great expansion to the prairies. Not being a lumberman himself, he went to the logging capital of the midwestern United States, Eau Claire, Wisconsin, for expert advice. Enterprising Americans listened to his story with considerable interest. They agreed that much lumber would soon be in great demand at Calgary to serve the needs of a prairie empire to be developed. Later a scouting party was sent from Eau Claire, travelling by rail, horses, boat and by foot to examine the timber births in the mountains.[20]

On June 25, 1883, in the office of North Western Lumber Company at Eau Claire, Wisconsin, a company was formed for the purpose of securing timber rights in the Canadian Rockies and eventually building a lumber mill at Calgary which was destined to become the largest in the North West Territories.[21]

The president of the company was Joseph G. Thorp, believed to have been Norwegian. The secretary was Vincent W. Bayless. Two of the original stockholders were Peter A. Prince who became the manager of the Calgary lumber mill and Isaac K. Kerr who later succeeded him. Between them the 14 stockholders raised $193,152.56. By June 30, 1883, they had tendered upon several timber births situated in the Kananaskis and Spray or Falls River in the District of Alberta, North West Territories. On July 14, 1883, the secretary for the Department of Interior at Ottawa wrote to the new officers of the company in part as follows:

> . . . I am to inform you that your tender ($104.20 per square mile) was the highest received for the birth in question, and that an Order in Council was passed on the 7th inst., granting you a yearly license to cut timber on the same.[22]

Thus, for a payment of $10,430.00 the Eau Claire Lumber Co. received the right to secure timber from 100 square miles of forested land in the mountains west of Calgary. The company also agreed to establish a lumber mill at Calgary by 1886 using the logs harvested from the leased timber land which flanked the Bow, Kananskis and Spray rivers. This was the beginning of the Eau Claire and Bow River Sawmill Company.

Early in 1886 the Americans dismantled a complete sawmill at Eau Claire and shipped it to Canada via Winnipeg, complete with a predominantly Norwegian crew of skilled workmen working under business leaders wise in the ways of developing new enterprises on the frontier.

When the American freight cars, loaded with a complete sawmill, arrived at Winnipeg, the CPR officials refused permission for the American railroad cars to travel west to Calgary. The Norwegian crew had to unload all the heavy machinery and reload it on CPR freight cars. This took one week of exasperating work. On June 6, 1886, they arrived at Calgary where they pitched their tents by the Bow River. Their first task was to unload the machinery again. On the south shores of the Bow River opposite an island named Prince's Island after their first manager, they worked long hours that whole summer and fall to build the mill and install the machinery. There they established one of Calgary's major industries, which soon would be producing three carloads of lumber daily not only for Calgary but for the surrounding territory some 100 miles in every direction. Many of the Norwegians eventually settled into newly built cottages on streets and avenues close to the mill and formed what is still known as the Eau Claire district. The avenue closest to the Bow River they named Eau Claire Avenue.

Martin Ulvestad, in his 1906 history of the Norsemen in America, reported as follows on these newcomers:

> It is in Alberta that we find the greatest number of Norwegians. The first Norwegian settlement in this province was established in the environs of Calgary in 1880 [1880s]. The founders of this settlement were: Bernt Thorpe, Conrad Anderson, Nils Anderson, I. Ness, L. Pedersen, Ole Foss, S. Soly all from Fredrikstad; Hans Green, A. Hurom and Hans Olsen all from Kristinia; Theodor Strom from Hedemark; C. Anderson from the area of Farsund together with Gilbert Berg. Peder Eide and Charlie Hammer. These men came to live among the Indians and the Canadians.[23]

These pioneers from Wisconsin who moved to the District of Alberta in the North West Territories had first come from Norway. Peter A. Prince, originally from Quebec, was manager of the mill from 1886 to 1916. Bernt J. Thorpe was the millwright. The homes of both Prince and Thorpe now stand transplanted in Heritage Park in Calgary. Theodore Strom was the mechanical engineer who operated the engines and later became much involved with the generation of electric power in Calgary.

Strom has left on record a few memories of when he and Calgary were both young. Here are some of his first impressions of Calgary:

> On our travels through the town we noticed there weren't any pretty women to look at and one fellow, Fred Farrow, said "If there aren't any women here this must be Hell!" Another chap, Charles Hammer, who didn't care for women, said this was the place for him and he would stay. They asked me what I thought about it and I told them it didn't concern me much. This Fred Farrow said if there weren't any girls to kiss he was going right back to Eau Claire. I advised him to stay and told him that kissing the girls was a bad habit anyway. It was like eating soup with a fork; you never got enough.
>
> But there is always a way around if you look for it, and in this case it was easy. We had the native daughters of that day. There were plenty of them and many lived in Elbow Park, too. They painted themselves just as the women of today do, but they did not wear silk dresses and silk stockings as the young ladies of the present time. They always kept themselves rolled up in a blanket. These blankets had black stripes on them, some having just one, and others two, three or four. The more strips these girls had on their blankets, the higher they were in society. So, if a fellow could make friends with a girl with four stripes on her blanket, he knew he had the cream of the land.

At that time there weren't any bridges across the river except the railroad bridges. There was a ferry boat at Fourth Street East, the fare being fifty cents each way, which was reasonable enough, but sometimes when it was in midstream it forgot which way it was travelling. There were very few settlers north of the Bow.[24]

In the fall of 1886, the crew kept busy driving piles, building platforms and setting up the mill machinery in the building erected during the summer. Strom continued to live in his tent beside the Bow River. He has recorded this incident also:

I was usually the first one up in the morning, and one morning when I went down to the river to get water I saw a nice, yellow keg floating there. Not knowing whether it had anything in it, I went out and got it. The contents were tasted and proved to be whiskey. Whiskey was not allowed in those days and when smugglers saw that they were going to be caught, they threw their loads into the river and then rescued them again as they floated downstream. This was one of these kegs. One man in camp offered me fifty dollars for the keg, intending to sell it in town.

There were several in camp, including the boss, that were opposed to liquor of any kind. A conference was held as to what should be done with it. The prohibitionists decided it should be poured down a gopher hole. I felt that it would not have done any harm to have let me have the fifty dollars and responsible human beings have the whiskey instead of drowning poor dumb gophers with it. The whiskey was dumped and the laugh was on me. In my opinion their reasoning was not very well balanced and I told them so.[25]

Strom reported that the young Norwegians had considerable contact with the Indians around Calgary:

We had heard lots of stories of the Indians and what to expect of them, but the scalpers did not come. There was a big Indian camp along the river near Shaganappi and they used to come over where we were working and pick up wood. There was one great six-foot Indian who would walk around and point out the wood for his squaw to pick up and carry. She carried two papooses on her back in her shawl and carried the wood in front. She was so loaded down that she could just wabble along.

Conrad, a big strong man in the gang, tied up a bundle of wood and hung it on the Indian's shoulder to make him understand that he should carry it and not pile it all on the squaw. The Indian took the wood off his own shoulder and hung it, also, on the squaw. Then Conrad took the Indian over to where we were loading logs on a sleigh. While I was lifting one end of the log, Conrad tried to make the Indian lift the other end on to the sleigh, but it was impossible to make him do it. He tried, but he would not lift. Then Conrad told the Indian he wasn't any good and to get along. He whirled the Indian around and kicked him in the back.

The Indian started down the ice yelling very loudly, with Conrad following after him, kicking all the time. The squaw with all her load also started to run and yell. I followed up with the team and enjoyed it all very much.[26]

The first logs were brought in from Banff by railroad. However, by the fall of 1886 the boom for holding the logs to be floated down the river was ready for the drive in the spring of 1887. Strom had recorded the difficulties in this task:

The first Eau Claire Company drive started in the spring of 1887 and as it was the first drive on the Bow River, it was a hard one. There were windfalls and obstructions on the river everywhere. It was a very sad affair as six of the drivers were drowned at Kananaskis Falls. The crew were crossing the river in a big boat above the falls, as they had done many times before, but this particular morning the current was a great deal stronger than they had figured on, as there had been a considerable amount of rain the night before. Before they reached the other side they lost control of the boat and were swept fast towards the falls.

There were nine men in the boat, and when they saw that they couldn't make it, they steered the boat right for the falls. The boat jumped the first falls and took in some water. It jumped the second falls and took in more water. When it went over the third falls it went under and six men were thrown out and killed against the rocks before they had any chance to save themselves. The three men who didn't strike the rocks came out without being hurt at all. The bodies of five of the victims were found later during the summer in log jams, but the sixth was never recovered.

It took all summer to get the drive into Calgary that year. It was so cold that there was thin ice on the still water every morning in the early fall and there wasn't much sawing done.[27]

In the winter of 1887-1888, the Eau Claire Company built the first traffic bridge over the Bow River which came to be known as the Bow Marsh Bridge. In the fall of 1888, Strom's company also drove the piles for the first traffic bridge across the Elbow.

In 1889 the Eau Claire Company started their first light plant in competition with a small company called the Edison System. Eventually, Eau Claire became the sole distributor and a forerunner of Calgary Power. In his record, Strom rarely complained but here was an exception:

In the early days there were no unions or government regulations in regard to labor. Long hours and low wages was one of Eau Claire Company's ways to success and when the old company went out of existence they had the advantage of being the only ones in business.

They raised the price of lights considerably but did not raise the wages of their employees.[28]

In those days both steam and water were used to generate the electric power. The steam plant was dependable but when the river was very low some of the needed power could not be supplied. This brought many complaints from customers, including a future prime minister of Canada, as Strom wrote:

The business lights were kept going but the residence lights were left off till the water came up again. The voltage was supposed to be fifty volts but sometimes the lights were pretty dim. The customers complained but no rebates were made. The only thing that could be done if the service was not satisfactory was to have the lights cut off.

I remember coming into the Eau Claire office one day when R.B. Bennett was there. He turned to me and said, "Your lights were pretty poor last night, Theodore. I could hardly find my bed." The manager spoke up and said, "Theodore couldn't help it. We had an ice jam somewhere on the river last night and we were short of water." Mr. Bennett said, "Short of water, that's funny; the lights looked as though they had too much water in them."[29]

The crew who worked on the mill for long hours had little available entertainment in the small town. Strom has provided this insight:

In those days Calgary was a very dull place, as there were no places to go. Then finally the Salvation Army came to town. They started their meetings in Boynton Hall on Eighth Avenue East. There were three fine girls that came to open up the meetings – a Captain, a Lieutenant, and a Cadet. Their meetings were well attended by men all the time. When the drivers got in, in the fall, there would be about thirty of us altogether, who would go down in a body, accompanied by Mr. Brown, an older man, who was our self-appointed guardian.

The officers of the Army were great beggars and were nearly always successful in getting what they wanted, including household goods and so on. One particular time the Captain was asking for a mirror. She said she did not want a small one, but a good-sized one.

Mr. Brown suggested that we, the thirty of us, should buy the mirror and he would present it. We all chipped in and bought a large one that required two men to carry it to the hall. The meeting had already started when we reached there, so we hid the mirror under the steps. At the close of the meeting the Captain asked if anyone had brought the mirror that she had asked for previously. Henry Brown went up to the platform and started to make a presentation speech, and asked some of the boys to go out and get the mirror.

In the meantime, some of us had taken the mirror around to the back. There was quite a good deal of commotion when the mirror was missing, and old Mr. Brown chewed his tobacco harder than ever, which was one of the evils that the Army was preaching against. However, the presentation was finally made by one of us who had taken the mirror and hidden it. The speaker, when making the presentation, said he admitted to being a sinner and not a hypocrite like some of the others.[30]

Several of the Norwegians who worked for the Eau Claire Lumber Company also homesteaded in the Shepard district. Even though they worked long hours at the mill, several could not pass up the opportunity to own land on the outskirts of Calgary.

One of these men was Conrad Anderson, born in Farsund, Norway, in 1858. At the age of 14 he took to the sea in partnership with his older brothers. Their sailing vessel took them to all the large ports of the world on five continents. For years these experienced ship wrecks, storms, scarcity of food, illness and hardships. After these years of adventure on the high seas, they returned to be told that both of their parents had died.

Conrad, now 22, worked his way across the Atlantic, arriving in New York in 1880. For two years he sailed ships on the Great Lakes. Then, he began working for the Eau Claire Lumber Company at Eau Claire, Wisconsin, for a small wage.[31]

In the summer of 1884, he bought an old covered wagon and two oxen. He travelled far into the northwest in company with Sevard Soley and Nels Anderson to "sun country." On this long trip they managed to reach the Calgary area in spite of the fact that the oxen became sick and had to be destroyed on the way. They returned to Wisconsin with little or no money and resumed work with the Eau Claire Lumber Company.[32] In 1885, Conrad married Jacobine Kristina Ness who had arrived from Oslo, Norway, several years before.

Then in 1886, when his mill decided to move to Calgary, he and his fellow Norwegians left by rail to the North West Territories. At the age of 28, he filed on NE¼ 14-23-29W4. The family lived in the Calgary Eau Claire District. In 1907, the family, now with six children, Anton, Martin, Harry, Gertrude, Clara and Gordon, left the mill and their home in Calgary to move into a new house on the homestead just west of the hamlet of Shepard.

Anton, the oldest son of Conrad Anderson has left this record:

> The original Blackfoot trail passed only a few hundred yards from our house. On one occasion a line of Indians with their travois passed on their way to the Calgary Exhibition. As they were passing our house, a storm was imminent, so they pitched their tepees in front of our house. After the storm passed, they gathered and pushed one another to every window. My mother was alone with Martin and myself. She was terrified and had locked the doors. Finally, the leader of the tribe came to the window and convinced her they meant no harm, so she let them in. They packed the house

61

full and looked into every drawer and corner, upstairs and down, then went quietly on their way.[33]

Anderson first ploughed with oxen. There were times of loneliness, discouragement and hardship, and the years from 1890 to 1894 were very difficult because of extreme drought. Because the CPR did not fence their right-of-way in the early years, cattle and horses were regularly killed by their trains. In 1892 a terrible smallpox epidemic struck the Calgary and Shepard district, and an isolation hospital was established at Nose Creek.

In 1906-1907 heavy snow and blizzards caused much suffering and the death of many cattle. In 1908, to get more land for his boys, he homesteaded also in the Hand Hills area in central Alberta. In 1918 the hotel in Shepard was converted into a hospital for influenza victims. Conrad Anderson died in 1928 and thus escaped the drought and depression that made life almost unbearable for his wife and children throughout the dirty thirties.

The old homestead, registered for $10, was sold in 1965 to a man from Texas for some $225 an acre. The big house and the driveway of red maples are still landmarks. Today, as the City of Calgary continues to spread, the Red Maple Farm of 817 acres is valued at 7.6 million dollars.[34] The good black soil will soon be swallowed up by the asphalt jungle and concrete block buildings of Calgary's industrial expansion.

The youngest son, J. Gordon Anderson, was a veterinarian in Calgary for years, also serving as the official veterinarian for the Calgary Stampede's chuckwagon races and the Calgary Zoo. Before he died, he wrote this tribute to his parents:

> . . . little reference has been made to mother who too was a product of Norway and who, like our Dad, typified the venturesome pioneer spirit of their forefathers. Those of us who survive are particularly proud of the contributions and loyalties generated toward the community in which they lived and served, and toward Canada, their adopted land. Their humility, their way of life, together with their devotion one to another, has provided for us a heritage that fills us with pride.[35]

Most of these early settlers of the Eau Claire colony chose to live in Calgary and here they established deep roots in both the early institutions and the community life of the growing town. However, Gilbert Berg (Gulbrand Berge) went on to Edmonton before the turn of the century and established the first general store there. Most of the Norwegians who followed in the next decade were primarily "sod busters" in a triple sense. The first furrows were usually made to plough up the grassy sod for building a home. The sods were about four inches thick, about 14 inches wide and at least 24 inches long. The walls of the sod house were built by laying the sods like bricks with the grass side down. Openings were left for doors and windows. Then either poles or boards were laid across the seven foot high walls. The roof would then be covered with tar paper upon which more sod would be carefully laid with the grassy side up. Sod barns were also very common.

As soon as these habitations were completed, it was usual to plow a fireguard, five or more furrows wide all about the place, to protect the home, the barn, equipment and feed stacks. Prairie fires were a real threat to the early settlers, especially in a dry spring or an open fall.

The third type of furrow in the virgin soil was plowed to provide the fields to grow gardens and grains. In order to receive title to the homestead, it was necessary to have 15 acres broken each year within a three-year period.

In the new land the problem of daily bread was an extremely important concern. In most districts there was enough hay and fodder to make it easy to raise cattle. In the early years there was an abundance of wild rabbits, as Anderson describes the situation:

> Snaring rabbits was much cheaper than shooting them. They were prepared in various ways and didn't taste too bad either. What we didn't eat was food for the cats, dogs and pigs. We were thankful for the rabbits especially in winter when snow lay deep on the ground. Many a settler would have starved without the rabbits because it was often impossible to travel far for supplies.[36]

P.B. Anderson's favorite rabbit story has been recorded:

> A missionary pastor who was plentifully supplied with rabbits on his menu, decided to give his landlady a gentle hint that he was beginning to tire of them. The next time he was invited to say grace he proceeded thus:

> "For rabbit roasted and rabbit fried,
> For rabbit cooked and rabbit dried,
> For rabbit young and rabbit old,
> For rabbit hot and rabbit cold,
> For rabbit tender and rabbit tough,
> We thank thee Lord, we have enough."[37]

INFLUX INTO CENTRAL ALBERTA

In 1875, the *Northwest Territories Act* provided for the survey and maintenance of Indian trails as recognized transportation routes. The earliest settlers followed these uncertain trails as they came by covered wagon, Red River carts, horseback or on foot. With all of their wordly goods piled high on a wagon and perhaps with spare horses or oxen tied behind, it was slow going.

While the CPR had reached Calgary on August 11, 1883, it was not until August 10, 1891, that the first train rolled into South Edmonton. The tracks from Calgary to Edmonton followed closely the old Edmonton trail upon which the stagecoaches had bumped along for several years. With the coming of the Calgary-Edmonton railroad, the prairie schooners, the horse-drawn stagecoaches and the Red River carts usually pulled by oxen soon fell into disuse. In any event, the coming of the railroad opened up the fertile regions of central Alberta and shortened the haul to the homesteads.

The trains stopped at several places such as Lacombe, Olds and Red Deer. For the Norwegians moving in from Minnesota and the Dakotas, Wetaskiwin became the most important stopping place. Here the first building was a large shed where settlers and their belongings were unloaded and protected until they could move to their homesteads. As the numbers grew, there was an immigration tent provided.

Among the first settlers were O. Didrikson and his family who settled just east of Wetaskiwin at Crooked Lake in 1892. Other Norwegians soon followed in 1893, including G. Bronken and his family and Edmund Thompson who later became well known as a land guide to hundreds of Norwegians who homesteaded most of the available land around Wetaskiwin and further east. As a Norwegian, Thompson was influential in persuading his kinsmen to settle in central Alberta.

In the early years, land seekers were few and provided little income for Thompson. For a time he worked with the CPR in the Crow's Nest Pass area both as a labourer and surveyor. Without previous experience, he took on the job of cooking for 80 men in a railway camp.

In the late 1890s, since land seekers were now coming in greater numbers, Thompson spent much more time as a land guide. His horses would haul wagonloads of land seekers out from Wetaskiwin, supplied with food and a spade to probe the virgin soil. Thompson was in demand by the Norwegians, for he spoke their language and was a forthright, informed man who inspired confidence.

Thompson bought and sold land and eventually became a man of considerable means. At one time he owned more than 60 quarters in the Camrose, Wetaskiwin and Cold Lake areas. He later became a partner in a ranching syndicate that purchased a large tract of land near Sexsmith, consisting of lake and lake bottom. After the costly project of draining this land, they kept 2,700 head of cattle, built sheds to house 700 calves and had eight flowing wells in the area. In 1919, after the war, the bottom dropped out of the cattle market. Thompson lost most of his money here, and returned to Kingman to make his home on his farm there where he died in 1926.

It was Thompson who guided the first Bardo settlers to their homestead in 1894:

It was not long until all the land seekers from Crookston were on their way under the guidance of Mr. Thompson who safely brought them to the lonely cabin on the banks of Amisk Creek. They put up their tent and by making use of the cabin managed very nicely while they were looking for homesteads.

Two or three men went with Thompson to a land office located at East Beaver Lake in order to find out which sections of land were open for colonization. They arrived at the land office late in the afternoon and were told that it was after office hours. Edmund Thompson began questioning the agent as to which parts of the various townships were still vacant. He persisted in his questioning so long that the agent finally looked at him and exclaimed, "Why man, how much more land do you want?" When they heard that the agent's name was Kildahl they asked him if he were Norwegian. He informed them that his ancestors had come from Norway . . . and settled in Ireland. The men decided that this Kildahl must be a Norwegian-Irishman.

The four men who first went out scouting were so pleased with the work of Edmund Thompson as land guide that a petition was drawn up requesting that he be appointed as a permanent guide. In due season, the Federal Government granted the request. Mr. Thompson was a born land guide and held this position for many years. He knew the country so well that he could locate any lake, creek or quarter section of land.[38]

Among the earliest Norwegians in that district which came to be known as New Norway were Evan Olstad and his brother Ludvik. As early as 1892 they filed on homesteads for themselves and a number of other relatives and friends still in Minnesota. In the fall of 1892 they returned to the United States. In June of 1893, Evan Olstad and Gullik Iverson came to Canada on a one-cent-a-mile excursion. After landing in Wetaskiwin, they rested a few days in the immigrant tents provided by the Dominion government for use by homesteaders. The tents contained long tables and benches, stoves and bunks filled with hay for sleeping. Then Evan Olstad walked the 25 miles from Wetaskiwin to Duhamel to get a team and wagon to bring the family to the new homestead. They lived in tents on the homestead until the cabins could be built. The tents were pitched along the old Winnipeg trail. Indians travelled close by, frightening the women and children.

Close to where Olstad and Iverson had homesteaded, the village of New Norway arose. Evan Olstad established the first store which served also as a post office. For a while it was thought the name of the place would be Olstad, but since for a long time the population was almost totally of Norwegian heritage, the name New Norway was finally approved.

Evan was one of three men elected to the first incorporated village council on May 19, 1910. Later, he operated a general store in Rosenroll which he moved to Bittern Lake using bob sleighs and 20 teams of horses. In 1915, he became the first United Grain Growers agent in New Norway and later in Duhamel. In 1921 he moved his family to the Peace River district where he homesteaded again. Most of his 10 children set deep roots in the Hines Creek district of the Peace River country.[39]

The story of the Bardo pioneers had been told beautifully in two books, *Pioneer Days In Bardo, Alberta* and *This Land is Our Land.* Both give testimony to a group of people tied together by bonds of a common faith even before they set out for Canada; it was a Christian community that migrated together with their pastor, Bersvend Anderson. Judging from the books, there was a warm current of Christian piety flowing through the lives of these early pioneers.[40] Founded in 1894, the Bardo settlement is still strong. Out of this group has come other settlements and congregations.[41]

There are many common threads that run through the histories of the Norwegian settlements. By selecting examples and incidents, this story begins to unfold.

In 1894 Edmund Thompson drove Ole Bakken out from Wetaskiwin. On the way Ole shared a dream that he had as a young man in Norway. From this dream he concluded that he was to own land by a stream of water and that later a city would be built on this land. After many hours of driving, Thompson brought Bakken to Stoney Creek. Bakken decided to file on SW 2-47-20 W 4th, for this was good land by a stream. The homestead shack of Ole Bakken was made of prairie sod but also dug into the hillside above the stream running through his land. His modest home became a centre of hospitality; many a wayfaring homesteader partook of his homemade bread. Ole's shack faced east on a small ravine which ran into Stoney Creek. Its actual location was on what is now 53rd Street in Camrose just below the Canadian Lutheran Bible Institute. The exact site has been obliterated by the filling of ravines, grading of streets, and various housing developments over the years, but the original site may be given as Lot 18, Block 13A, Plan 6778 AB. A historic marker has yet to be erected.

After engineers surveyed his land for the village then called Stoney Creek, Bakken sold one-third interest in his land to Edmund Thompson and one-third interest to John Paulson, another Kingman homesteader. Paulson immediately opened a real estate office with a view to selling townsite lots. In May of 1904, Ole Bakken had brought Duncan Sampson from Wetaskiwin with a load of lumber and helped him to erect a small store with an upstairs dwelling. Later Duncan Sampson bought Lot 4, Block 2 for $200. Thus, the first lot of Ole Bakken's homestead was sold onto which the first store could then be moved. K.O. Eggen opened a harness shop, Stoney Creek Lumber Company was soon in business under François Adam, A. Tretvold built a "Stopping House" and Ole Bakken began to build the Arlington Hotel which he completed in the winter of 1905. Mail for the early Stoney Creek settlers was driven by coach from Wetaskiwin and left in a soap box in Sampson's store for the settlers to pick up.

By the summer of 1905, the steel had been laid from Wetaskiwin to the new village of Sparling. Typically, the CPR established its headquarters in a low level place so that its heavy cars would not roll away. Thus, the first action of the village overseer, Frank P. Layton, was to borrow $100 under the provisions of the Village Act so that deep furrows could be plowed on each side of main street to drain off slough water from the townsite into Stoney Creek. Thus the duck pond up from Ole Bakken's shack was drained. Now Ole had to go further afield for his fresh meat.

Ole Bakken's dream was being fulfilled. His land was becoming a town, but not with his name upon it nor even the later name of Oslo. The village name of Sparling was also rejected because it was so often confused with Sperling in Manitoba. When the village became a town, those in high places approved a beautiful name – Camrose, a hill of roses. Camrose is now a city and remains the hub for the largest settlement of Norwegians in Canada.[42]

Prior to 1894 most of the land east of Wetaskiwin was virgin land except for the odd squatter or Indian camp or isolated homesteader. Many of the Norwegians who came from the States were relatively well off and well equipped. Thus on May 17, 1894, the Thore S. Grue family and his parents brought with them a wagon, a team of horses, four cows, a plow, flour mill, saw mill and planer, a 12 horsepower stationary steam engine, and a separator for threshing grain. All of this was most useful in opening up the new land around Armena and Hay Lakes into which more Norwegians came to claim thousands of acres of fertile homesteads. These people were resourceful and co-operative and soon built a solid Norwegian community known for its generous hospitality to wayfaring pioneers and the spires of its many Lutheran churches. The Grues are remembered by many for their hospitality. Their house stood by the side of the old Indian trail that came to be known as the Erling trail in the pioneer era.[43] Today this house stands on the Camrose Museum grounds.

The bulk of these Norwegian pioneers that settled in such great numbers in central Alberta had chosen to be homesteaders again. They came by colonist car often attached to the freight train carrying their settler's effects. Haakon Stolee has described their typical arrival in 1902:

> It was about mid-summer when Brynjel and family came to settle in Alberta. . . . Brynjel sold his Dakota farm, half a section for $2,200. Some price for 320 acres! He shipped his horses, cows, implements and furniture in a CPR freight car as was the custom. The car was loaded in Pollock and kept intact until it reached Wetaskiwin, duty free.
>
> I think it is worthwhile to describe such an emigrant car. . . . The few pieces of furniture and household goods were piled high in the rear end of the car and partioned off. In the front end of the car

were stalls for the four horses. Then the stalls and pens for some cows and young stock. In the center of the car were hay, grain, and feed boxes. In some emigrant cars the man in charge of the livestock had his bunk also in the center of the car. The families rode in passenger coaches. These were "special" third class or less. The people had their own cooking utensils, bed clothes and wearing apparel in these coaches. Immigrants did not look for luxury; they looked for economy.[44]

Thus, after some 15 years on the Dakota plains 11 members of the clan left by train to arrive finally at Wetaskiwin. After a stretch of extremely dry years, a wet cycle had again established itself and soaked the land. Stolee described the trip from Wetaskiwin thus:

I shall never forget the trip from Wetaskiwin to the homestead. The families and livestock had to be transplanted. Brynjel and Tom Vikse drove the wagons with their families, clothing, groceries, etc. It was my job to drive the cattle. That meant that I rode bare-back those fifty miles for about four days. It was also my privilege (?) to scout ahead, whenever we came to a mud hole or creek, to find a place to get across. Otherwise we got mired hub-deep. There must have been at least ten thousand such bottomless pits on the way. We built "corduroy" bridges across some of the sloughs. That is, small bush was cut and laid down across the road in the mud. That kept the wagon wheels up.

On the afternoon of the second day out we had crossed several swamps. We had to double up the teams in some places. . . . In fact, the lead team often had to be hitched by chain 20 feet or more ahead of the others so that the lead horses could be on solid ground while the near team was still in the mud or the water. Then when one wagon was safely across, the process was repeated to get the next load to "shore". . . . That afternoon I had been in charge of the lead team as usual, wading after the horses. We came to a Mr. Iverson's farm in the New Norway settlement. I rode up to the house and asked for permission to camp there that night. The girl who met me at the door stared as if she were seeing a ghost or an outlaw. I didn't know what was wrong, but when Mr. Iverson came, he laughed out loud. Then I realized that my face and hat were entirely covered with mud . . .

The men, women and children – eleven in all – were welcomed to the Iverson home that evening. And we surely needed a rest. So did the horses and cattle. The next day we got to the home of Eskil Sand, about 12 miles from the homestead . . . and so in the afternoon of the fourth day we reached "home."[45]

Even though the families, wagons and livestock had been brought to the new homestead in July, the machinery and most of the household goods had been left in Wetaskiwin. It was decided to "raft" these heavy goods to the homestead. Stolee has recorded the saga of "The Battle River Sailors" thus:

The first job was to haul the freight and lumber from town to Pipestone Creek, about six or seven miles north-east of Wetaskiwin. There three rafts would be built and loaded in the creek. This creek led into Battle River and on to Dried Meat Lake and again to Battle River. Ferry Point is on Battle River, a place five miles northwest of Brynjel's home. That would be the place to unload.

With two wagons it took us less than two days to get the machinery and lumber out to where we would launch our "ships." All the groceries and other perishables for the two families Tom Vikse brought home in the two wagons. He drove one team and trailed the other. Brynjel and I started our shipbuilding. The material was cedar lumber 12 feet long. Also a few 2 × 4 spruce studdings. This lumber, plus a quantity of shingles, was to be for building a good-sized barn with hayloft.

The rafts were made eight feet wide, sixteen feet long, and ten inches deep. It was not a difficult matter to build them, using the 2 × 4's as cross-pieces at the top and bottom. The rafts could not be deep because we were told that there were sand banks in the lake. Pipestone Creek is narrow and crooked. That is why we made the rafts only eight feet wide. When they were finished, the machinery, a binder, mower, rake, grain seeder and "brush-breaking" plow plus smaller articles and the bundles of shingles were piled onto the rafts. The rafts were fastened by ropes to float after each other about two feet apart. We did not make fast progress the few miles to Battle Lake. The creek was so crooked in places that when the front and rear rafts touched the bank on one side, the middle raft would rub against the bank on the opposite side. But eventually we made it to the lake. Dried Meat Lake is really a wide stretch of the Battle River, very shallow in places with sand bars at the upper end of the lake.

Those sand bars were tough! At one place we had to take the rafts, one by one, and push across the sand banks. We lightened their loads by throwing all the shingle bundles into the water and setting some of the other things on the sand bars. It took hours of hard work to get everything across the worst sand piles. Fortunately, the weather was sunny and the water warm, just right for wading. It took us four days and nights to transport the stuff this way. Once we tried to keep going all night, but otherwise we anchored at night. We slept on the rafts the first two nights, or rather we tried to sleep, but shingle bundles are not ideal pillows. . . .

Finally we anchored near Ferry Point. It took us two days to get the stuff to B.J.'s place. It had been a hard week, but profitable, and we were not worse for wear.[46]

Jacob Vikse was born in 1850 on the Vikse farm in Haugesund, Norway. After marriage to Aasa Stolee in 1885, he emigrated to Hillsboro, North Dakota, with three of his wife's brothers. Then in 1903, Jacob and Aasa Vikse with their six sons, Torkel, Rosenberg, August, Michael, Conrad and Alfred, decided to be pioneers again in Canada. In 1936, he left a pencil-written account in Norwegian in which he said:

It was in 1903 that we left South Dakota and came to Alberta, N.W.T., Canada. Wetaskiwin was our nearest town, and the homestead I had taken the year before was 63 miles south-east from it. It was not pleasant to travel this long way at that time. It had rained for a long time before we arrived and so it continued to do both day and night much of the time afterwards. It was not possible to take any load to amount to anything. For the family we had a large buggy with a good team of horses, and they set out with one or more of the young boys riding a horse each to follow along with the cattle, and the horses not in harness or saddled. I took a team and wagon with the most essential things we needed to start housekeeping. Finally, we reached our destination, merely a log house, 14 × 16 feet, thatched with sod. There was only a soil floor. The thatch allowed rain water mixed with soil to drop down inside long after the showers were over.

I spent a week in the woods [Spruce Coulee] to get logs to saw for lumber for the floor. It rained every day. When I came home Saturday night, the family had set the table in the middle of the floor and the children sat under it, some crying and some laughing. My parents-in-law were there too and how it looked inside the house you may well imagine.

Monday morning I set out to buy tar paper to put on the roof of the log house, which was again covered with sod over the tar paper. Then for almost a year I spent almost every day in getting logs to saw into lumber for the rough construction part of a frame house. I began to build in the spring, 1907, but then I had to go to Wetaskiwin for shingles, and siding, and the better lumber for top floors, as well as for doors and windows. That was no pleasure jaunt in those days. We were six families that came here at the same time, and when we wanted to go to town for supplies we had to go several of us together so that there would be help to be had when the wagons sank into the deep mud. We would hitch several teams on the wagon that was stuck, and this was repeated time and again and day after day. I made two trips to Wetaskiwin for the materials I needed for the house, and when walls and roof were finished I didn't need to invite the family more than once to move into the new dwelling.

Next was the setting up of fences, and for these we used willow posts and rails cut in the poplar thickets growing all around. Then there was brushing to clear the land we wanted to break for fields. But six of my best horses died of a sickness that was called swamp fever, so I had to buy oxen. In the beginning breaking them was a real circus, but finally it went very well, with three oxen and two horses on the breaking plow. Often the plow got so solidly stuck in a stump of willow or poplar that we couldn't manage to get it loose, and then we had to hitch a team back of the plow to pull it out. Then it was a matter of setting out once more full speed forward, after using an axe on the visible stump. Often the plow would jump out of its furrow with the root fixed to it. . . . This went on day after day that summer.

The next great problem was to provide shelters in the form of log barns for horses and cattle before the coming winter. Haying didn't pose much of a problem for there was an abundance of grass everywhere. Some years later when all the land was taken I had to buy more land, both for pasture and for hay . . . In 1929 I rented the farm to one of my sons. My wife and I moved to the village of Donalda. My wife died December 26 eve, 1935, 74 years old. I am now 86 years old, and will not have too long left before I too will be permitted to move from here. But I must thank the Lord for his goodness and grace that he has shown me to this day.[47]

In 1942, at the age of 92, Jacob T. Vikse was laid to rest in a parkland grave adjacent to Bethany Lutheran Church near Donalda. He was one of the 10 charter members of this rural church. His tribe had multiplied and prospered. His sons and their wives had built enduring homes, farms and businesses. They continued to serve the pioneer community in church, school, business, municipality and civic organizations. They too sense the fulfillment of an ancient prophecy: "The Lord thy God is bringing you into a good land . . . a land of wheat and barley . . . a land in which you will eat bread without scarcity . . . and you shall bless the Lord your God for the good land he has given you."[48]

Among the Norwegian pioneers there were many who could easily be described as "giants upon the earth." Gabriel Dahl was such a man. In 1902 he left Norway on a sailboat over the rough North Sea to England. From there he came across by steamer to America. In Milwaukee, he obtained employment operating a steam hammer for the Allis-Chalmers Machinery Company. From his earnings, he helped all his brothers and one sister to come across. In 1908, he went back to Norway to find his wife.

By this time, he had heard of the plains of Canada where a man could get free land to raise wheat at a dollar per bushel. Late in 1908, he came directly from Norway to Hanley, Saskatchewan, where he first worked as a blacksmith. He soon moved out to a homestead in the Kindersley area of Saskatchewan but continued his blacksmithing in nearby Flaxcombe. In 1915, he moved into Flaxcombe after some tragic losses by fire on his farm. In 1922, he attended the annual "Camrose Week" – a series of evangelistic Lutheran services conducted by the Inner Mission Society of Central Alberta which was largely under lay control. He decided that what he needed most for his family was to live and work in a strong Christian community. Thus, he moved to Camrose where he established both a machine and blacksmith shop.

In those years, the Norwegian settlers in central Alberta were buying more land to support their growing families. It was a Herculean task to remove all the brush from the virgin land yet to be broken into more fields. Dahl saw the need for an improved type of axe to do a better job of clearing the land. Hence he developed an axe in which the blade was fixed to a sturdy axe handle so that it cut a horizontal swath along the ground. When swung by a determined pioneer standing relatively upright, this axe cut a wide swath of bush in clean strokes. So popular did the axe become that over the years Dahl imported vast amounts of expensive Swedish steel which he forged and tempered into these unique axes.[49] In fact, this was the axe that was used to clear much of the bush in central Alberta during the 1920s and the 1930s. Dahl "tailored" an extra wide axe with a very long handle for the big Swede, Uddo Johansson, who stood six feet ten inches tall. The effective use of this special axe by this giant in clearing much land developed into a district legend.

In the early years of settlement, there was little cash income from the homestead fields. Early frosts were a hazard to the heavy crops on the fertile soil. Extra money was earned by building grades for the burgeoning railway lines in the summer and working in logging camps or lumber mills in the winter. However, it was still necessary to spend six months of the year "sitting on the homestead" in order to meet the residence requirement. Also in the early years, money could be made by trapping and skinning muskrats. L.J. Hoveland reported that in 1910 a muskrat skin would bring from 30 to 60 cents. There was also a market for weasel and coyote skins. Later there was money to be made in raising cattle. At the time of World War I, good wheat was selling for over $2.00 per bushel. Under these conditions, the farmers prospered. The race was on to get more land to raise more wheat to get more land to raise more wheat.
. . .[50]

Through all of these years, settlers continued to pour into Alberta. There were many hardships, but the pioneer spirit was equal to the challenge. Most pioneers are able to look back with a sense of victory and a capacity to recall that which was humorous in the midst of trials. Clarence Magneson has left this account:

In the spring of 1910, on my way to my homestead, I stopped at Craik, Saskatchewan, to see my uncle and aunt and there I met two of my old friends, C.M. Wold, and Ole Kasa. They were also heading west and they persuaded me to ride in the boxcar with them and their oxen, instead of riding in the questionable comfort of the passenger coaches of those days. We unloaded our oxen and supplies at Kindersley, remained there for three days and then headed west with loaded wagons pulled by oxen. During the 90-mile trip, we camped on the open prairies except for the last night, when we stopped at Gullikson Brothers (now Excel). This was our first bed rest in 6 days, and these people were most hospitable. We left early the next morning, arriving at our destination at Cereal the same evening, pitching our tent on Ole Kasa's homestead. This was the 1st of June 1910. During the night it started to snow, dumping 8 inches of wet snow on our tent. The tent was not calculated to stand this strain and collapsed. What a mess! The snow did not disappear until June 6th.

The next day we parted company as my homestead was 3 miles south of theirs. I stayed with my future father-in-law, E.O. Bergh, in a sod shack on my homestead. There were no lumber or trees available for roof supports for sod shacks, so four of us went with 4 yoke of oxen and wagons to the Red Deer River valley to get some poles. There was just a trail to follow across the prairie, and the trip took 10 days. In the party were Ole Branes, Gilbert Kasa, Herm Larvik and I.

On the way back, we stopped to visit with a rancher for a few minutes and he offered us some buttermilk. I didn't care for any but my three companions drank several glasses each. About eight miles from the ranch the three buttermilk drinkers got so sick that we had to put up camp. I was actually afraid they were going to die. We finally got some sleep, and the next morning, they felt better. We didn't have any bread left by this time, but I spotted a shack about ½ mile away and thought that perhaps he could spare us a loaf of bread. The occupant, a bachelor, refused to part with any bread, even though I offered him a $1.00 for one loaf. When I got back to camp, one of the boys said they heard cow bells, so we went in search of the herd hoping there would be a cow or two among them. We managed to hold one of the cows still long enough to get a half pail of milk. To this we added our last food supply, two tins of tomatoes, heated it and had a meal of home-made tomato soup. Some salt and pepper would have helped, but nobody was in a position to argue about it. We had nothing more to eat until we got home about 14 hours later.[51]

It was not uncommon for the pioneers to seek "comic relief" especially among the pioneer bachelors who lacked wives to keep them out of mischief. For days, Ole Loken's kitchen stove had refused to burn wood properly. In fact, it smoked so badly that he had to open both doors and windows to clear the choking smoke that spread throughout his little shack. In desperation he found a ladder, climbed up on the roof to check his stove pipe, only to discover that it was plugged loosely with a burlap sack. Instinctively he knew that it could have only been done by his good friend and neighbour, Ole Krogstad. The burlap sack was saved and at the first opportunity when Krogstad drove to the village of Bawlf, the sack was placed in Krogstad's stove pipe chimney. Both men often laughed about this over the years. The incident was usually recalled with the question, "And how has your stove been drawing lately, Ole?"

Others were not fortunate in their first choice of land in Alberta. John Lefsrud, born in Norway, migrated to the United States in 1888. In 1902 the family came to Wetaskiwin but moved to the Lesser Slave Lake a year later. The party included the Lefsrud family with six children, Mr. and Mrs. Soren Fevang and their four children and Anton Lefsrud. At old Strathcona in South Edmonton, they purchased horses and wagons to take them as far as Athabasca landing. From there they travelled the rivers to Lesser Slave Lake by York boats or running ships. These were pulled by Indians, wearing harness, running along the shore of the river. When open water was reached, sails were raised and the breeze carried them along.[52]

After pioneering in this northern area for some years, John and Karen realized the need for more adequate schooling for their large family of 11 children. The return journey to Edmonton was made in 1907 travelling by horses. The family left in January averaging 25 miles per day. By February they were back in Edmonton. Eventually, the Lefsrud family came to the Viking district which had become a place of Norwegian settlement as early as 1902.

Many other settlements were established throughout the province. In the Eagle Hills district near Sundre a settlement of Norwegians was started in 1902. These homesteaders too had first come from Norway in 1885 to Thief River Falls in Minnesota. Eskrick has described some of their early experiences:

> For the first few days they lived in shelters made from boards nailed to trees. Days and days of hard incessant work faced them, building log shacks, bringing in their scanty equipment, their furniture and extra supplies from Olds. Every step of those weary miles of country they battled impossibly muddy trails, and when one wore too deep to get a wagon through, they cut another road around it. Thomas Ronneberg had a big team, one horse weighed 1,800 and the other 1,700 pounds, but there were times when his wagon was stuck solid going up the hill toward home, and he would have to unload and make the grade leading from the river . . . but shacks were completed on each homestead by August, and they began the task of

putting up winter feed for their livestock. They cut wild hay by hand that first year with a scythe. Living within a two mile radius of each other, the homesteading Norwegians worked as one unit, and many hands made those first back breaking months bearable.[53]

The influx of Norwegian settlers after the turn of the century was often diffused. However, another important settlement was established in the Claresholm district and south and east of this early centre.

Ole Jacob Amundsen who was a cabinet maker in Oslo, Norway, emigrated to North Dakota in 1894. After seven years of bad drought in this state, many of the settlers there decided to consider a future in Canada. Claude J. Amundsen has written this about his father:

My father was a first cousin of Capt. Roald Amundsen, who dis-covered the North-west Passage and the South Pole. Some of the same blood was in his veins and when he came to Canada in 1901 it was to see what Canada could offer by way of good and cheap land. He was on a train from Fort Macleod to Calgary when they came to a siding without a name but there was a CPR section house on the right-of-way and a large water tank. He got off the train at this point and went over to the section house, where the section fore-man, a Mr. Fields, and his family lived. After looking the land over he went back to Lethbridge and filed on the quarter section of land where the section house was located. He then went back to N.D. and advised everyone about the land flowing with milk and honey, and in the spring of 1902 they came in droves . . .

I may say that twenty-five cars of settlers' effects arrived in Claresholm from North Dakota in one day. This, of course, would not be a usual day. . . .

Subsequently, in 1910 my father was appointed Land Agent for the CPR for the Kingdom of Norway and spent some time over there selling land to prospective Norwegian settlers, and they settled, if I remember correctly, around the Bassano area. . . .[54]

In tribute to O.V. Amundsen there now is in Heritage Park, Calgary, Alberta, a building named "Amundsen's General Store." Like many early buildings, this one was used in several different ways over the years. First it was a family home, then a boarding house for railway workers. For 26 years it was the Claresholm Town Hall, and for 23 years the head-quarters of the Royal Canadian Mounted Police in Claresholm. It has been made into a typical small town General Store of the early West.

The great influx of Norwegian settlers especially after the turn of the century was not confined to central Alberta alone. The Norwegians did not hesitate to seek land in many isolated corners of the province. In order to secure free homesteads, they often had little choice. Ronning underlined this problem when he wrote:

Often on my visits to new settlements, I was grieved that our Norwegian people seeking new land scattered so widely. Neither church nor government lent them any guidance. It was very difficult to organize congregations which might become self-supporting.

I felt fully convinced that our church ought to do more to guide and gather our people in the founding of new settlements. Then I began to think about the Peace River district, where there was said to be grand opportunities. Strangely enough, the decision to go there was formed in my mind before I knew it.[55]

Thus it was that in 1912 this elderly missionary and minister took his large family from the pioneer settlement at Bardo and travelled over 400 miles through a vast wilderness to found the Norwegian settlement at Valhalla in the Peace River district beginning the first journey there in 1912.

The 1901 Census of Canada reported only 304 Norwegians in the Alberta area. By 1911, there were 5,761 who had been born in Norway living in Alberta. By 1921, there were 17,614 people of Norwegian origin on the rural front and 3,709 classified as urban dwellers for a total of 21,321 persons. By 1931, there were 21,615 in rural areas and 5,745 in urban centres for a total of 27,350 in Alberta.

After 1930, the immigration of Norwegians to Canada became a mere trickle. In 1931 only 66 arrived in all of Canada from Norway and the number diminished thereafter until the end of World War II.[56]

PENETRATION INTO BRITISH COLUMBIA

The first son of Norway to become a permanent resident of British Columbia is believed to have been Hans Helgeson who settled near Victoria in 1860 during the gold rush era. In that area he became a well-known and influential man who was later elected a member of the legislature. He was also a pioneer of the Queen Charlotte fisheries in partnership with Alfred Magnusson, a fellow Norwegian.

Another isolated settler was John L. Brae from Iowa who settled near Matsqui as early as 1884. In the following years other Norwegians came to join him in that area. Fillip Jacobsen pioneered at Clayoquot on Vancouver Island and was a correspondent to the immigrant press. By 1897 there were some 40 Norwegians at Clayoquot.

Significant Norwegian settlement in British Columbia came after 1893 as a consequence of the activity of land companies and the offer of governmental assistance to colonists. When this became known to discontented Norwegian farmers in Minnesota, they were ready to investigate the situation in British Columbia. The rigorous winters of northern Minnesota and depressed conditions in the 1890s led them to send Pastor C. Saugstad and A. Stortroen to tour the Pacific Coast with an eye to securing land suitable for settlement.

Some years before, a Norwegian anthropologist, F.B. Jacobsen, had made extensive explorations of the coast of British Columbia and his writing caught the attention of Pastor Saugstad who was favourably impressed by the young scientist's description of the land.[57] Saugstad and his companion travelled up and down the coast on steamers, fish packers and Indian canoes. At Bella Coola they met a countryman, Captain Thor Thorsen, who with his family had settled there some years before. They were taken up and down the valley. It seemed to them that the rivers were black with salmon, and they were very impressed.

When they returned to Victoria, they met with the Minister of Immigration, Colonel James Baker, who promised to reserve the valley at Bella Coola for settlement if at least 30 families would locate there. Each family would receive 160 acres free and a road would be built when 30 homesteads had been established.

The two delegates went back to Minnesota. Pastor Saugstad presented a glowing report to the depressed settlers. The news spread widely. In all 84 people from five states joined the pioneering band. Leaving homes in Minnesota, Wisconsin, Iowa, North and South Dakota they departed on October 17, 1894, for Winnipeg and from there by CPR to Vancouver. The colony had been formed under the laws of British Columbia and loyalty to Canada and the British Empire declared as part of their code. A constitution with by-laws was written for the new colony by Pastor Saugstad. Paragraph Two read: "The purpose of this colony shall be to induce moral, industrious and loyal Norwegian farmers, mechanics and businessmen to come to Bella Coola and make their homes there under the laws of British Columbia."[58]

These Christian pioneers of the Lutheran Free Church, aware of the abuse of alcohol both in Norway and on the American frontier, also included in their constitution: "Every member of this colony must abstain from import, manufacture, export or in any other way whatever, the use of intoxicating drinks excepting sacramental, medical, mechanical and chemical uses."[59] The other clauses were regular and secular in tone stipulating name, officers, membership, co-operation, and rules for meetings. The annual meeting could change the by-laws but it was stated that "any alterations shall be submitted to and approved by the Minister of Immigration before coming into force." Membership in the Bella Coola Colony required "satisfactory evidence of good moral character, working ability and possession of necessary means to cover travelling expenses and provisions for one year."[60] The membership fee was set at $500 dollars and it was agreed that the expenses of the trip be equally divided among the colonists.

From Winnipeg they obtained two sleeping cars on the CPR at a reduced rate. One evening while the train made an extensive stop, the Governor-General of Canada, Lord Aberdeen and his Lady, with guests, boarded the cars of the colonists and bade them welcome to Canada. In concluding his remarks he said: "And I would like to personally urge upon you the necessity to hold fast to the fine religious principles which have brought you together. The Christian religion is the foundation for all success in life. Your efforts and your colony of Bella Coola will be a success with the help of God.''[61] On October 20, they arrived in Vancouver and spent the greater part of a week buying tents, tools, stoves and other supplies. The next day the *Victoria Daily Colonist* printed the following news item:

> A party of very desirable immigrants arrived in Victoria by the steamer Charmer last evening. They number 80 persons, and are the advance guard of over 300 Norwegians, who are taking advantage of the settlement terms offered by the Provincial Government to emigrate from Crookston, Minnesota, to Bella Coola, where a good tract of land, already surveyed by the government, is available. The intention of the government is to establish colonies of desirable immigrants on the available lands on the coast of the island and mainland.

Editorializing about the colony, the same *Victoria Daily Colonist* remarked:

> We trust that the expectations and hopes of the Norwegians who are on their way to settle in Bella Coola will be more than realized. Scandinavians make good settlers. They are intelligent, sober, pious, industrious and self-reliant. They do not expect too much. They come from a country where nature is not very generous – where men have to work hard and continuously to gain a comfortable livelihood, and they therefore will not be discouraged when they are required to fact the difficulties and endure the hardships and privations incident to pioneer life.

On October 26, the colonists were summoned to the office of Hon. James Baker who handed each family head a copy of the agreement with the government and concluded his presentation by saying: ''We wish to express our appreciation to you for coming west to help us develop this great province and I speak personally and for our government, when I say as you do in Norwegian, ''Ha saa mange tusen tak'' [have many thousand thanks].[62]

The side-wheeler *Princess Louise* had been chartered to take them to Bella Coola. On the morning of October 27, most of them were aboard when a very drunk Ole Olsen walked up the gangplank shouting ''Hurray for Bellah Houla.'' The pastor firmly ordered him to go below and stay down until he was sober. However, Ole insisted he was not sleepy but needed some more drink from the bottle he hauled out from his pocket as he was going to be dry for a long time in the new colony. In the struggle that ensued, the drunk man was overpowered.

Ole Olsen never got to Bella Coola. A meeting of the managing committee of the colony was held aboard the ship still in harbour. It was unanimously agreed that Ole be expelled from the colony on account of drunkenness and disorderly conduct. Ole was helped ashore, his goods and baggage with him, and his fee of $500 thrust into his pocket. A sympathetic colonist said, "Poor Ole, he never got to the promised land."[63]

On October 30, 1894, Captain John Irving, skipper of the *Princess Louise*, cast anchor at the mouth of the Bella Coola River. The colonists gazed with awe at mountains which rose out of the sea to lose themselves in the clouds. There was no wharf nor sign of human habitation. The land appeared mysterious, with feet in a thick dark forest and head above the clouds.

The crew lowered the lifeboats which were to be used in making the landing, but they leaked so badly that they had to be pulled up again. Captain Irving then blew the ship's whistle. As it echoed between the mountains, the shore came alive and a flotilla of small boats came shooting towards the big ship. To the colonists they first appeared as logs but as they came closer they beheld a swarthy people rowing furiously and calling to one another in gutteral voices. "There are your new neighbours coming to greet you or eat you," observed a crew member.[64]

As the colonists worried about trusting their lives and belongings to the frail Indian dugout canoes, a larger boat approached the ship with a tall slender white girl standing in the bow and calling to them in their own language, "Velkommen til Bella Coola." Ivar Fougner, the first teacher of the colony, never forgot this dramatic moment. Over 40 years later he reported:

> You can imagine our feelings, then, when out of this dusky crowd of red men, chattering in a strange guttural language, there appeared the figure of a ten-year old girl, fair hair flying in the breeze, and with her light dress for all the world like the figure on the prow of a Viking ship.[65]

The beautiful girl was the young daughter of Captain Thorsen, one of the few white families of the valley. Because she had no fear of the Indians, the fears of the colonists subsided also. A rousing cheer went out from the hearts of strong men and women for they felt as if they had come to their own native land.

On the first trip most of the group were men, but on May 6, 1895, women and children followed. In later years more Norwegians came until there were over 200 in the colony. They carved their homes out of the forest and cleared the land by removing more of the heavy trees. In order to fulfill his post as teacher, Ivar Fougner attended Normal School, and became the holder of the first Normal School diploma issued in the Province of British Columbia.

On Sundays, in this jungle of backbreaking work and alternating fear and hope, Pastor Saugstad led his flock in devotion. From a huge spruce block used as a pulpit, he preached the Word of God but only for a few years. He died on March 17, 1897, from a severe kidney infection – the first of the colonists to die. Just above his homestead and for over 10,000 feet rises a mountain – the highest in the valley for many miles. To this day it is named Mount Saugstad as a memorial to a rare pioneer.[66]

The colony struggled through growth and disaster, hope and failure but it remains. Where the wilderness prevailed, there now stands an organized settlement. Articles, chapters and books continue to be written about this unique colony where people still bear Norwegian names. But many have left, including Oscar and John Lokken, now well-known pastors in the Evangelical Lutheran Church of Canada.

Another planned Norwegian colony was established in 1895 at Quatsino at the upper end of Vancouver Island. It came to be known as the Scandia settlement and was headed by Chris Nordstrom. The government provided legal surveys and some roads but failed to provide early boat and mail service to this remote area. Hence, the colony failed to grow or to develop into a permanent settlement.[67]

After 1890, sailors and fishermen began to make their homes in coastal towns. The gold rush to the Fraser River in 1858 had first attracted dozens of Norwegian Americans, but most of these returned to the United States. However, as time went on more and more Norwegians obtained small holdings along the coast, and with their limited farming combined such activities as fishing and logging. Many became involved with large fishing and canning industries. Soon Norwegian settlers began to penetrate far into the inner valleys of British Columbia as a scattered people.

The concept of planned colonies exemplified by Bella Coola and Quatsino was not continued. Rather the Norwegians were scattered in all directions like sheep without a shepherd. Before 1901 it is estimated that there were fewer than 500 Norwegians in British Columbia. Ulvestad has offered this explanation:

> The Norwegians are a seafaring people who first look around along the coast. Then, when some of them have become tired of life on or by the sea, they go inland. Furthermore, some of them have such a love for adventure that they are not satisfied before they have tried what the inland has to offer as well as the sea on the coast. They want to see and try everything under the sun.[68]

In 1901 the Canada Census reported only 365 Norwegians born in Norway living in British Columbia. By 1911 this had risen to 3,732. In 1921 the Canada Census reported that there were 6,570 people of Norwegian origin in British Columbia. The number had increased to only 8,258 by the time of the 1931 Census. In British Columbia, people of Norwegian descent are most numerous in New Westminster, Vancouver and Prince Rupert, but there are some in almost every community along the coast where they have been integrated into the mainstream of Canadian life.

The great growth in the number of Norwegians in the Province of

80

British Columbia started after 1930. During the Great Depression many prairie Norwegians moved to the favourable climate of the West Coast. Thus the number of Norwegians here more than doubled from 1931 to 1941. This internal migration did not stop in the decades that followed. The beautiful setting of British Columbia is in many respects like Norway. Norwegians consider it to be an ideal province in which to live during retirement years. Naturally, it is a province with special appeal for immigrants directly from Norway. In 1971, of the 16,350 Norwegians born in Norway and now living in Canada, the greatest number by far, 7,075, live in British Columbia.[69]

FIRST SETTLEMENTS IN SASKATCHEWAN

Saskatchewan got its name from the Indian words *Ki-Sis-Kah-Chi-Wun*, meaning "the river that runs swiftly." Through this vast territory, often referred to as "The Great Lone Land" in the early days, flow both the North and South Saskatchewan rivers. For 200 years it was a part of Rupert's Land. In 1870, it became part of the North West Territories. In 1882 the District of Saskatchewan in the north and Assiniboia were organized within the Territories. Not until 1905 were these districts realigned to form the Province of Saskatchewan.

This area attracted relatively few settlers before the coming of the railroads and the quelling of the last Riel rebellion in 1885. For many decades the population consisted of Indians, fur traders, explorers, halfbreeds, trail freighters and buffalo hunters. Then came the early railroaders, militiamen, missionaries, Mounties, bone dealers, aristocratic promoters and pioneer ranchers. It was not until around the turn of the century that the tide of homesteaders and townsmen from many lands began to flow into this open land. The Canada Census of 1901 reported only 14 national Norwegians in the District of Assiniboia and 14 in the District of Saskatchewan. As in the other areas of the West, the flow of Norwegians came from the United States, started slowly, and then gained momentum as the new century progressed.

That the early Norwegian settlements in Saskatchewan were few and far between at the turn of the century was attested to by Dr. H.C. Holm, Home Missions Superintendent for the United Norwegian Lutheran Church. In the fall of 1903, he spent some time in the Districts of Assiniboia and Saskatchewan. Upon his return to the United States, he filed this report:

> The first place I visited was Hanley, Assiniboia. To my surprise I found between 20 and 30 families in and about Hanley. I spent some time there organizing a congregation, conducting services, and taking steps to set up a parish. During my stay a call was sent to Pastor S.H. Njaa of Hanley Falls, Minnesota. Upon an urgent request from the Department of Missions, Pastor Njaa visited the congregation at Hanley, as well as other mission parishes.

From Hanley I travelled north to Saskatoon, Sask. In Saskatoon I found very few Norwegians; but 20 to 30 miles west of the city are three settlements: Thue, Eagle Hill and Minnesota Settlement. Here the Saskatchewan church was organized and plans were made for a parish.

From Saskatoon I continued north as far as the railroad goes, namely to Prince Albert. In this city there were but a few Norwegians, but east of Prince Albert, from 50 to 100 miles, there are several large Norwegian settlements: Birch Hills, Glen Mary, Carrot River, Star City and Melfort. To give an idea of the extent of the immigration to Canada, permit me to single out one of the above named settlements, Glen Mary, where 150 Scandinavian families have filed on homesteads. I spent some time here; found people who had come more than five years ago – all this time without church activity. Here we organized the Norden church.[70]

Ulvestad, in his early history, wrote:

The first Norwegian settlement in Saskatchewan was founded near Glen Mary in the nineties by the brothers Christian and Ole Boe from Solor, Norway. They came [to Canada] from North Dakota. However, it was not until 1901 and 1902 that the real immigration began. Among those who settled at Glen Mary were Carl C. Larsen from Honefos, Tollef Kjontvedt from Nore, Nummedal, and Carl Hovdeby from Kongsberg. Raising cattle is the principal source of income. Prince Albert, about 40 miles away, was the Norwegian settler's market during the earliest period.[71]

The diverse Lutherans who settled at Glen Mary established a congregation on September 10, 1903. When they celebrated the 25th anniversary of this congregation, the original corner stone of the church was opened. Herein was found a history of the settlement and the church written in Norwegian indicating that the first Norwegian settlers came in November, 1894. There were nine families and five single people who joined the church as charter members for a total of 74 members in this Norden congregation. This area north of present day Weldon remained an isolated outpost of Norwegian settlement for many years.[72]

One of the early homesteaders in the Assiniboia District of the North West Territories, R.R. Reinersten, has written:

I and some friends and relatives filed on land here in the spring of 1902, and later, in the summer my wife and I came here to live on our homestead. Our land was about 40 miles from the nearest railway station. Our first winter in Canada was very severe. There was a great deal of snow, and lacking roads it was impossible to get about. Our cabins were not the best either, and it was far between neighbors. Once when a couple of us were to fetch some cattle from about 50 miles away, an extremely strong snow storm broke at sunset. We rode into the wind as best we could, and finally saw a light, far in the distance. We headed for this, but happened to get out on a lake, where we were nearly lost since there were many holes in the ice. When we came to the place, our noses and faces were frozen. It was eleven below zero.

The nearest post office was 18 miles away. Once when my wife and I had been to a neighbor 4 miles from our place to get the mail that he had brought for us, we got lost, and mucked about in our moccasins until late at night when we found our snow-covered cabin. The following day was one of storm and drifting snow; we were lucky to be able to get home.

The following spring my brothers-in-law, O.G. Knudsen and Haakon Holmendal came from South Dakota with their families. I went to town to get them. When we set out home over the bad roads we were often stuck with our heavy loads. Over the worst sloughs and creeks we had to carry the womenfolks, children and all that was in the wagon, in snow water to our knees. Sometimes we had all we could do to get our horses out of "the slough of despond." But we got through that time also. Now things have improved so that it is quite possible for folks to live here.[73]

Many of the Norwegian pioneers who came from North Dakota or even Montana simply loaded their wagons and drove across an uncertain boundary line into Canada. In those early years in the big wide country there was little "red tape" and customs officials were few and far between.

From a far vantage point, the prairie appeared flat and safe for wagon travel, but this illusion soon proved to be a false one. The heavy grass obscured the stones, the piles of buffalo bones, deeply grooved animal trails and the holes of burrowing animals, all of which pitched the wagon from side to side, jarring the bodies of the passengers to the bone.

As they travelled on they would suddenly find that the flat prairie dropped off into deep ravines and coulees that somehow had to be circumvented. Then they would come to fast moving rivers and streams often flowing in beds of soft mud, gravel or quicksand. They learned too late in some cases that they must note where the Indian trails led across. Again it was one thing for experienced Indians to ride nimble horses across the rivers and quite another matter for the new settlers to drive over with a loaded wagon and nervous horses. In going down steep inclines, it was necessary to chain some of the wheels to act as a brake. On occasion spokes or chains would break. More than one pioneer was injured or killed as the wagon and horses sped wildly down the steep inclines scattering and smashing precious cargo over the hillside.

Seasonally, the whole outfit would be surrounded with clouds of hungry mosquitoes that rose from the deep grass to torture both man and beast day and night. Often there was no escape from the blazing sun and the steady winds that further tired the passengers and drivers on their endless journey. Then there were sudden showers, persistent rain for days on end or even hailstorms. Safe water was often hard to find and when children cried for milk or water. Neither of which was immediately available, the mothers began to wonder about the long trek into the new land.

When they reached the homestead, they often found little but more flatness and endless grass. Perhaps they would start life in a tent, tether the horses and set up the cookstove out on the bald prairie. Then they had to find a slough where a hole could be dug alongside to filter the slimy water and make the taste a bit more agreeable. After many weeks of major effort, there could be a sod shack and a shelter for the horses all circled by a narrow fireguard. It was a beginning, and for many a beginning never to be forgotten.

A major Norwegian settlement was started in the Outlook district by Hans Mollerud from Sigdal, Norway, who had lived at Grafton, North Dakota, for 10 years. In 1960, at the age of 86 his wife wrote:

> In 1903, Hans went to look for homesteads for himself and seventeen of his neighbors and acquaintances. He got a quarter section for them all right around in one place. We got to be neighbors again like we were in the States and everybody was satisfied. Hanley was our nearest town then twenty-seven miles away. Now our town is Outlook, Saskatchewan, ten miles away.[74]

Mrs. Mollerud recalled that her husband went back to Grafton later in 1903 but that after spring's work he went back up to Canada to build a small house. Because of the lack of materials on the bald prairie, he bought the first homestead shack that had been built at Grafton, tore it down and shipped all the materials to Hanley, Assiniboia, North West Territories. Here he rebuilt a one-roomed shack with "a small upstairs room, big enough for a bed and clothes." After breaking some land on his new homestead, he seeded his first crop of wheat in Canada. Then he again returned to Grafton for the harvesting there.

In the spring of 1906, Hans went back up to Hanley with a carload of machinery, a team of horses and a cow. The family came later by passenger train. Mrs. Mollerud has recorded these memories:

> Hans was already in Hanley to meet us. We stayed in Hanley that night and early next morning we started off for our homestead. It was a beautiful day in the last part of April. We went with horses and a democrat. . . .
> I enjoyed that trip so much and so did the children. When we were halfways we stopped to rest the horses and have lunch. The prairie was green all over and so many flowers I had not seen before. It was like a green flowered carpet. The children had a great time running around picking flowers.

We came to our homestead, our future home, about 7 o'clock in the evening. The furniture we had brought with us was all in the house . . . stove, table, a few chairs and an old rocking chair that by now must be one hundred years old. Hans bought it at a sale when we were getting married. So it was old then. We still have it. I have rocked all my babies to sleep in it. I though that was the nicest time I had when I could sit down with them. We had three children when we came here. Five were born after we came here.[75]

Hans Mollerud had been a trail blazer for those that followed to this prairie land west of Hanley and north of Outlook. Most of the people that settled were Norwegians from Minnesota, North Dakota, Iowa, Illinois and Wisconsin. Only a few came directly from Norway later on. Most of the settlers had been farmers in the United States but some had been business men. They still considered themselves to be Norwegians even though some had already taken out citizenship papers in the United States and several had children who had been born there. Agnes Kolden has prepared the list of all the people who came to the Outlook area in 1903 and 1904. It is a long list of over 40 families, many with children, and over 30 single people.[76] There were many strong community builders in this group, one of whom was P.M. Henricks, who at the age of 60 was instrumental in bringing the large numbers of settlers from Minnesota.

In due course Henricks built up a successful farm and started a Norwegian newspaper, *Norden*. The Government of Norway appointed him as Norwegian consul for the area. He was able to assist many young men to emigrate from Norway. The whole area from Outlook to Hanley and the surrounding areas became a major Norse settlement. By 1915, they had built the Outlook College and established numerous thriving congregations in the area.

In the years that followed up to the beginning of World War I more and more Norwegians poured into this area, mostly east of the South Saskatchewan River and south of the City of Saskatoon. With Outlook College as their educational and cultural centre, some 20 communities of Norwegians established local Lutheran congregations. They began with Larson Post Office east of Hanley but in a few years railroad branch lines were established and villages and towns sprang up all over the area – Hawarden, Strongfield, Loreburn, Elbow, Macrorie, Ardath, Conquest, Bounty, Swanson, Delisle and Pike Lake. Today, this area of some 500,000 irrigable acres is bounded on the south by Lake Diefenbaker, created by the building of the Gardiner Dam on the South Saskatchewan River. It is a land of good soil, much sunshine, water for irrigation and fertilizer available from nearby potash mines. The land is in possession of people of Norwegian origin. The optimism of the early pioneers who moved west of Outlook was reflected in the names of many of their towns and villages: Conquest, Bounty, Sovereign, Rosetown and Plenty. During the Depression their faith wavered but in recent years it has been restored again. Outlook was an area where they always had a crop on July 1 but what they had on September 1 was another matter. With the advent of irrigation, the threat posed by dry, hot summers is largely overcome for many.

There were many Norwegian settlers whose prairie experiences in the United States drove them to seek the shelter of trees and the evidence of abundant rainfall. Opening such land in northern Saskatchewan was back-breaking work, swinging the axe, grubbing roots and breaking a sod full of tough tenacious roots. On some homesteads the brush was so thick that it was impossible to turn a team and wagon around. As long as the driver kept going, small trees could be driven over but to return the driver would have to take his axe and chop out a circle for turning.

It was into such territory that Andreas Hagen came in 1903 from Kenyon, Minnesota. He had made a good start in the United States but he needed more land for his large family of 11 children. He came to Canada by freight cars loaded with machinery, cattle and horses. Hans Hagen, a son of Andreas, has recalled the long trip:

> When we came up we had an immigrant car on the train. . . . It cost us $35 from Kenyon about thirteen or fourteen hundred miles. . . . When a passenger train came along we would swing on a side track. . . . But after one or two stations we would have to swing to the side track again. That's the way we got up here. It took about ten days to get to Prince Albert. I didn't mind it at all. I stayed on the freight car with the stock and horses. We couldn't let the horses down. . . . If they lay down they would get under the planks and couldn't get up. . . . I had a whip and would yell at them and kept them up for ten days. They were big Percheron horses, sixteen or seventeen hundred pounds. . . .[77]

In all the Hagens brought 10 good horses to Canada, but soon these all died due to swamp fever. Hagen then thought it best to buy oxen and break up the new land with these animals. Only after the country was opened up did he return to horse power.

In due course this area around Birch Hills, Brancepeth, Weldon, Kinistino, Melfort, Gronlid and Domremy became another strong Norwegian settlement. To honour the pioneering work of Hans Hagen, the nearby village was named Hagen.

After a three week trip across the Atlantic in 1900, Peder A. Anderson landed in Philadelphia with only 10 dollars in his pocket. This he split with his partner who had no money left. The next four years were spent in Minnesota working on farms, in logging camps and sawmills at low wages ranging from 15 to 20 cents per hour.

Then in the spring of 1904, he heard that there was free land in the North West Territories of Canada and that the Canadian government had been successful in gaining control over the Indians. He and his friends left by train to Regina. After delays due to a Lumsden River flood, balky horses and a spring blizzard, they all filed on homesteads in the Bulyea district north of Regina. Later they built their sod shacks. In his autobiography he has recorded this about the eventual settlement:

Most of us Norwegians were settled in one district. There were a few Englishmen and Scotchmen as well. The railroad track was completed that fall; the first train arrived in Bulyea in November. There were now two stores in Bulyea and they sold almost everything required in the way of food, clothing, hardware and machinery. These two storekeepers opened for business in the spring of 1905; they brought their goods from Lumsden by horses and wagon until fall when the trains started to come. It would be of interest to note that as well as building the first frame houses in Bulyea, I also purchased the first article sold in the store, namely a plug of tobacco. I make this first purchase on a Sunday morning as I happened to be in the store when the storekeeper came with his first load. I begged him to sell me a plug of tobacco. He did, but at the same time informed me that he would not make a practice of selling things on Sunday.![78]

Before leaving for America, Peder had become acquainted with Laura Masseidavog who eventually made her way to Saskatchewan in 1905. They had not seen one another for six long years. Anderson has recorded their reunion:

She had my picture so that she would recognize me when she saw me. I felt at this time that things would be much better if only I had an opportunity to change clothes. However, I purchased the necessary stuff we needed at the store; we had some coffee; and then we set off for my shack out in the country, which was about three miles distant from Bulyea. Things went well as we drove along the crooked roads amongs the poplar groves, but when we arrived at my shack, my young girl friend was most amazed. She asked if this was what I called "my home"? She had never seen a house made of sod before.

We went inside and lit the lamp and a fire and things took on a better atmosphere. I had put a wall of boards on the inside and had put paper over the boards. I had also made a cupboard, plenty of shelves, and I had practically everything in the way of household utensils that was necessary. I had four chairs, one sofa, and one home-made table. I had cut a hole in the floor and dug a small cellar to keep things in. This cellar had to be very tight in order to keep out snakes and other pests. I had four sacks of potatoes in this hole. I also had two small shanties built alongside the house, one to have clothes in, and the other was to be used as a place to keep meat, vegetables, and fruit. It was with a good deal of pride that I showed her my possessions. The future looked very bright for us – as bright as a star. We were two young people starting out in life with the hope that we would one day have a good home, and that soon this wilderness would be tamed and would become a fruitful land.

Next day I went to get our marriage license. We set our wedding date for the twentieth of December, and set about getting things ready for the wedding. All our neighbors were invited to the wedding, which was the first in the neighborhood. . . . Before the day got too far underway, George Nealle arrived with two lively horses hitched to a sleigh to take the young couple to the preacher to get married. The preacher was a Scotchman, and lived seven miles south from where we lived. The wedding party consisted of eight people. The snow was deep and the horses became very tired with such a heavy load in the sleigh. There were packs of wolves in front of us, back of us, and on both sides – a cheerful setting for a wedding. They seemed to be singing a wedding march as we arrived at the preacher's place.

Luck was with us as we found that the preacher was at home. Everything went well, except for the fact that the bride was unable to speak English, and the preacher was equally unable to speak Norwegian. However, we used an interpreter, and that worked very well. We were treated to cake and coffee before starting home again.[79]

One of the earliest attempts to navigate the uncharted waters of Long Lake was made in 1904 by a group of plucky Norwegians who constructed a scow on top of a lumber pile in the flooded town of Lumsden. They paddled their way the 60 mile length of Long Lake to the northern extremity where they debarked after adventures of shipwreck and storm, and dismantled their sturdy craft.

The party of 12 Norwegians arrived in Lumsden from Minnesota in May, 1904, during the big flood. They lived in a tent pitched in the hills because the water on the main street was six ft. and one inch deep. Each day, they rowed to the lumberyard, where they constructed a flat bottomed scow measuring 24 ft. in length, four ft. in width and about two ft. in height. For a mast they utilized two 4 by 4 studding, 14 ft. long. With tar which they used to waterproof the bottom, they christened their scow, "From," which is a Norwegian word meaning to search or to seek.

Finally on Norwegian Independence Day, May 17th, 1904, they launched their craft from the lumber pile in Lumsden, loaded it with equipment, plows and personal effects and set off up the lake for their homesteads. The party of nine who travelled aboard the scow included Gustav Glomlun, John Glomlun, Amund Tunold, Peter Johnson, Rasmus Gredung, John Swenson Brun, John Watne, Gilbert O. Undseth and Thorvald Lakness. Gundar Lakness, Joe Tunold and Martin Masters journeyed from Lumsden by horse and wagon, bringing two teams of horses. They encountered adventures of their own and eventually met the water *voyageurs* at their homesteads at the north end of the lake.

The journey northward in the scow took about a week in all, and was uneventful enough at first. The men rowed much of the time because their sail proved too elastic to be practical. It consisted of two double blankets, sewn together. Like the hardy Vikings of old, this young and courageous group of Norwegians were in their glory sailing the scow up the flooded waterway. "Hard times," exclaimed one of the men, with a touch of scorn. "Why when I was young and strong and when I got on my quarter section, I was sitting on top of the world."

West of Bulyea, they lay windbound for four days. They were forced to unload their goods on shore and wait out the storm. Finally, the strong gusts of wind and snow abated, and the wind changed in the early evening of the fourth day. They started off again, homestead bound. A short distance from Arlington Beach, they ran aground on a big rock just below the surface of the water. They feared their scow would break apart, and they suffered anxious hours before they managed to free themselves and proceed north. The next day, they beached on what is now Knute Hagan's land, and there dismantled their strange craft. The wood was used in the construction of their sod shacks. Some years later in Joe Tunold's sod home, Thorvald Lakness saw a board on the ceiling bearing the name "From." They built the first sod shanty on Gundar Lakness' homestead.

As they beached the scow at their destination, the stove sat in the front end. The first one in to shore took the stove with him, and John Watne, the cook, baked pancakes for the party. Until the sod homes were built, the men lived in their tent. Of the group who made this bizarre journey to their homesteads only Gilbert Undseth and Thorvald Lakness lived in Govan in 1955. One of the original oars used to paddle up the lake is on display in the Govan Jubilee exhibit room.[80]

At the turn of the century, there were many Norwegians who had made an early beginning in North Dakota. Confronted with persistent drought and depression, they began looking for better opportunities. Just across the border, there was the hope of better living in southern Saskatchewan. Through aggressive land agents, Canada was beckoning experienced settlers. The lure of free homesteads was compelling.

Ole Tenold was one of many Norwegians who made the move to Canada. In 1902 he filed on his homestead, built a sod shack and dug out a spot in the side of a coulee hill to serve as a temporary barn and chicken house. Then in 1903 he brought his wife and six children by wagon from Ashley, North Dakota. The youngest child, Ina, now Mrs. Elvin Kvammen, clearly recalls how glad the children were to dismount the wagon and run freely on the homestead now their new home.

It was a lonely and isolated life. Ole had to travel all the way to Portal for groceries and all the way to Estevan for coal. These trips took three days by horse and wagon with nothing but a trail to follow, including the cumbersome crossing of Long Creek.

On one of his long trips, while stopping overnight on the trail, he awoke from his sleep in the wagon. The smell of smoke was very strong. Against the western far horizon in the region of his homestead, he saw the billowing smoke and the bright orange glames of a distant raging prairie fire. But he was many miles from home and there was little he could do but pray that his family and his new home were safe.

The fire did not reach him but as he anxiously travelled on, he soon came to the black smouldering prairie region where all the grass was now burned. For many long hours, he travelled over the blackness not knowing if his family was safe.

One can imagine the relief that Ole Tenold felt when, as he neared the homestead, he saw grass and greenness surrounding his home. Mrs. Tenold and her boys had worked all night carrying buckets of water from the well and had soaked the grass around the house. That, along with the fireguard they had plowed, had saved their belongings.[81]

The terror of prairie fires for the early homesteader has been vividly described by Arthur Bergum:

> Many of these were started when people were trying to burn off grass before breaking. The fireguard was often inadequate and with mile after mile of dry prairie grass the flames would make an eerie sight in the western sky. This was a signal for everybody to get busy; first, to plow fireguards around the buildings, then to gather sacks and water containers and go to fight the common enemy – the Prairie Fire!
>
> This could last for days and was a time to watch and hope for calm weather and the welcome rain. This was also a time when a sudden switch in the wind, when the fire was almost under control, could mean that the monster was off again, in another direction, and miles and miles of rich prairie grass and perhaps some settler's home would be gone before its appetite for destruction was appeased. Then it might burn itself out against a backfire, along someone's thin ribbon of breaking.[82]

In spite of prairie fires and isolation, more and more Norwegians came to Saskatchewan from North Dakota. Mr. and Mrs. Axel Vinge had come to the United States in their late teens, obtained jobs on farms but eventually saved enough money to get married at Sioux Falls, South Dakota. From there they had moved to a homestead at Ashley, North Dakota. Because of an uncertain future in North Dakota, Axel made two trips to the territory which later became the Province of Saskatchewan, travelling by horses about 400 miles each way. In 1904, he discovered after he had returned to North Dakota that the quarter he had filed on some 12 miles from Estevan was only a partial quarter. By proxy, Ole Tenold filed on another homestead for Axel Vinge. Plans were made to dispose of the land in North Dakota. Then in the spring of 1905, a railway car loaded with some stock and settler's effects was shipped to Estevan. The father and his son Arne went with the railway car – a trip which took four days. The mother and eight children came later.

Before leaving for the homestead, he purchased sufficient lumber for the roof and floor of a proposed 14 × 30 sod house. The lumber, door and windows cost about 70 dollars. After the house was built, a coat of plaster made of clay and water was put on the inside walls. This was finally covered with a finishing coat of clay, sand and lime to make the walls white. The sod walls were three feet thick and were plastered with clay mixed with straw on the outside. The roof was made of lumber, tar paper and sod in that order. As soon as the tar paper rotted, the roof leaked. Otherwise, the sod house was warm in winter, cool in summer and always sound-proof.

Axel purchased three oxen to pull a walking plow in order to break the prairie sod. In a long day he was able to break one-and-a-half acres. His first crop was flax which was threshed with a horsepower outfit and put into bags. It took a whole day to haul the bags to Estevan with oxen. When he arrived, the elevators were all filled. Fortunately, he found a place in Estevan to store his bags of flax until the elevator could take his first crop.

The Vinge home became a meeting place in the community, and many bachelors came for meals. Mrs. Vinge baked bread for a number of bachelors, charging only one dollar for baking 100 pounds of flour into bread. Her work was never ending, raising a large family in the midst of poverty and primitive conditions. She was another of those pioneer mothers than never received a medallion of honour in this life. In all she bore 11 children including two sets of twins. Ten were born in North Dakota and three died there; one was born in Saskatchewan and died at the age of twenty. The remaining seven all married and together raised 33 children. The seven children and 33 grandchildren are scattered and include pastors, missionaries, teachers, nurses, homebuilders, druggist, doctor, salesmen, social workers, municipal secretaries and farmers. From pioneer Norwegian stock came a large family that has contributed already to making the Torquay district and the province a better place to live.[83]

Of these, Arne Vinge was one who came with his parents as a young boy to the Torquay area. When he was 18 he decided to try to get one of the few remaining homesteads. Thus in 1912, he stood holding the door knob of the Estevan land office through a long cold night. By the morning hours, he had to fight off, with police help, a group of toughs who tried to push him out of line. But he soon tired of farming, and in 1914 entered the municipal service at Torquay as assistant to Ben Johnson, the secretary. He didn't make very much money, but won the secretary's daughter as his wife. Two years later Arne was named secretary – a post he held for over 50 years.

Arne Vinge also served as secretary of the larger Southeastern Municipal Association. For over 40 years he served as secretary of the Torquay Rural Telephone Company. In 1965, at the giant Diamond Jubilee convention of the Saskatchewan Association of Rural Municipalities, Arne was honoured by the convention for 51 years of service, exceeded at that time by only one other man in the history of Saskatchewan.[84]

He was a dedicated public servant who "had to use tact, diplomacy, common sense and infinite patience as he helped guide the affairs of the municipality and its people through crises that have included fire, famine, droughts, economic depression and insect scourges."[85] His life in Dakota began in a dugout. He started in Saskatchewan in a sod shack. In his lifetime he witnessed the transition from oxen to horses to steam engines followed eventually by diesel tractors. Roads developed from trails to dusty or muddy country roads followed by gravel and eventually by smooth asphalt highways for increasingly efficient automobiles. Before he died there were non-stop jet flights to Norway and the magic of television bringing the world to his comfortable cottage in Torquay. In his first home they burned cowchips and twisted grass to keep warm during prairie blizzards. Then came coal from Estevan mines followed by oil or propane furnaces where a turn of a thermostat kept the home at controlled temperatures without having to carry out ashes.

The above examples have been selected from typical settlements of Norwegians in Saskatchewan. The settlements around many other centres have had to be by-passed; for example, Lake Alma, Macoun, Midale, Moose Jaw and Viceroy; Admiral, Cabri, Chaplin, Frontier, Kyle and Swift Current; Hanley, Langham, Saskatoon and Watrous; Buchanan, Melville, Naicam, Norquay, Preeceville, Rose Valley and Southey; Birch Hills, Fairy Glen, Melfort, North Battleford, Parkside, Prince Albert and Shell Lake. And there were more. Community histories and congregational anniversaries tell much of the local history of these settlements and the part played by the Norwegians. For lack of space, it has been necessary to be selective. Further, this history has aimed to focus attention on the earliest settlements on the frontier.

After the turn of the century more Norwegians came to Saskatchewan than to any other province. Soon Saskatchewan overtook Alberta in its total of Norwegian immigrants. By 1931, there were 39,755 people of Norwegian origin in Saskatchewan; 27,360 in Alberta; 8,258 in British Columbia; and 5,623 in Manitoba. However, during the Great Depression, the number of Norwegians in Saskatchewan declined from the 1931 peak of 39,755 and this peak has never been regained. (See Table 14.)

EARLY NORWEGIANS IN MANITOBA

As has been pointed out earlier, Norwegians came as isolated settlers to the area of Manitoba as early as 1814 in association with Lord Selkirk's project at Norway House and became a part of the Red River settlement shortly thereafter.

The Manitoba Census of 1870 contains information about two other Norwegian families. In the parish of St. Andrew lived "Henry Erasmussen, age 40, born in Norway, son of Bastian Erasmussen." His wife, the former Jean Stead, age 31, was born in the North West Territories. They had five children, all born in Manitoba. The Hudson's Bay Company had granted them lot 540. In the parish of St. Pierre the 1870 Census reports Alphonse Christianson "age 45, born in Norway." His wife Elsie, age 21, and their three children had all been born in Norway. But this is all that is known about these families.[86]

According to Ulvestad, the first Norwegian settlement in Manitoba was established in 1887 in the area of Brown Post Office, Stanley district, by B.O. Holo. He was originally from Saga, Norway, but had first settled in Pembina County in North Dakota and had fought in the American Civil War. This was the lone family to homestead in Manitoba close to the North Dakota border. Soon more Norwegian settlers arrived: Jacob Spangelo, Nila Vigen, Ole B. Nelson, Knud Halvorsen, Gisli Gundersen, Halvor Halvorsen, Kittel Halversen, Thore Halvorsen and Lars H. Lien. Because so many of these had originally come from Numedal in Norway, their first post office in the settlement was named "Numedal." Today no trace remains of this first settlement.[87]

Ulvestad also reports that Ole H. Gilman, originally from Telemark, came to Morris, Manitoba, via North Dakota in 1899. Johannes Johnson and others also settled in this area. Later, Norwegians settled on some of the best farm land in the province, especially in the Starbuck area near Winnipeg.

Before the turn of the century, the Dominion government set aside a large reserve of land for Scandinavians in townships 17-18, ranges 17-18, west of the first meridian on Otter Lake in the Riding Mountain district near the town of Minnedosa. It consisted of 80,000 acres of excellent soil, with good water and ample timber. To woo the Scandinavians, this large reserve was named "New Scandinavia." It was widely advertised in Norway, Sweden and Denmark and through the ethnic press on the American continent. The colony was founded in 1886. While it was settled predominantly by Swedes, several Norwegian families also became a part of the settlement. By 1891, seventy-seven families occupied substantial homes in the new colony. The settlers had also developed large herds of cattle and had 600 acres in crop.[88]

After 1900, the Norwegian population of Manitoba grew rapidly. The 1901 Census reported only 121 Norwegians, while the 1911 Census reported 1,434 Norwegians in Manitoba as born in Norway. At this time the Canadian Census reported all immigrants from the United States as "Americans" irrespective of racial origin. Thus, the 1911 figure above includes only those Norwegians who came directly from Norway. The extent of the Norwegian migration via the States to Canada can be ascertained to some degree by reports from the Canadian Immigration Office at Winnipeg. For example, the 1900-1901 report indicates that about twice as many Norwegians came via the United States as came directly from Norway:

> Mr. J.W. Wendelbo, our Scandinavian interpreter, submits his report for the past fiscal year . . . showing that . . . 194 Norwegians have arrived here from European countries . . . and 377 Norwegians . . . from the United States. . . . The Dominion Land agents report 276 Norwegians to have made homestead entries in western Canada. . . . They are a fine class of immigrants, and any effort to secure them will be much appreciated by the Canadian people of the West.[89]

Winnipeg was a point of embarkation to many other regions of Western Canada. Thus, many who first came to Winnipeg soon moved on to the other western territories, principally Alberta and Assiniboia. Some who first came to Winnipeg from Norway later moved on to the United States. A. Hallonquist, who succeeded Wendelbo as Scandinavian interpreter for the Department of Immigration, reported that for the year ending June 30, 1902, about 10% of the immigrants moved on to the United States. Of those who remained in Canada, about 50% took homesteads. The others found work on farms or in railroad construction.[90]

By the spring of 1903 the influx of settlers was so great that for a time transportation companies had difficulty in coping with the numbers. All immigrant trains were accompanied by Canadian officials who tried to meet the needs of the travellers and offered aid in settling. However, not all arrivals came in this manner. The Commissioners of Immigration estimated that about 25% simply crossed the border in their own wagons at some remote spot and thus were never recorded in official statistics. Nearly all were experienced farmers, with considerable equipment and in many cases considerable cash.[91]

An example of the many who came to Manitoba in the early twentieth century was Ludwig Benjamin Gusdal. He was raised on a homestead in Benson, Minnesota, in a family of 11 children. After completing high school, he attended seminary at Wilmar, Minnesota. But in May, 1905, driven by wanderlust, he bought a ticket on the Great Northern Railway and travelled to Winnipeg. From Winnipeg he took the CPR train to Minnedosa. From there he and another young man, G.M. Strand, walked some 25 miles to Danvers, where he filed on a homestead and also purchased an adjoining quarter section which had a log cabin on it for $700. Danvers was a small colony of people mostly of Norwegian descent but there were also people from Denmark and Sweden. On this trip he stayed long enough to make improvements to the log cabin but then returned to Minnesota.

Just days prior to his nineteenth birthday in November, 1905, he returned to Canada. His daughter Lenore has written about the final leaving:

> His was the first carload of settler's effects to be unloaded by the Canadian Northern, now Canadian National Railway, in the town of Erickson, five miles from his farm in Danvers. In the carload were two horses, three cows, five sheep, a binder (bought for $25.00 from a widow), a small machinery and the usual things to help a young homesteader get started. His enthusiasm of a young country resulted in all members of the Gusdal family moving north.[92]

The area settled by the Gusdals became known as Viking Valley, served today by No. 10 Highway. L.B. Gusdal soon expanded his homestead quarter to a total of 640 acres and later purchased more property near the town of Erickson. In the early 1930s the Government of Manitoba secured the land just north of Viking Valley and established a park. Close by also is Riding Mountain National Park established by the Federal government at the suggestion of L.B. Gusdal.

In 1916, L.B. married Gunilla Hall from a Swedish family:

> Ludwig and Nellie Gusdal raised four children, two girls (Martha, 1917, and Lenore, 1923) and two boys, (Leonard, 1931, and Delmar, 1934) and there are twelve grandchildren. Lenore married a Salvationist and Leonard married a girl raised in the Seventh Day Adventist tradition. Members of the family are reminded of the statement Dad Gusdal made – "that all his kids were marrying funny religions!" Martha and Delmar, however, remained within the fold and all the grandchildren are baptized in the Lutheran Church.[93]

The Gusdal family were charter members of the local Norwegian Lutheran Free Church, an institution which "forms the heart of the Danvers community." The Fiftieth Anniversary booklet of Bethel Church printed in 1957 records that L.B. Gusdal was elected to the first Board of Trustees although he was still not twenty-one. When the Danvers Young Peoples' Society was organized earlier in 1906, he was elected the first president of what is now the Bethel Luther League. All members of his family have been active Luther Leaguers.

Ludwig Gusdal was a community builder. He served the local school board both as trustee and secretary-treasurer. At this school his four children took Grades one to nine. From 1910 to 1916 he served the Municipality of Harrison as councillor for Ward Six. A typical Norwegian, he was a leader in co-operative farm organizations – the local United Grain Growers, the Wheat Pool, and Rural Credit which was a forerunner of the present day credit unions.

In the late 1930s, Mr. Gusdal changed from mixed farming to producing registered seed for the Canadian Seed Grower's Association. In 1966, he was honoured by the Association for outstanding services to the Association and to Canadian agriculture. Viking Valley seed grown on the Gusdal farm has included Thatcher, Selkirk, Marquis Pembina and Manitou wheat as well as Ajax oats and Red Wing and Dakota flax. The wall in his home is adorned with certificates and awards for accomplishments as an Elite Seed and Foundation Grower.

L.B. was known to neighbours, but especially to his family, as a notoriously early riser. When a member of the family made reference to a lovely sunset, he would quickly counter by saying, "It's nothing; you should see it rise."[94]

L.B. Gusdal was not the first Norwegian to marry a Swede in Manitoba, for in 1916 there were 7,571 Swedes compared to 3,367 Norwegians in this province. There were also 1,647 Danes and 11,833 Icelanders.[95] The latter group of Scandinavians had formed large settlements in the area of Manitoba as early as 1876.

As will be discussed in a later chapter, there were major sex inequalities in provincial populations in the early years. Immigration was responsible for a large surplus of males also in Manitoba up to 1931.

IN RETROSPECT: 1886-1930

The span of years from 1886 to 1930 was a time of major developments in the opening of the Canadian West. Roughly, this span of 45 years can be divided into three periods of 15 years each: (1) From the establishment of the first Norwegian colony at Calgary in 1886 to the turn of the century. Essentially, this was a time of early probings and beginnings on the frontier; (2) From the turn of the century to World War I. During these years there was a rapid influx of Norwegians both from the United States and from Norway; and, (3) From 1915 to the end of the 1920s. During these 15 years, agriculture was rapidly expanded and established. Likewise, numerous Norwegian settlements were consolidated during the war years and the "roaring twenties," assisted by a further influx in the late 1920s.

The building of the CPR introduced the first period. After 1900, in the second period, railroad branch lines brought about a mushroom growth of villages, communities and towns all over the West and the greatest influx of settlers that this country has ever experienced. For example, in 1913 Canada admitted 400,870 immigrants mostly from European countries. Of these, 1,698 were Norwegians from across the sea.

In the third period from 1915 to 1930, World War I drastically reduced immigration from all European countries. In the span from 1915 to 1922, the Department of Immigration reported that only 2,381 Norwegian immigrants came to Canada, fewer than 300 per year on the average. This lull in immigration allowed for more permanent building and consolidation. From 1923 to 1930, the flow from Norway increased to new levels, totalling 19,275 for this eight-year period. The peak year was 1927 when 5,102 persons came, mostly to Western Canada. This large influx was due to a severe depression in Norway and the optimistic and favourable economic conditions in Canada. Again, there was the push of adversity and the pull of new hope to a new land. Also for the first time, Norway encouraged some of her people to get off county and city doles by offering help from the government to emigrate. In contrast to earlier Norwegian immigrants, these people had no chance to gain experience or money on the American frontier. They came directly to Canada, usually with limited means and few skills.

From 1927 to 1930, the Norwegian Lutheran Church of Canada stationed Pastor T.J. Langley at Winnipeg to serve as Director of Migration from Norway to Canada. Of the thousands who came to the West via Winnipeg, Pastor Langley reported a new indifference by these Norwegians to the church. He estimated that only some 500 souls joined the Norwegian Lutheran Church in Canada. The rest located in districts where there was no Lutheran Church or else showed no affinity for this institution.[96]

During the 1920s, some 80% of the Norwegians were involved in agriculture in the Prairie Provinces. In British Columbia most were engaged in logging, fishing and ocean transportation. Because this was a time of expansion, the new immigrants found work on established farms or in other extractive industries. There were also developing opportunities in the growing urban centres. Those who sought new land moved to the northern stretches of Saskatchewan or into the fringes of the great Peace River country covering both northern Alberta and British Columbia.

When the Depression struck without warning in the 1930s, many of these newcomers to Canada were sorely pressed and displaced. For the next 15 years, including World War II, emigration from Norway slowed to a trickle.

The Census for Canada reports that there were 93,243 Norwegians in Canada in 1931. Of these, 39,241 were born in this country, 31,451 in the United States, and 32,551 in Europe. Only 27% were classified as urban dwellers with 11% living in cities 30,000 and over. In 1931 the Norwegians in Canada were predominantly rural and scattered far and wide. The greatest concentrations of Norwegians were in the four western provinces. Although in fact there were almost as many Norwegians in Ontario as in Manitoba, they were so scattered and urbanized in the former province that Norwegian settlements were difficult to identify by 1931. Several early settlements had ceased to exist.

All of the Norwegians who came to Canada were influenced by a planned and aggressive advertising campaign conducted by government agencies, railroad, steamship and land companies. Particularly after the completion of a transcontinental railway, it was possible to lure the homesteader to free land and opportunities to earn money in building railway lines, homes and businesses. Besides land there were many opportunities for the labourer.

It was paradoxical that the Norwegians who first formed the major settlements of the Canadian West were usually people who had first passed through Canada on their way to the midwestern United States of America. However, the economic and social squeeze that later developed for the Norwegians in these areas caused them to seek virgin land and new opportunities in Canada. They found this land to their liking but requiring strength, experience and some capital and equipment. So successful were their efforts in these first years that soon they were able to attract an equal number directly from Norway. Together they all became Canadians but maintained many links with both the United States and Norway. In this first half century or so, Norwegians were a significant part of the ethnic mosaic in Canada, particularly in British Columbia, Alberta, Saskatchewan and Manitoba.

It took more than an act of Parliament to open and build this country. It took strong hands and straining backs of many races coupled with iron wills to fell the trees, to break the soil, to plant the seeds and to provide the services sustaining community life. It took unique vision for thousands of separate communities to grow into one nation stretching from sea to sea.

NOTES

1. Arthur Doughty and Chester Martin, *The Kelsey Papers* (Ottawa: Public Archives of Canada, 1929).
2. *The Western Producer,* June 28, 1962.
3. John Franklin, *Narrative of a Journey to the Shores of the Polar Sea* (London, 1824), I, p. 314.
4. Hjalmar R. Holand, "An Early Norwegian Fur Trader of the Canadian Northwest" in *Studies and Records,* V (Northfield, Minnesota: Norwegian-American Historical Association, 1930), p. 2.
5. L.R. Masson, *Les Bourgeois de la Compagnie du Nord Quest, Lettres et Rapports Inédites Vol. I* (Quebec, 1889), pp. 105, 135-151.
6. *Ibid.,* pp. 73-96.
7. Franklin, *op. cit.,* p. 314.
8. Holand, *op. cit.,* p. 13.
9. *Selkirk Papers* (Ottawa: Public Archives), Vol. 79, p. 131.
10. *Ibid.,* Vol. 70, p. 76.
11. Census Reports on the Red River Settlement, 1831, 1834, 1838, 1846 (Ottawa: Public Archives), Series M, Vol. 399.
12. Also see Paul Knaplund, "Norwegians in the Selkirk Settlement 1815-1870" in *Norwegian-American Studies and Records* (Northfield, Minnesota: Norwegian-American Historical Association, 1931), pp. 1-11.
13. Reported by Pierre Berton, *The Last Spike* (Toronto: McClelland and Stewart, 1971), pp. 237-8.
14. *The Calgary Herald,* 1975-03-18.

15. The Camrose *Canadian,* October 11, 1972.
16. Norman Macdonald, *Canada: Immigration and Colonization: 1841-1903* (Toronto: 1966).
17. *The Calgary Herald,* June 4, 1885. This harsh editorial was headed "Drive Them North" in reference to the Indians.
18. *Ibid.,* November 13, 1886.
19. *Ibid.,* March 18, 1975.
20. Glenbow-Alberta Institute Archives on Eau Claire Lumber Company.
21. From the files of Northern Eau Claire Lumber & Building Supplies, Calgary (W.M. Smith).
22. *Ibid.*
23. Martin Ulvestad, *Nordmaende i Amerika* (Minneapolis, 1907), p. 238. Ulvestad states that this first colony was established in 1880 but research indicates that most of these men came in 1886 even though some had been in and out earlier as in the case of Conrad Anderson.
24. Theodore Strom, "A Few Memories of When Calgary and I Were Young" (Calgary: Glenbow Institute Archives), p. 1.
25. *Ibid.,* p. 2.
26. *Ibid.,* pp. 3-4.
27. *Ibid.,* pp. 4-5.
28. *Ibid.,* p. 11.
29. *Ibid.,* p. 13.
30. *Ibid.,* pp. 5-6.
31. Information based on a biography of Conrad Anderson written by his children and kept by Irene Anderson of Calgary.
32. *Ibid.*
33. Anton Anderson in *Tale of Two Townships* (Dalemend Community Club local history).
34. Ad in *North Hill News,* September 22, 1976.
35. *Saddles, Sleighs and Sudirons* (Chestermere Historical Society, 1971), p. 29.
36. P.B. Anderson, translated documents from the family files of Magda Hendrickson, Camrose.
37. Ragna Steen and Magda Hendrickson, *Pioneer Days in Bardo, Alberta* (Tofield, Alberta), p. 79.
38. *Ibid.,* pp. 23-24.
39. See *Memory Opens the Door* (Local History of New Norway and District, 1972), pp. 60-61. Similar local histories provide much useful information.
40. See editorial "Canada Pioneers" in *Lutheran Herald,* August 29, 1944.
41. The author taught in the Bardo district from 1940-42.
42. See *That Golden Trail* (Camrose *Canadian,* 1955), pp. 116-133 which also reported that Norwegian homesteaders adjoining the new town site were: Jacob Elner, Ole Spiedahl, C.G. Erickson, John Jubberness, Lars Larson, John E. Spokke and John B. Larson. By 1906 application was made to the Provincial Government for incorporation as a town. Among

the many new businesses were: Scandinavian General Store by Charles Peterson; Camrose Photograph Gallery by Chris Langbell; Camrose Millinery by Mr. Hoyme; The Otteson Company, C.O.D. Store; Blacksmith Shop of Haugen Asp and Jacob Langbell's Hotel which later came to be known as the Heatherbrae.

43. Dorothy M. Lyseng, *History of the Armena District* (local history).
44. Haakon Stolee, *Stolee Family* (from the personal files of Jacob B. Stolee, Camrose), p. 52.
45. *Ibid.,* pp. 52-53.
46. *Ibid.,* pp. 54-55.
47. Family record as supplied and translated by P.B. Stolee, Edmonton.
48. Deut. 8:7-9.
49. Based on an interview with Ralph Dahl of Camrose.
50. Taped interview with Ralph Dahl of Camrose.
51. From the local history of Cereal and district, 1975, pp. 51-52.
52. Based on the *Lefsrud Story* supplied by Ragna Stolee of Edmonton.
53. See Muriel Eskrick, The Norwegian Settlements: Eagle Hills and Bergen.
54. Excerpts from a letter to Glenbow-Alberta Institute written by Claude J. Amundsen, November 15, 1971.
55. H.N. Ronning and N.N. Ronning, *The Gospel at Work* (Minneapolis, 1943), p. 88.
56. Extracted from Canada Census reports. See Appendix for Tables.
57. For an interesting and detailed account see *Bella Coola* (Vancouver: Mitchell Cliff Kopan, 1970), pp. 219-240.
58. *Ibid.,* p. 246.
59. *Ibid.*
60. *Ibid.*
61. *Ibid.,* p. 248.
62. *Ibid.,* p. 248.
63. *Ibid.,* p. 250.
64. *Ibid.*
65. Clifford R. Kopas, "Norse Canadians" in *MacLean's Magazine,* April 15, 1935.
66. *Ibid.*
67. For a full account of this colony see Kenneth O. Bjork, "The Founding of Quatsino Colony" in *Norwegian-American Studies (Northfield, Minnesota: Norwegian-American Historical Association, 1972),* pp. 80-104.
68. Martin Ulvestad, *Nordmaendene i Amerika* (Minneapolis, 1907), p. 236.
69. 1971 Census of Canada Vol. I, Pt. 3, Table 34.
70. Reported by Harold Engen in his history and quoting in translation *Den Forende Kirke's Aarsberetning* (Minneapolis, 1904), pp. 160-161.
71. Ulvestad, *op. cit.,* p. 239 (Translation).
72. Engen, *op. cit.,* p. 24.
73. Ulvestad, *op. cit.,* p. 240 (Translation).
74. Mrs. Hans Mollerud, *Memories* (Saskatoon: Saskatchewan Archives Paper, 1960), pp. 2-3.

75. *Ibid.,* pp. 4-5.
76. Agnes Kolden, *Recollections of Pioneer Days* (Saskatoon: Saskatchewan Archives Paper), pp. 21-24.
77. See edited transcript of a taped interview with Hans Hagen of Hagen, Saskatchewan, by Dr. G.O. Evensen on September 25, 1972, available from archives of Lutheran Theological Seminary, Saskatoon.
78. Peder A. Anderson, *Pioneering in Western Canada: An Autobiography,* p. 8.
79. *Ibid.,* p. 10.
80. From *The Nokomis Times* (Golden Jubilee edition), August 24, 1955, p. 4.
81. See Carol Mossing, "The History of Tenold School District" in *Our Diamond Heritage* (Local History project of the Rural Municipality of Cambria, 1965), p. 90.
82. *Ibid.,* "The History of Maple View School District," pp. 59-60.
83. *Ibid.,* "The History of Haata School District," pp. 23-24.
84. *Ibid.,* p. 24.
85. *The Leader Post,* March 13, 1965 (Article by Harold Longman).
86. Reported by Paul Knaplund, "Norwegians in the Selkirk Settlement 1815-1870" in *Norwegian-American Studies and Records* (Northfield, Minnesota, 1931), p. 11.
87. Ulvestad, *op. cit.,* p. 239.
88. See Norman Macdonald, *op. cit.,* pp. 205-206.
89. Canada, Sessional Papers, Vol. XXXVI, No. 10, p. 117.
90. Canada, Sessional Papers, XXV, No. 2, p. 103.
91. See Kenneth O. Bjork, "Scandinavian Migration to the Canadian Prairie Provinces, 1893-1914" in *Norwegian-American Studies, XXVI* (Northfield, Minnesota, 1974), pp. 16-17.
92. Lenore G. Dinsdale, "Biographical Sketch of Ludwig Benjamin Gusdal, A Manitoba Pioneer," August, 1962. Mrs. Dinsdale is a daughter and has written this account for the family.
93. *Ibid.,* p. 4.
94. *Ibid.,* p. 17.
95. Census of the Prairie Provinces 1916, Table VI.
96. Stolee, *op. cit.,* p. 42.

FOUR

Black Blizzards and Dark Years

The present generation has difficulty in comprehending the travail of that era known in the West as the Dirty Thirties. That decade was followed by five years of devastating war. Since World War II there have been over three decades of much prosperity and unprecedented progress with only minor slumps or pauses in the growth of the economy. For those who can remember the Depression, the current spectres of inflation, mounting debts and much unemployment present ominous warning signals. Perhaps it is well to recall that there was an era that almost crushed the West.

During the Great Depression, the farmers converted their cars to horse-drawn vehicles, calling them Bennett buggies in derision of broken election promises that under the circumstances could not be kept. Others took two wheels from their cars to make comfortable carts drawn by one horse. In hard-hit Saskatchewan, they called these Anderson carts, named after the premier whose Conservative government had the misfortune to be in power at that time. Then came the war with gasoline and tire rationing to prolong the use of these slow means of transportation.

The agony of the Depression was also prolonged by the dark clouds of World War II. Both the Depression and the war created intense deprivation and destruction. The nation survived, but the losses were cruel and devastating. Not until the heavy clouds of war were lifted in 1945, did the nation heave a sigh of relief and return to new hope and normal pursuits.

In Canada the 15 years from 1930 to 1945 were times of testing and transition. During these unsettling years many ethnic groups, including the Norwegians, could never be the same again. Ethnic groups found one another because in the Depression all faced a common disaster and in the war that followed all faced a common enemy. These commonalities served to promote Canadianism among the various ethnic peoples.

PERSPECTIVES ON PRAIRIE PRODUCTION

In the early centuries the cash crop from the Canadian West had been furs brought by the Indians to various trading posts. This was followed by the export of thousands upon thousands of buffalo hides, many of which were used to make belts for the industrial machines of America. Then with all the buffalo slaughtered before 1885, tons and tons of buffalo bones were gathered from the vast plains and shipped out for use as fertilizer or for refining sugar. For years this harvest of bones was an important cash crop for the West.

In June, 1857, the British government sent an expedition under Captain John Palliser to survey the vast territory lying between the Red River and the Rocky Mountains to determine its future. After three years of thorough work, Palliser described a vast triangular-shaped region of the prairies as too arid for agricultural settlement. A Canadian expedition under H.Y. Hind and S.J. Dawson started in the same year and reached the same conclusion about this area; that it was comparatively useless for agriculture. Both of these surveys were made in very dry years. With this information, the route for a transcontinental railway was projected to run from Winnipeg into the northwest via Battleford and Fort Edmonton. Concerning this more northern area, Palliser reported:

> Almost everywhere along the course of the North Saskatchewan are to be found eligible situations for agricultural settlement; a sufficiency of good soil is everywhere to be found; nor are these advantages merely confined to the neighborhood of the river. . . . In almost every direction around Edmonton, the land is fine, except only the hilly country at the higher level, such as Beaver Hills.[1]

Then in 1879, the Dominion government authorized the railway company which it then owned to send John Macoun to study the resources and potential of the prairie region. At this time rains were unusually abundant throughout the region. Early in 1880, Macoun published an enthusiastic report of the potential of the West in which he classified over 150 million acres as suitable for agricultural settlement. It was this report that led a CPR syndicate to reconsider the route for the new transcontinental railroad.[2] The eventual decision to build the new railroad across the southern route spawned such prairie centres as Regina, Moose Jaw, Swift Current and Medicine Hat. It also opened up vast areas of dry land only marginally suited for grain farming.

As viewed by Macdonald's government, the chief purpose of the CPR was to promote the settlement and development of the West as a part of Canada. Also, the CPR was envisioned as the means of bringing out the potential resources of the West. Thus when Manitoba was made a province in 1870, Ottawa kept control of Manitoba's resources "for the purposes of the Dominion." Similarly, when Alberta and Saskatchewan were formed in 1905, Ottawa retained their resources "for reasons of high public policy." It was not until 1930 that the resources of the Prairie Provinces were returned to the provinces, and then only after a long and persistent struggle.

The early settlers on the prairies had faced several discouraging years

103

of drought and depression from 1890 to 1899. However, the period from 1900 to 1915 was one of sufficient moisture and rising prices for wheat. There was a great rush of immigrants and a rapid development of the means of transportation. The period from 1915 to 1930 opened with the call for greater production of wheat and livestock to meet the exigencies of World War I. When peace came, satisfactory prices for wheat, the manifest advantages of diversified farming, and the development of co-operative methods of marketing produce – all contributed to yet greater production. The acreage in wheat in 1920 was 15,856,391 acres for the three prairie provinces; in 1925 it was 20,942,590 acres, and in 1929 it was 24,277,116.[3] As crop after crop was marketed, with tolerable satisfaction, no one raised questions about over-production or a disastrous fall in prices. Tempted by the ease with which larger and yet larger areas could be cultivated and harvested by means of machinery, the farmers doubled and even trebled their estates and bravely went heavily into debt. All envisioned a bigger and better future for the West.

STRUGGLE, FAILURES AND SURVIVAL

At the end of the 1920s the average Norwegian-Canadian farmer in common with all others was loaded with debt and optimistic about the future. Without warning the Depression struck. It was on October 24, 1929, that the New York Stock Exchange gave one final shudder and collapsed. The whole world awakened to the realization that the abundance and enthusiasm of the late 1920s were but nostalgic memories. The Great Depression was on. During the next 10 years and more the whole world would suffer from its effects.[4]

Those who had gambled on the futures or stock market lost beyond all expectations. Those who held on to their 1929 grain crop in anticipation of higher prices were eventually forced to sell for a fraction of the earlier prices. Suddenly there was little or no money to meet current debts and ongoing mortgage payments. For many it was a struggle even to pay the interest and often this was accomplished by various types of borrowing again at high rates of interest.

Drought and pestilence settled over the West but were particularly devastating in the Palliser Triangle area. The scorching sun of summer burned the spring growth to little or nothing. What was left was often consumed by black clouds of grasshoppers. In some areas of the southern regions hordes of army worms came, stripping every green spot. Overnight, precious gardens were consumed. The ground was so covered with the crawling worms that it was impossible to walk outside without crushing dozens of them in a few steps.

Strong prevailing winds blew the dust so high and so far that it choked both man and beast. Regions hundreds of miles from the Dust Bowl would find that their snow of winter periodically turned grey overnight from the dust settling from a strangely-coloured sky. So strange and dark were these days that people looked and declared, "Here comes another black blizzard."

Drought, depression and dust led to eventual despair, and thousands deserted their homesteads. It had been dry in the prairies before, but the drought of the 1930s was more severe than any which preceded it during the eras of the white man in the West.

There were thousands of Norwegian settlers in the triangular area extending from Lethbridge to Provost and then down to Outlook to Moose Jaw and extending east of Estevan and including the southeast tip of Manitoba. It is impossible now to list or even to total the number of Norwegian families that were forced to leave this area in the 1930s. But some idea of the exodus can be gained by what happened to the many Norwegian Lutheran congregations in the region. In 1920, the Norwegian Lutheran Church had 140 congregations and preaching places in the area roughly described as the Palliser Triangle. In 1945 only 75 remained. Evenson has reported:

The attrition that had begun in the twenties was most pronounced in the thirties. There was almost mass migration from some communities. (In a conversation, one pioneer settler who "stuck it out" said of his community that when it was first settled there was a family on every quarter section [144] of the township; but in 1950 there were four families in the township.) Some took homesteads in northern Saskatchewan and Alberta; some moved to cities of the prairie provinces; some moved to the west coast. (It is related that a Vancouver pastor was praying for a few new singers who would improve the congregational singing. One summer he added a whole choir from a Saskatchewan community!)[5]

In fact, the entire Norwegian Lutheran Church suffered heavy losses from 1929 to 1939. The total membership dropped from 14,108 in 1929 to 10,930 in 1939 exclusive of the membership in the coastal areas of British Columbia and exclusive of the smaller synods of the Lutheran Free Church and the Lutheran Brethren.

The struggle during these years was not limited to those who experienced it most intensely in the dry belt. Death often claimed one or both of the pioneer parents at an early age.

Sten Stenson is typical of those pioneers whose years were hard and short in the new land. In 1899 at the age of 17 he left Norway. After landing in Halifax, he travelled by train to Canton, South Dakota, to work for a cousin there. Here he chose the surname "Gunderson" after his grandfather's first name of Gunder. Many Norwegians were flexible in their choice of surnames, often basing the selection on the name of the farm in Norway or by adding "son" to the grandfather's or father's first name. Nor did they have any hesitation in shortening a long name.

In 1901 Sten Gunderson in company with Severin Olsen left South Dakota for the North West Territories. By feeding and watering animals

105

on a cattle train and sleeping in the grain bin on this train, he gained a free ride to Calgary. From Calgary he proceeded to Wetaskiwin. From here he walked some 30 miles to the future Camrose area by following old buffalo and Indian trails, but having to circle the numerous sloughs and lakes now a part of this parkland region. Here he found his homestead and built his sod house. In 1902, he returned to the United States to marry Marthaellen Olsen, and to bring her to the sod shack on the homestead.

By 1911 he had prospered enough to build a two-storey frame house with nine rooms. The family was growing and by 1919 there were eight children. One daughter died in 1917 at age of nine, and the mother died of influenza in 1919 at age 33, three days after giving birth to her last baby. The two youngest children, Sten and Morris, were raised for a few years by their grandmother, Mrs. Severin Olsen, who was confined to a wheelchair. She died in 1924. Then the father of the family died in 1926, leaving seven orphans on the farm six miles northeast of Camrose. Under the terms of the will and the laws of Alberta, the farm could not be sold until 1940 when the youngest would be twenty-one.[6]

Together this family survived loneliness, isolation and many inconveniences. With pioneer help, hard work and patient endurance, they worked together in a spirit of faith and co-operation. Agnes, the oldest, was only 20 when the father died. Morris, the youngest, was seven, and there were also Stella, Mabel, Clifford and Gunnar. The struggle and survival of this family through the Depression years is a pioneer story in itself.

In the middle of the Depression the brave group gathered enough money to send Sten to the Normal School in Camrose. After a short stint of teaching in rural schools at extremely low salaries, he joined in Canada's war effort. In spite of war injuries, he returned to become an outstanding teacher of music in Alberta schools.

In the three Prairie Provinces, Norwegian immigrants from the United States were predominantly rural people who for the most part settled in those sections which suffered most from drought. Many of them had also experienced dry years in the United States. They were used to adversity and tough going but the drought and depression of the 1930s was for most of them the greatest challenge ever faced. Carl Magnus Houg is typical. As a young man of 25, he filed on his homestead in 1908 at Enchant, Alberta, situated in the drybelt country. He has recorded some of his trials in the family history which he wrote:

> We moved to our homestead in Alberta, Canada in 1910 with our daughter Ellen and our second girl Lillian, who was born on the homestead the same summer. Our first crop year was an absolute failure, with no rains all season. . . . 1912 became a domestic disaster year for our little group, as wife and mother was found to

have contracted T.B. and left with our two little girls for South Dakota. I had to remain to harvest the crop and also to prove up in the land so as to procure a loan to provide funds for taking my wife to some sanatorium [but] the grim reaper prevailed and she passed away March 6, 1913.[7]

The sorrowing father and husband did not return to his homestead until the spring of 1914 when he sowed another crop which was never harvested. Again, he went back to South Dakota but returned in the spring of 1916 bringing his two girls with him for the summer. In the fall of 1918 he married another woman from South Dakota and in the winter of 1919 he once again set up housekeeping on the homestead in Alberta. The first crop year in 1920 was again a total failure. In desperation he moved to another dry farm in the district.

In 1916 he obtained his first threshing rig as crops and prices were good in that year. As Houg puts it, "My threshing activities extended into the early 1930s and embraced a wide and dusty circle around and beyond the Enchant district. Threshing was my life at its best."[8]

Throughout the many dry years the only dependable biennial crop was of another type. Houg eventually had a family of 10 girls and one son. He has written:

What about babies? O yes, they were plentiful and omnipresent. They were strictly a home product, born and raised at home. The mother was shackled to the cradle. Where mom went around the house the cradle went. Sure, they spoiled the youngsters, but what giants they became in their pursuits of the survival of the fittest.[9]

By 1935 the dry years had been so persistent that Houg tried for greener pastures by renting a farm near Hussar, Alberta. His hard luck continued and the crops both dried out and froze out. He returned to Enchant where he purchased an option on a quarter of irrigation land. Irrigation turned the tide for Houg and in the next years he was able to pay off the debts accumulated in the earlier years.

Then the war came. In 1943 his only son enlisted and paid the supreme sacrifice on July 25, 1944. It was then that Houg lost interest in farming which he says "became more and more irksome after that." In the spring of 1949 he and his family moved to Calgary and entered the real estate business in which he prospered. Five years later his second wife died but Magnus Houg still had 10 daughters, 33 grandchildren and eight great grandchildren. At the age of 95, he still survives in his own home in Calgary, living alone but regularly worshipping with the congregation at Trinity Lutheran.

When Houg retired, he decided to write the family history extending back to include six generations. After all he had gone through, and at the age of 82, he penned this poem entitled "Recompense":

We make no claim to prominence
In Science or Art nor noted works;
But there's a priceless recompense,
With us no noted wanton lurks.

By law of gravity we know,
While there is ample room on top,
Still someone has to stay below
With strength to hold the elites up.

Foundations are not built on clouds
But down below on solid rock.
No faulty timbers there allowed,
Naught but the best from proven stock.[10]

Early in the 1930s the government set up a Relief Commission to handle assistance through the appointed relief officers. But before long this responsibility was assigned to the various municipal secretaries who issued relief orders for food, coal, clothing, feed grain, hay and straw, seed grain, machinery repairs, tractor fuel and chicken feed. Applications were taken from those in need and notes signed and liens taken. The food orders were issued monthly at a set date each month. The order would be turned over to the merchant, the merchant would pay the wholesale company with orders. These orders would often pass through a number of hands before they would be returned to the municipal office for payment. Finally, the government provided the money to pay for the various orders. All the orders issued were charged to the individual family head and scores of ledgers were filled with charge accounts recorded by the municipal secretary. One secretary said he had to move the little amount of cash on hand out of the vault in order to have room for all the notes.[11]

Municipalities were compelled to guarantee hospital accounts, doctor's bills and drug prescriptions so that people would get medical attention. At last it got to the stage when hospitals would not accept patients on a municipal guarantee. They could no longer carry on without some cash. Vinge has reported:

> There were times when discouragement and burdens became too heavy and men broke down and wept. Land values dropped so low that no land changed hands. In fact, one non-resident taxpayer wrote to the Municipality and said "do not send me any more tax notices. I am trying to forget that I ever owned this land."[12]

Dust storms came with such sudden blackness that lamps would have to be lit in the early afternoon. Cars became stuck in the sandy dust on prairie roads. Chris Linn, a farmer of the Mount Green district, told how he and his father were working on a field when a severe dust storm blew up. They became separated. Chris did not want to go home until he found his father and kept circling the field for some time. Finally, he gave up and found his way home to discover that his father had returned just ahead of him. Forty years later, the dust banks are still evident on that farm.

In another recollection from southern Saskatchewan, Mrs. Elvin Kvammen told about driving to her sister's home and having to stop many times on the road because visibility was zero. Inside the home, wet cloths were laid along the window sills to trap the fine dust. Blankets were hung over the windows. The plates had to be wiped off before eating as in minutes they would be covered with dust.

Andrew Tenold while plowing a field could not see the furrow after he had completed a round for it was completely filled with fine dust. Horace Johnson recalled that his white chickens became grey after the dust storms.[13]

Under these conditions it was impossible to produce grain crops. Russian thistles did grow. When cut green and flavoured with salt and molasses, they could be used to feed livestock. Mostly, they dried out and rolled across the land, coming to rest along fences only to tumble again when the strong wind changed directions. The author recalls a Christmas visit to Frontier, Saskatchewan, in 1937. Very thin horses were pawing the prairie to get at grass roots. Along the CPR snowfences there was very little snow but haystacks of Russian thistles. Dust was piled in long tapering drifts extending into the piles of thistles. When I came to Frontier I found that one of the jobs for the caretaker of the outside rink was to remove regularly the Russian thistles that rolled over the banks and onto the ice surface. The door to the Post Office lobby had inadvertently been left open and large Russian thistles had blown into the far end of the lobby.

It was remarkable how the farmers and townspeople managed to keep up a courageous spirit and even manifested humour under these trying circumstances. One farmer maintained that it was so dry on his farm that he had four year-old frogs that did not know how to swim. Another declared that his gophers were digging up into the dust to make holes because the hardpan below was much too hard. Then there was the farmer who brought a pail of eggs to town but when he found that all he could get was five cents a dozen, he took the eggs back home. Here he became irritated at the rooster who was perched on a post crowing, began to fire the worthless eggs at the rooster and said, "You have nothing to crow about."[14]

Prices fell so low on farm produce that the farmer refused to sell. It was hard work to shovel a triple-box wagon full of wheat and it was a long haul to town over frozen roads in a bumpy wagon. But it was harder still to have your wheat graded as No. 6 damp and to be offered only nine dollars and a few cents for the total load. In dismay, oue Bawlf Norwegian hauled the heavy load back over the eight miles to the farm. Before nightfall, all the wheat had been shovelled back into the granary. As it turned out, the grain was fed to the farm animals.

Eventually prices on farm animals dropped as well. One farmer shipped a cow and several pigs to Regina. When the cheque came back, he learned that the payment for the cow was not sufficient to pay for its freight and that this charge was the sum deducted from the payment for the pigs. Ferdinand Carlson shipped two sheep. He received a letter stating that he owed a little money on the freight as the sale price of the sheep did not cover the freight charges. "Would he please send the amount by return mail?" Mr. Carlson wrote back, "I don't have any money, but I've got more sheep." Horace Johnson remembers shipping a steer weighing 2,600 pounds. His cheque was $6.00. A five gallon cream can often brought as little as $1.50.[15]

By the fall of 1937 many farmers in southern Saskatchewan were asked to reduce the number of cattle down to a schedule related to the size of the family. The farmers received one cent a pound for the surplus cattle that they were forced to sell. This was done in order to reduce the amount of hay, straw and feed that had to be shipped into various areas. It is safe to say that over 100 carloads were shipped into the municipality of Cambria alone. This had to be carefully portioned out by a municipality that now had so little money that it could not pay wages and eventually could not afford to purchase stationery.[16]

Many loyal and faithful pastors stuck by their flocks in these difficult years. They suffered with their people and did all they could to keep hope alive. Stolee has left this record:

> I preached in Central Lutheran Church in Moose Jaw, Saskatchewan, in 1937. That was the bleakest of the dry depression years on the Prairies. After the service, Mr. Tysdal, Sr. came to me and asked whether our church would be doing anything to supply relief clothing for our people. I could only tell him that I would do what I could to bring this matter to the attention of our church leaders. Dr. Aasgard certainly did do great things for us. As a result of his appeal to our church people in the States, thousands of pounds of good used clothing were shipped to our Canadian people. I remember the shipment of 2400 pounds that I cleared through customs in Estevan which was re-shipped to the pastors of ten parishes. Later, several more shipments came so that the total amount came to several tons. The pastors who were serving here at that time remember the problem of distributing these dresses, shirts and not least of all the high-heeled shoes for the women.[17]

By 1936, 60% of the Norwegian Lutheran parishes were receiving Home Mission Aid from the United States, and others had to be sent

110

emergency aid. During these depression years, the budget ingathering of the churches was a financial disaster. In the wake of economic stress, there was also considerable evidence of moral and religious breakdown in many communities.[18]

In his master's thesis, P.B. Stolee has illustrated an aspect of the problems that developed:

> The dance is not conducive to good morals . . . in the western pioneer settlements. Often it is the only form of social entertainment available, or the almost invariable accompaniment of every gathering, from that of Farmers' cooperatives to Christmas tree programs. These dances are held in the local school houses, or in barn-like halls, and here no one and nothing is barred. Drinking is common, and the worst louts of the countryside as well as those from great distances gather here. The influence upon young and old may readily be surmised. Fighting and "rough house" of a sort impossible in town and city became common for the police are far away, and usually not anxious to take a hand unless it becomes absolutely necessary. In one settlement, more Norwegian in its composition than average, and filled with dancing and drinking young people, eight babies were born out of wedlock in one year. . . . The boom years . . . attracted a great many people to Canada who did not have physical or moral stamina to endure the hardships of the depression years which followed. This was also true of the Norwegians.[19]

In those years there were many who sought solace for at least a day and a night in another prairie institution, the village beer parlour. Here fathers, neighbours and sons lingered long over their beer sharing their mutual woes and idle boastings while they drank themselves into mental stupor. Money so sorely needed for family items and long-term obligations was poured into the coffers of the brewing corporations. Thus, the beer parlour became an elusive galaxy that further compounded problems for many families during the Depression. The Norwegians were far from immune to this approach to problem solving. Many of them drank like fools so that in the process they had the courage to be fools.

The years of the Depression were not all gloom and doom. Neighbours reached out to one another to bear one another's burdens. Somehow when problems were shared the load seemed less heavy. There was time to visit and to plan co-operative approaches to community problems. Everyone seemed to be in the same boat and it was not difficult to reach the conclusion that all would have to pull together to overcome. The hard times were especially difficult for the many immigrants who had come from Norway in the years just before the Depression; but even here there were those that sought to help.

The peak year for Norwegian immigration was 1927, when 5,102 persons were admitted to Canada. This dropped to 2,241 in 1928, rose slightly in 1929 to 2,549 and dropped in 1930 to 1,049. In the whole 15-year period from 1931 to 1945 inclusive only 379 people came to Canada from Norway. Of the 10,941 Norwegians who came to Canada from Norway in the years from 1927 to 1930 inclusive, many had not been able to establish themselves fully before the Depression struck. Some of these found that they could exist by working for board and room on various farms. However, many of those who had found employment in cities and towns soon found themselves unemployed and a part of various city breadlines. Randi Halvorsen has recalled what the Norwegian Lutheran Church at Calgary did for these displaced Norsemen in this time of crisis:

> A lot of immigrants had come in those years and our church base-ment became such a lovely, warm and cosy meeting place where everybody was welcome and good friendships established.
>
> Most of all I remember Christmas Eve 1930 in the church. Times were very hard with so much unemployment and many had nothing. A little group of us got together, and decided we would try to make a Christmas Eve for the lonely that had no place to go and no chance to celebrate the important event. We talked to Pastor Jovaag about the plan, he gave it his blessings, announced it from the pulpit and asked the congregation for help. For several Sundays we stood by the door after service, received donations of money from some and promises of Julekake, Lefse, cake, cookies, pickles and jam from others; everybody shared something. For dinner we would have something that was good and filling so we decided on meatballs, creamed cabbage with a dash of nutmeg and potatoes. Oranges would be a nice dessert because they were not so plentiful at that time. Of course, coffee we had to have and together with all those promised goodies it would be an evening fit for kings. Two of the boys went out in the streets to invite lonely Scandinavians, and gave a personal invitation. Little Christmas Eve the 23rd, Mrs. Nellie Mc-Clung who I worked for, let me have the whole afternoon off, thus I was able to do all the meatballs, and cut up the cabbage. In the eve-ning the committee came together and set up the tables horseshoe-shaped so we could have the feeling we all were sitting together. The decorations were pyramid-shaped piles of oranges, (that was our dessert), with pieces of fir sticking out here and there. The boys decorated the tree they had chosen. The potatoes were peeled and all that was possible to do the day before was done.
>
> Next day some of us were lucky to come to church early to do the rest. Everything got done in time. The evening started up in church where Pastor Jovaag told the beautiful Christmas story. I was sitting in the kitchen looking after the stove and dinner, wondering how many had come. Suddenly I heard, *Gladejul, Hellige Jul* sung by many voices; different Christmas songs followed loudly and clearly.

It was like the roof would lift – what a beautiful sound. I was so happy, the tears streamed down my face. All I could say was Thank you God, Thank you!

The dinner was enjoyed by all, together with the Pastor and family; then it was singing around the tree followed by a variety program by all that would like to contribute to it. I remember an old Swede that sang about his life in verses. Of course coffee and goodies were served as long as they lasted. It was such a cosy, warm and happy evening. The guests had a hard time to leave, but some of us had jobs we had to tend to next day. Those that needed got money for beds when they left. It was many that thanked Pastor Jovaag afterwards. They hadn't had such a nice Christmas Eve since they had left the old country. We that had worked with it felt good and that made us happy.[20]

INTERNAL MIGRATION

Under haphazard land settlement policies, and pulled by selfish promoters, and with little or no guidance from government agencies, many Norwegians settled on homesteads or bought land that should never have been opened to wind erosion. The fact that the CPR had been built on the southern route promoted early settlement of a vast dry belt which was subject to cycles of drought and destruction by grasshoppers. Without irrigation and lacking knowledge of proper management of the dry soil in the Palliser Triangle, thousands of Norwegian families barely survived during the Great Depression. An equal number were forced to move before the decade was over. This tragedy has been underlined by Magnus Bjork:

> Much of the land now held as grazing lease by the ranchers along the Red Deer was broken up by homesteaders at one time, for cultivation. These people, many of them immigrants, invested everything they had in their homesteads, and spent many back-breaking and sometimes heart-breaking hours breaking and working the land. More eloquent than words in describing the labor invested, are the huge rock piles, picked by hand, still standing beside what once were plowed fields. For most of these pioneers, tragedy struck with the drought and depression of the thirties, and the farms were abandoned as many of the farmers moved on, seeking a living for their families, while their land reverted to the Crown. Others, more hardy or more fortunate, were able to stay on until their deaths or retirement, when their land was purchased and added to nearby ranches.[21]

The exodus of people from the general area of the Palliser Triangle was extensive and sad. MacGregor has illustrated that this problem began even before the depressing 1930s:

As many of the homesteaders on the lands extending east from Brooks had found out a decade earlier, that area should never have been settled by small scale dry-land farmers. In 1911 some 2,400 families had lived in it, but by 1926 that number had been reduced to 1,500. Then with incentives provided by the provincial government's Re-settlement Scheme farmers continued to flee until by 1930 only five hundred people – not farm families – were left cringing as the hot winds swept across the shadeless prairies.

North of the Red Deer River a similar migration had carried farmers out of the Youngstown-Alsask area. For in the whole of the Palliser Triangle all of the dry-land farmers' climatic foes had begun to mount a combined campaign. . . . To add to the burden of financial disaster, all of these plagues had been visited in the Palliser Triangle. And these visitations had merely begun, for indeed in a physical sense the Dirty Thirties had only started to strike.[22]

In the whole of the Palliser Triangle six million acres of once-cultivated land drifted unchecked and totally out of control. Fences disappeared under drifts of soil. Road allowances deeply buried in loose sandy soil became impossible stretches as much as when plugged by the snow of winter blizzards.

The Great Plains of the West even today provide evidence of a region where time, work and money were tragically lost and wasted. The area is still dotted with the stark evidence of deserted homes, broken windmills and collapsed barns. Unattended graveyards in many areas are loaded with markers of stone carved with the pioneer names of Norwegian settlers. Each in its own way speaks of shattered dreams and blasted hopes.

Kristian B.L. Jacobsen had a family of four boys and seven girls in 1933. The depression and drought in Saskatchewan forced him to consider relocating. He has written of his experiences in moving to northern Saskatchewan:

In the spring of 1933 we decided to leave the homestead in the Loreburn district and move to about 250 miles farther north. Two four-horse wagon loads, driven by my oldest son, Erling, and myself and a triple boxload driven by Corbett took our necessary machinery needed to operate a farm we had rented from Rev. Njaa at Weldon. The first mishap came before we got as far as Saskatoon when an axle on one of the wagons broke. However we got it repaired without too much delay. Near St. Louis one wheel of my wagon hit a soft shoulder on the road and the load went over. I felt it going so jumped to safety. The only casualty was a small casting on one of the drills. Even the alarm clock I had with me ticked away as good as ever. We arrived at Weldon without any more trouble, and went back for the family and household goods after we had put in some crop. This time we put everything on two trucks. Arne came down from P.A. with his truck to help us move. We were really loaded skyhigh, what with sixteen people big and small, some sacks of flour, furniture, a crate of chickens and the family cat. We left Harold and Hilda after staying there overnight, and all went well until after dark when both trucks bogged down in the Hagen district. A farmer living near by, pulled us out with his tractor and we were soon on our way again. It was now nearing 11 o'clock at night so when we came to a place we thought was where Christian Ganes lived we knocked at the door to ask permission to camp there overnight. We received a warm welcome, and we slept all over Mrs. Ganes' front room floor that night on her soft rag rugs. The men were put up in a granary, and all slept well for we were mighty tired. Next morning we started out again and came later in the day to the farm that was to be our home for the next nine years. I might say here that Erling, Dagny with Agna and the Kaldor boys drove the cattle up, and I think it took them thirteen days. The boys on horseback, and the girls drove the covered wagon.[23]

More people left the sandy brown soils of the prairies to seek the grey wooded soils of northerly regions. Again, many found themselves in pioneer isolation where there were no Lutheran congregations and very few community services. It was a case of starting all over again but with little strength or enthusiasm for the titanic struggle ahead.

The Norwegian Lutheran Church of Canada tried to help in this situation. At its 1937 convention held at Saskatoon it passed the following report for implementation:

In view of the very severe drought conditions which has affected a large part of our Church in Canada, and knowing that members of our church body will be forced to move, and in view of the fact that we as a Church are concerned with their spiritual welfare, therefore we recommend that a committee of three be elected for the northern district of Saskatchewan, also for the northern district of Alberta, to gather the available information and advise intending settlers, as to conditions both as regards church affiliations and suitable places for settling. We also recommend that we have a key man in Southern Saskatchewan, Central Saskatchewan, and Central Alberta, to advise and guide intending settlers to the best of their ability.[24]

The persistent crop failures scattered the people; congregations and institutions faded. People from the prairies moved to such places as Crooked River and Chelan in Saskatchewan, to Sexsmith, Dawson Creek, Montney, Doe Creek and North Rolla in the Peace River block of Alberta extending into British Columbia. Small Lutheran congregations on the west coast received scores of new members, especially from the southern regions of Alberta and Saskatchewan. Thus, Norwegian Lutheran congregations at Prince Rupert and Vancouver grew in the

1930s because of a great influx of prairie people. So many at an older age left their Norwegian settlements to homestead again in isolated regions and to do battle with stumps and roots almost beyond their strength.

Anton and Bertha Odegard, originally from Norway, came to Canada in 1909 via cattle car after spending several years in the United States. Their wagon, along with the horses, was unloaded from the train at Bassano, Alberta. With all their earthly belongings in the wagon, the father and mother and their three young daughters started across the prairie to their new homestead. They settled in the Lomond area, where drought and abandonment of farms began early.

Annie Odegard will never forget those years of searing winds and grey clouds without moisture:

> We tried to strip farm to prevent soil drifting. The seed would blow out of the ground, or if it did root the scorching sun would shrivel it, since there wasn't enough moisture in the soil to give it life. These long, hard years absorbed all the pioneer spirit from most of us.
>
> The Morgan boys, who batched over on the east side of the coulee, brought us some English chocolate one day. It was a treat I shall never forget. Mother, in turn, made some cake out of it and sent it over to them. They saw how needy we were and gave Mother two red flannel shirts, which they could have still used, to make dresses for us.
>
> One time I was a little tardy coming to dinner; when I sat down at my place I found that my brother had eaten my serving of beans. I missed my meal because there just wasn't any more. Often Mother would say that she had already eaten, so that we could have a little extra. . . .
>
> I can still see my mother out beside the house leaning against the siding, which was rough for the want of paint, and looking out across the sand-covered stubble, weeping in silent desperation.
>
> Dad knew that to make a living there for such a large family was futile. They moved back to the States. He found work on the Coulee Dam project. . . .
>
> I was married before they left Canada, so of course was the only one of the family to remain here.[25]

I Remember

When the Depression first struck, I was a lad of 12 in Grade 8 attending the rural school of Scandia No. 2913. I was the oldest of five children raised on a homestead eight miles from the village of Bawlf situated in the midst of a predominantly Norwegian settlement.

For my parents the latter years of the 1920s had been more rewarding than earlier years. In addition to the homestead on which Dad had filed in 1905, he had been able to secure and pay for another 80 acres of good land and had added to both buildings and equipment. The long trips to town had been shortened by the purchase of a Model-T Ford. With a growing family and new confidence in the future which seemed much brighter and more promising, he decided that the time was ripe to buy the other 80 acres of the northeast quarter of section eleven. Therefore, in 1928 he mortgaged the homestead to secure the cash to pay for this land. The mortgage was firm at eight per cent compound interest.

The summer of 1929 was so dry that in the fall he harvested only 600 bushels of wheat, most of this from the field of land just broken in the previous year. Most farmers felt that the shortfall in wheat production in the West would cause wheat prices to rise rapidly. The Alberta Wheat Pool had been organized in the fall of 1923 and the Saskatchewan and Manitoba Pools in 1924. New stability in prices seemed assured under this system that the Norwegians and their neighbours had fought so hard to establish. Under the open marketing system the average piece of No. 1 wheat had dropped from $2.63 in 1919-20 to $1.07 in 1923-24. With the advent of the Pools, prices immediately went up to just over $1.60 per bushel in 1924-25. In the decade from 1919 to 1929 the average price of wheat at Fort William exceeded $1.40 per bushel.

Dad was an enthusiastic charter member of the Alberta Wheat Pool. He completely mistrusted the speculative grain selling of the Winnipeg Grain Exchange. Every fall the wheat prices used to fall to their lowest levels, but he and his neighbours usually could not wait for the markets to improve. There was an urgent need for cash each fall to pay for the twine, repairs, farm debts, threshing and a host of other bills that had piled up over the summer. For him it happened all too often that the wheat prices would rise soon after he had been forced to sell. He suspected that the speculators were getting rich without raising a single bushel of wheat by the sweat of their brows.

In the years before the establishment of the Wheat Pool, he failed to understand the daily fluctuations in the wheat prices. If the elevator agent quoted a favourable price in the morning, he would start out for town with a wagonload of grain. On more than one occasion, by the time he had reached the elevator eight miles away, he would be told that the noon quotations had dropped by as much as five cents per bushel. He had missed the morning prices by an hour. To him it did not make sense that the price of wheat should fluctuate in this way from hour to hour. Nor did he or his neighbours appreciate coming to the elevator with a load of their best wheat only to be told that there was room only for No. 4 or 5 wheat and that these lower prices would have to prevail that day. Dad was also suspicious of the whole grading system, the spread in prices between the grades of wheat, and the fluctuating spreads between the prices quoted at the terminals at the Great Lakes and the actual price on the open market at the Bawlf elevators. He was confident that all of this had been changed for the better under the co-operative marketing system of the Wheat Pools.

Thus in the fall of 1929 he determined to sell very little of his slim crop

117

at the prevailing price of about $1.25 per bushel. With the short crop, he assumed that prices would soon reach the 1925 levels at least. Some of Dad's bachelor neighbours agreed with him and since these bachelors had some extra money they ventured into the futures market and purchased "paper wheat" on the speculation that they could thereby reap where they had not sown. But this was not to happen.

Suddenly the bottom seemed to fall out of the stock markets. The price of wheat fell to unbelievably low levels. By 1930, the price of No. 2 wheat was down to 43 cents per bushel at the local elevator. Because the Wheat Pools had offered as much as $1.00 per bushel in the down payment, all the provincial pools completed the year with many millions of dollars of debt. The general management of the pools was suspended and from 1930 to 1939 the farmers were again subject to the open market system and the Winnipeg Grain Exchange. From 1930 to 1935 inclusive, the average price of No. 2 Northern wheat at the local elevator was about 47 cents. From 1930 to 1942 inclusive the average was about 60 cents. With such prices and the slim crops of the dry years, Dad found himself in real financial trouble especially to meet the payments on the mortgage to which he had so optimistically bound himself in 1928. It was not long before he could pay only the interest. Later the old homestead was saved by legislation that suspended foreclosure on the home quarter. The homestead remained a haven for the whole family throughout the extended depression.

Meanwhile the mortgage hung over the farm like a dark cloud for some 15 years. Every financial decision had to be tempered by the priority of some kind of payment on the mortgage.

By the fall of 1931, I had taken as much high school as could be obtained at rural Scandia. To continue it would be necessary to attend the Bawlf High School. After much discussion and negotiation, it was arranged for me to have room and board with the K.O. Eggens at 75 cents per day on the understanding that most of this could be paid for by bringing in eggs, cream, butter, vegetables and meat. To reduce the charges to $3.75 per week, it was important that I spend Saturday and Sunday on the farm. Thus in the winter time I would ski the eight miles back and forth on the weekends.

In order to have money for books, clothes and incidentals it was essential that I go threshing each fall. This meant pitching bundles for several weeks at $2.00 per day and coming to school as much as a month late each year. Catching up in the various subjects was a real challenge.

By the fall of 1935, I had graduated from the Bawlf High School and desired to attend the Normal School in Camrose. The intensity of the Depression had not lessened and it seemed impossible to secure the $100 tuition fee which had to be paid in advance.

Dad had exhausted his cash resources. By borrowing on his insurance he had been able to purchase a quarter of land for $475 at a tax sale. This was deemed necessary to provide hay and pasture for a large herd of cattle including some dozen or so milk cows which had to be tended and milked twice a day. At least there was some cash income from the cream and butter, but not enough to raise the lump sum of one hundred dollars. Eventually the sum was quietly borrowed from a "private banker," the local Scottish hardware merchant who trusted Norwegians and believed that there was a future in teaching.

A room at $4 per month was rented from Mrs. Norvick in Camrose. Every week a large box of food was brought in from the farm – a distance of about 25 miles. Money saved from trapping weasels and snaring rabbits would pay for books and clothes. Then, just as Normal School opened there was a province-wide polio epidemic. As a result, I found a job threshing again on September 15. This chance to make extra money ended when the Normal School opened again on October 1. Here, Principal Haverstock made the announcement "that time lost will have to be made up in the amount of work covered each day."

When I graduated from Normal School in the late spring of 1936, it was difficult to secure a school since there was a surplus of teachers. After numerous contacts made by driving all over the country in Dad's Model-T Ford, a contract was finally signed late in August to teach Grades 7 to 9 inclusive at Salt Lake No. 979 for $500 for the year. Thus the gross cheque was $50 per month for the 10 months of school. After paying $25 per month for board and room, there was roughly a balance of one dollar per day for the heavy load of teaching both junior and senior high school and serving as principal of a two-roomed rural school in central Alberta.

In spite of the fact that the government school grant of that time was only $1.20 per day per room for a school year of 200 days, before that first year was over the Department of Education ordered the Salt Lake local school board to raise the total salary to $600 for the year retroactive to September 1, 1936. I remember the consternation of the Board in contrast to the jubilation of the principal. Happy day!

After seven years of high school teaching in Alberta, I accepted the principalship of the high school department of a Lutheran college at Outlook, Saskatchewan, for a yearly salary of $1200. By this time I was married and supporting a family with two children. Each summer I would return to the University of Alberta to work on completing a B.A. degree. As often as possible, I would visit my father and mother at the old home.

I remember returning to the farm in the fall of 1944 and that Dad made a dramatic announcement at the supper table that first evening. "Well, Gulbrand, the mortgage has been paid in full . . . but I paid for that land three times." To emphasize this last point, he gave the table a resounding blow with his big hand.

Actually, that mortgage which had prevailed for 15 years was paid for also with "blood, sweat and tears" extending even into the seasons of the night. It seemed to all of us that a long dark threat had been withdrawn and that a new day was on the horizon. And it was.

THE STORM CLOUDS OF WAR

On September 1, 1939, Hitler's bombers and panzer columns began their sweep into Poland. The horror of subjugation descended as a black cloud upon free peoples. In dismay and anger, the rest of the world rose up to crush the monstrous war machine created by Hitler and his gang. On September 3, 1939, Britain was in the war and on Sunday, a week later, Canada too declared war on Germany. In the process the Allies found one another and Canadians discovered their identity and nationhood in a new way.

The general course of the war and its ultimate consequences need not be recounted here. What is less known and of greater interest in this history is the partnership that developed between Norway and Canada during the course of the war as a result of Hitler's attack on Norway.

On April 9, 1940, without warning or provocation the Nazis broke the peace that had lasted for more than 125 years between Norway and Continental Europe. By sea and air they came, bent on the quick collapse and early subjugation of a northerly neighbour. Thousands of Germans, who as children some 20 years before had been saved from starvation by Norwegian help, now returned to kill, capture and enslave those that had treated them as their own children. Hundreds of planes bearing their black Swastikas dropped bombs indiscriminately upon the Norwegians attempting to shatter and demoralize resistance.

The small Norwegian navy and coastal fortresses sank several German warships. A handful of dauntless Norwegian pilots, hopelessly outnumbered, shot down many enemy planes. Unaided the Norwegians stopped the German army for three weeks but German superiority in tanks, artillery and planes forced a withdrawal to northern Norway. Here the fighting lasted another month before active resistance on Norwegian soil came to an end on June 7, 1940.

At the time that Hitler made his attack, Norway's merchant marine was the fourth largest in the world. It seems that Hitler's main purpose in attacking Norway was to strengthen his own diminishing fleet with the Norwegian. However, the 25,000 Norwegian seamen manning Norway's ships, both private and government-owned, needed no coaxing to join the Allies. The Norwegian merchant fleet became a most important help to Britain during the 12 months that she was left to stave off the Nazi attack virtually alone. During the last months of the Battle of Britain which followed the collapse of France, the ships of the Norwegian merchant marine brought in about half of the nation's supply of oil and gasoline and more than one third of all her foodstuffs and war materials from abroad. "Norway's contribution to the Allied merchant fleet has been of decisive importance," declared Sir Ronald Cross, British Minister of Shipping.[26]

It cost the Germans more than 60,000 men and one-third of their fleet plus a precious two months of time. Later events in the war have indicated that these losses were even more decisive than was believed at that time. After 62 days of fighting, the Norwegian Air Force flew to England at the request of the RAF commanding officer and the Norwegian government already in exile. The Norwegian government immediately made plans for the reorganization and strengthening of its air force. The plans for a training base in France were abandoned with the fall of France in June, 1940. Instead negotiations with Canada led to the choice of Island Airport on Toronto Island, Ontario, as the combined training base for the army and naval air force. Some of the trained pilots and mechanics were put straight into the Royal Air Force units in Europe, but during the summer of 1940 more of the personnel were sent to Canada aboard two small steamships, *Iris* and *Lyra*. In the beginning no other facilities than Island Airport were available. Upon arrival in Toronto in August, 1940, barracks had to be obtained for the recruits until a camp could be completed. Lakeside Home was formerly a summer home for the Sick Children's Hospital. It was situated on Toronto Island and very conveniently available at that time. It was not usable in the winter, but in the summertime it was used as a school for recruits. The *Iris*, which had been able to navigate the Saint Lawrence Seaway, was also used for temporary accommodation.

Camp "Little Norway," Toronto, was the first unit to be built in Canada. It was situated at the foot of Bathurst Street, directly across the western channel from the Island Airport. The land, property of the Toronto Harbour Commission, was included rent-free in the contract with that body for the use of the Island Airport. Building had been started immediately upon arrival of the staff in Canada and on November 10, 1940, the camp was officially opened.

In 1940, the camp consisted of the following: an administrative building, an equipment building, a group school, a building housing mess hall, kitchen and canteen, a hospital, two barrack blocks, an officers' mess, an NCO's mess, two officers' quarters, two NCO's quarters, a guard house and garage. These buildings were all standard block size of the single H-type. In January, 1942, a two-storied block was erected. Because it housed the Wireless and Radio School it was popularly known as "Radio City." Shortly afterwards another building was added with a gymnasium and sauna on the ground floor and a reading room and library on the second floor. This building was the pride of the camp. It was named "Haraldshallen," christened and officially opened by HRH Prince Harald. The Royal family regularly visited Little Norway. Their participation contributed greatly to the "Spirit of Little Norway" which

121

also became the name of the training aircraft financed by the personnel themselves. Christening of aircraft and unveiling of names was always a Royal act.

In the late spring of 1941, a property of some 430 acres, situated between Oxbow and Long Lakes and known as Interlaken, was acquired through funds owned by personnel of the air force. Buildings were set up to accommodate 150 personnel including staff. Later it was used as a training camp for recruits. After the war this property was sold to the Kiwanis Club of Toronto and it is still in use.

Throughout the war years young men continued to escape from Norway by devious routes to join the armed services. Because of the particular hazards involved in leaving the coast of Norway and crossing the North Sea to the United Kingdom, this was known as the "hard" route. The "easy" route was to go via Sweden and across Europe and Asia by various routes and thence to the United States and Canada. At a much later date many Norwegian recruits left Sweden by air. The average strength of "Little Norway" was about 700 persons throughout the war years from the the end of 1941.

Having finished elementary training in Little Norway the students were accepted within the British Commonwealth Air Training Plan and were posted to various schools in Canada, such as Service Flying Training School, General Reconnaissance School, Operational Training Unit, Bombing and Gunnery School, Air Gunners' School, Flying Instructors' School, Bomb Aimers' Course and various conversion courses. It soon became apparent that the camp area and the space available for aviation on the Island Airport would be too small to house the personnel and activities needed to carry out all the educational duties and to support the overseas forces. Recruiting continued as young people were still coming out of Norway and making their way to Toronto.

A contract dated January 1, 1942, was entered into with the Department of Transport for the use of the Muskoka Airport or Dominion Airport, Muskoka, near Gravenhurst, Ontario. A hangar was built and a log building was designed and constructed under the supervision of a Norwegian architect who had arrived in Toronto. It was officially opened on May 4, 1942, as an elementary flying training school. From then on the elementary flying training was carried out at this airfield.[27] A recruiting and recreation centre was set up 60 miles further north again, called *Vesle Skaugum.*

Little Norway was unique, for here was the first alien air force training camp in existence on Canadian soil. From this modest beginning in exile, Norwegian volunteers began to flow in from Europe and from all parts of the world including Canada. Those who came can now be counted in four figures.

The training the Norwegians received at Toronto was synchronized with the British Commonwealth Air Training Plan because the Norwegian squadrons fought as independent units but within the Royal

Air Force of England. The first Norwegian unit went overseas to Iceland' in April, 1941, and operated from a base there. The first all-Norwegian fighter squadron complete with air and ground crew arrived in England in June, 1941. These squadrons stationed in both England and Iceland proved to be excellent units and effectively fought back against Germany in numerous brave bombing raids and clashes with the enemy in the sky.

Today there are many Norwegians who remember those critical years of World War II when they were suddenly transplanted from the fjords of Norway to the shores of Lake Ontario, transformed from peaceful, freedom-loving citizens to become determined army pilots trained on Canadian soil at Little Norway. Overall, these special Norwegians in Canada received a warm response from Canadians and Americans alike and were welcome guests in many Canadian homes. Many married Canadian girls. Others returned to live in Canada after the war.

Since the end of World War II, the many veterans from the Royal Norwegian Air Force who have visited Canada have naturally found their way back to Toronto, a city which provided the early home for their training base during the war. Toronto has grown and a visitor will not recognize any sign of the war-time establishments of the Royal Norwegian Air Force training camp, Little Norway, that Canada so willingly housed during the dark years when Norway was occupied and fighting for her freedom.

In order to preserve the history of Little Norway and of Norwegian-Canadian co-operation for future generations, a memorial stone has been brought over from Norway and erected at the Toronto harbour front. The initiative was taken by Norwegian Air Force veterans and the stone was presented to Canada in gratitude for the help and hospitality which made it possible to establish Little Norway and carry out the formidable task of rebuilding and training a Norwegian air force.

The memorial stone is a granite boulder from Lista in southern Norway. It is engraved and carries a plaque well known to most of the people who knew Little Norway, showing two airmen walking on the top of the globe, one standing in Norway and one in Canada, 4000 miles apart. This also represented the distance Norwegian escapees had to travel to reach Canada.

The memorial stone, located just off Bathurst Street on the Toronto waterfront, was unveiled by HRH Crown Prince Harald on September 18, 1976. The meaning of the Indian word "Toronto" – meeting-place – remains a reality for the Royal Norwegian Air Force. The monument is a memorial to the fact of Little Norway in Canada and a permanent symbol of the friendship between Norwegians and Canadians who fought together to preserve principles basic to democratic nationhood.

IN RETROSPECT: 1930-1945

The story of the Depression in the Canadian West is the story of the most tenacious struggle for existence in our history. In this era, the prairie

123

homesteader discovered the tenuous nature of his setting. Suddenly, he was painfully aware that he was a peasant legally tied to the mortgage companies and that taxes and debts were shackles that he could not shake. He thought that he was a free man but now conjectured that his future and his income were being determined by people in the East who seemed to lack understanding of his western problems. A system of tariffs designed to protect the eastern manufacturer forced the price of his machinery and trucks to unreasonably high levels. The more he learned about the freight rate schedules, the more he realized that these had not been designed to build the West but rather to exploit it. He fought to be a part of his own grain marketing system and learned to despise both the Winnipeg Grain Exchange and the sordid practices of the grain speculators who became rich because of his sweat. He spurned the national political parties and voted with others in the West to send political mavericks to Ottawa. He fought with those who saw injustice in the fact that the Prairie Provinces alone were denied control of their own natural resources. Not until 1931 did they gain the control granted to all the other provinces from the beginning. This alone bred real distrust of the central government.

And so in the struggle came the co-operative stores, the credit unions, the Wheat Pools and the medical insurance schemes. The record shows that Norwegians were often leaders and generally active members in these battles. They fought hard for egalitarianism and hence were often dubbed radicals by the elites.

Prior to World War II, the typical Norwegian in the West was a hyphenated Canadian but when the war came, he gave freely of his sons and daughters to defend freedom. In addition he had become closely identified with the spirit of the Canadian West. Stanley has provided this insight:

> The history of the Canadian West from the earliest days of which we have knowledge by written word and oral tradition, has been one of survival and adaptation to environment. Hence my suggestion that the characteristic spirit of the Westerner is that of independence, self-reliance, willingness to strike out on a new path. These are the essence of adaptation and the secret of survival. If a settler did survive in the Canadian West, "far from markets, burned by drought, beaten by hail, withered by hot winds, frozen by blizzards, eaten out by grasshoppers, exploited by capitalists and cogened by politicians" as W.P. Webb puts it in *The Great Plains*, "he survived because of his own efforts."[28]

NOTES

1. See J.W. Grant MacEwan, *West to the Sea* (Toronto: McGraw-Hill, 1968), p. 56.
2. For elaboration see Pierre Berton, *The Last Spike* (Toronto: McClelland & Stewart, 1971), pp. 11-23.
3. Seventh Census of Canada, 1931.
4. Also see James H. Gray, *The Winter Years* (Toronto: Macmillan, 1966) and *Men Against the Desert*.
5. G.O. Evenson, *op. cit.*, p. 115.
6. Based on a letter from Sten Gunderson in author's file.
7. C.M. Houg, *Our Hougs in America* (family history printed in 1965).
8. *Drybelt Pioneers* (Local History of Sundial, Enchant, Retlaw, 1906-1967), p. 169.
9. C.M. Houg, *op. cit.*, p. 63.
10. *Ibid*, p. 65.
11. See A.G. Vinge, "The History of the Rural Municipality of Cambria" in *Our Diamond Heritage* (Torquay, 1965), p. 3.
12. *Ibid*, p. 4.
13. See Carol Mossing, "The Drought Years" in *Our Diamond Heritage* (Torquay, 1967), p. 107.
14. A.G. Vinge, *op. cit.*, p. 4.
15. Carol Mossing, *op. cit.*, p. 108.
16. A.G. Vinge, *op. cit.*, p. 4.
17. J.B. Stolee, *The Evangelical Lutheran Church of Canada* (unpublished history, 1959), p. 7.
18. Harold Engen, *op. cit.*, p. 108.
19. P.B. Stolee, *op. cit.*, pp. 52-53.
20. Randi Halvorsen, "Memories of Christmas in 1930 in the Norwegian Lutheran Church."
21. Magnus Bjork to Robin Krause, *Seventy-Five Years Along the Red River* (Calgary, 1971), p. 15.
22. James G. MacGregor, *A History of Alberta* (Edmonton: Hurtig, 1972), pp. 266-267.
23. From "The Jacobsen Jubilee Journal" (a 1955 family history in possession of Dr. S.T. Jacobson).
24. 1937 *Annual Report of the Norwegian Lutheran Church of America*, p. 387.
25. *History of Lomond and District* (1966), p. 98.
26. Material in this section from the archives of the Royal Norwegian Embassy at Ottawa.
27. Based on information from the Royal Norwegian Ministry of Foreign Affairs, Oslo, Norway.
28. G.F.G. Stanley, "The Western Canadian Mystique" in *Prairie Perspectives* (Toronto: Holt, Rinehart and Winston, 1970), p. 23.

FIVE

Quest for Identity

An ethnic group has ties of ancestry, culture, language, race, nationality or religion or a combination of these characteristics. Ethnic groupings provide members with a sense of belonging and a feeling of security in sharing a common heritage and mutual aspirations. Thereby ethnic groups manifest collective identities in their declared identification with a particular ethnic association. The ethnic press communicates particular ideas, traditions and styles of life which are unique and treasured within the group. Hence, patterns of identity and common bonds develop which are most readily discernible in the institutions sponsored by the ethnic group.

For Norwegians, the church was not a remnant but a universal, as exemplified in the Church of Norway. Traditionally, it was monolithic, societal and inclusive, touching life from the cradle to the grave. In spite of difficulties, the Norwegian immigrants struggled to establish the Church in the new land. For them, the Church offered not only spiritual life and nurture, but the refuge of ethnic inclusiveness and social appeal. Hence, among Norwegian pioneers, the Lutheran Church became the primary and prominent organization of their ethnic identity also in Canada.

Because cultural and religious roots were in Norway, they found their models in tradition. Even in the material realm, they promoted old peoples' homes, hospitals and co-operative approaches, as in their mutual insurance societies, all indicating the depth of their social consciousness anchored in Christian concepts and expressions of their faith.

The quest for identity among Canadian Norwegians cannot be separated from the larger continental associations and institutions first established on the American frontier. Both have deep roots in Norway. It must be remembered that Norwegian colonies in Canada began usually as an overflow from crowded American settlements. Strong bonds have been maintained over the years. Thus American example and leadership

126

have had a significant influence upon Norwegian ethnic institutions in Canada.

PURVIEW OF MULTICULTURALISM

Canada is still a young country. Peoples from other nations have continued to come to Canada throughout the years with relatively few interruptions, thereby injecting a steady stream of ethnic variety. Because these peoples from a multitude of nations have not yet been assimilated fully, both federal and provincial governments have been forced to recognize that we are a multicultural nation. Here ethnic groups preserve a sense of uniqueness and consequently make distinctive contributions to a young nation still seeking its own identity and integrity.

Declarations by the Canadian government which flowed out of the Royal Commission on Bilingualism and Biculturalism brought these issues to the fore but also created a backlash within the nation. Native peoples felt that they have been overlooked again; surely they were among the founding peoples. Many ethnic minorities, who were numerically greater than the French in most of the provinces of Canada, felt that they had been minimized. They soon made their position known.

Obviously, Canada is not just a melting pot for fusing people into one new mould but rather a setting for the existence of identifiable cultures of considerable variety. Stability is given in the Canadian setting by the common cement of government, laws, language, education and economic patterns. Uniqueness and distinctiveness are most readily found in churches, colleges, the ethnic press, and in particular clubs and societies. In Canada there still remains much evidence of cultural pluralism in these areas.

Therefore, it is necessary to examine in historical perspective that which is unique and distinctive within the Norwegian ethnic group. Here those institutions, associations and activities which are foci of ethnic identity and solidarity are most significant. In the case of the Norwegians, religious institutions have played predominant roles over the decades.

THE NORWEGIAN LUTHERAN CHURCH HERITAGE

The prophet Isaiah exhorted the people of Israel to "look to the rock from which you were hewn, and to the quarry from which you were digged." The spiritual complex of the Norwegians is the result of significant and often diverse developments anchored in the history of Norway alluded to in earlier chapters.

Officially, over 96% of the Norwegian population belongs to the Lutheran Church of Norway. In Canada in 1941, of the Norwegians

127

born in Norway, 84.7% adhered to the Lutheran Church, 5.4% to the United Church of Canada, 2.6% to the Anglican Church, 1.5% to the Presbyterian and 5.8% to other miscellaneous groupings.[1] It is also known that Norwegian individuals born in the United States were also predominantly Lutheran.

Because of the close relationship between church and state in Norway, the clergymen there were largely identified with the ruling classes. In the nineteenth century, the pastors of Norway were highly educated and sophisticated civil servants paid by the government. They often failed to relate to the common man. Thus the traditional religious hierarchy remained estranged from the *husmann* and the *bonde* classes, and a secularistic and rationalistic climate prevailed in the official state church.[2]

More importantly, orthodoxy had put an indelible stamp of churchliness upon the solid and unchanging people of the rural areas. Rohne has explained this phenomenon:

> The Bible, the Lutheran doctrine, the clerical office, the church, the liturgy, the hymns, yes, even the vestments, and practically everything connected with the Church and its service were given a very elevated position. But mere intellectual orthodoxy lacked the power of changing the hearts of men; while Christianity was robust and strong at the top, it was anemic and powerless at the bottom.[3]

Then came the evangelistic Haugean movement which violently shook the established church and the religious elite. All over Norway people were "awakened" and the fire of religious revival moved the common folk of Norway under Hauge's strong leadership. Rationalistic clergymen violently opposed all that Hauge was doing and instigated a shameful persecution of him which included a long and barbarous imprisonment. But this did not stop the evangelical movement. More and more Norwegians shared in the great awakening. These deep religious convictions united the common man in Norway against the aristocracy and eventually led to the dissolution of the estate society in Norway and the establishment of an egalitarian society.

Many of the immigrants who came to the new land in the early years were both religiously and politically products of the Haugean revival, for this religious conflict also led to political position. Hauge was a *bonde*, and it was indelibly stamped upon the popular mind that he had innocently suffered at the hands of overbearing officials and clergy.

The followers of Hauge were critical of high church and aristocratic tendencies but they were not separatists. However, they did gather informally in various homes for mutual edification under lay leadership and lay preaching. They did not despise the sacraments or the doctrines of the Lutheran Church, but their new life and earnest piety gave personal testimony to an awakened faith anchored in the Scriptures and as taught in the historic confessions of the Lutheran Church. It was a new day of

Christian living and a new spirit which had political, social and intellectual implications.

The Hauge movement rejected worldliness in teaching and practice. It preached that men should repent and believe in Jesus Christ. It called for personal experience of the power of the Gospel to provide peace with God, and promoted Bible reading, prayer meetings and lay preaching across Norway. Unfortunately, many of the high church leaders opposed the low church tendencies of the Hauge movement. As a result some of the followers of Hauge became extreme in their position and assumed very negative attitudes to the structured church of the state.

Many Norwegians were caught in the middle of this battle between the high church group and the low church group. In a sense, they were those with a broader church view accepting the ministry and ceremonies of the church but acknowledging also the need to live by the true teaching of the Word and declaring that there should be room for lay people to "show forth the excellencies of Him who called them out of darkness into His marvellous light."[4] Therefore, three main tendencies developed in Norwegian church life.[5]

Most of the early settlers were interested in the work of the church, but in varying ways. The most ardent Haugeans had grown suspicious of clergymen and church ritual on account of the persecution they had experienced. Placed in a new country without any state church, they felt no particular need to perpetuate the outward forms of the church in Norway. At the same time they yearned for the warm friendliness of the fraternal groups in which they had shared in the homeland.

Another large group desired to have the forms of Norway's Lutheran Church reproduced in the new land as far as pioneer conditions would permit, with a properly appointed house of worship, the accustomed liturgy, and a "regular" clergy, but in addition they wanted also the free right of lay witnessing maintained. This was the middle or broad group.

A third group longed for the forms of worship that they were used to from Norway, but were largely indifferent toward lay activity and somewhat intolerant of lay preaching.

These three attitudes found expression in the work of the Lutheran Church in both the United States and Canada. They caused the church life of Norwegian Lutherans in this country to flow in three fairly well differentiated channels but not without considerable friction for decades.

The outstanding pioneer of church work in America was a Hauge lay preacher who arrived from Norway in 1839. He began at once to preach among his scattered countrymen and eventually formed the people into little fraternal groups, later united into a federation or synod by 1846. In 1843, a group of believers in the Fox River settlement of Illinois called Elling Eilsen to become their pastor. He was then ordained and became the first Norwegian Lutheran pastor in the United States.

In these early years there were many differences of opinion as to how to proceed with the church in the new and strange country. Norwegians were strong in their views and their independence led to the establishment of a variety of synods and varying emphases within each. The transition from Norway's State Church to the establishment of a free church was accompanied by prolonged controversies and numerous fragmentations among the scattered settlers. In fact, at one time the total Lutheran Church on this continent was divided into more than 150 synods along national, doctrinal and geographical lines. Today there are only three major divisions containing 99% of all Lutherans.

Mergers started as early as 1890, but the major one affecting the Norwegians was the union of the Hauge Synod established in 1846, the Norwegian Synod established in 1853, and the United Norwegian Lutheran Church established in 1890. In 1917 these combined to form the Norwegian Lutheran Church which kept this ethnic identity until 1946, when it chose as its name the Evangelical Lutheran Church. In 1960 this church merged with the United Danish Church and the American Lutheran Church of German background to form the American Lutheran Church. In 1963 another Norwegian group known as the Lutheran Free Church also joined this group. All of these church mergers were of singular import to the Norwegians in Canada for, prior to 1967, the Norwegian Lutheran Church in Canada was just one of many districts attached to a larger continental church body with headquarters in Minneapolis, Minnesota.

In the Lutheran tradition all children were taught early to read and write. All Norwegian children had to be confirmed, and that meant Christian instruction in the Bible, Bible history, catechism and hymnal. This began in the home, was continued at school and climaxed in two years of intensive memorization and review from about the years of age 14 to sixteen. This was the period often referred to as "reading for the minister." Upon confirmation, a youth was accepted as a full member of the church and treated as an adult.

Even the early immigrants were generally literate and placed high value on education for their children in the new land. In general, the Norwegians were faithful patrons of public school education from kindergarten to university. Nevertheless, many Norwegian settlements established parochial schools to supplement the compulsory secular education given in the public schools. In the parochial schools the subjects were mainly religious along doctrinal, historical, Biblical and practical lines. Here the Bible became a familiar book, with cardinal doctrines outlined in Luther's small catechism and major aspects of Bible history carefully mastered. Select hymns and tunes were committed to memory.

Parochial teachers were carefully selected and approved. For some, this type of teaching became a respected profession, but with little pay. In the early settlements, the instruction was carried on in the Norwegian language, usually during the summer. To promote such instruction, the

130

pioneer lay pastor, Elling Eilsen, was the first Norwegian American to publish a book in America. In 1841 he walked to New York to have a translation of the small catechism of Luther published in English "with plain instruction for children and sentences from the Word of God to strengthen the faith of the meek."[6]

Because the State Church of Norway was opposed to Norwegians leaving the homeland, the colonists experienced great difficulty in securing an adequate supply of pastors from Norway. They were forced to discuss the problem of building Lutheran higher schools to prepare teachers and pastors. There was also the problem that the public schools did not teach the cultural heritage of the immigrants nor the Christian faith. The Norwegian pioneers wanted to pass on their national heritage and establish their children in the Christian faith. From the beginning the Norwegians proceeded to build church schools. In the United States, in the period from 1850 to 1890 the Norwegians founded about 40 educational institutions – seminaries, colleges, academies and special schools such as deaconess schools, normal schools, Bible schools and business schools. Many of these had humble beginnings and limited enrolments.[7]

In the era from 1890-1930, there was considerable expansion, growth and consolidation. Norlie has provided this insight:

> The period started with practically every Norwegian believing in the whole school system as an absolute necessity – parochial schools for children, academies for the youth, and colleges for young manhood and womanhood, besides the theological seminary for the training of ministers and missionaries, normal schools for the training of parochial teachers and deaconess homes for the training of deaconesses.[8]

During the period, Norwegian Lutherans founded 38 new schools, of which 22 were academies. This period is of special interest to Canada, for in 1911 Camrose Lutheran College was established in Alberta and in 1915 Outlook College was established in Saskatchewan. Later many of these academies were closed because of the competition from public high schools. Norlie estimates that in the period from 1852 to 1922 the total attendance at these various Norwegian Lutheran schools was about 150,000 student places and concludes that "the Lutheran Church is an educational church."[9]

The schools that were established in Canada were a combination of the heritage from Norway and the organizational example of the United States. In fact, these pioneer church schools, including parochial instruction, were fostered and nurtured in the beginning by the larger total synod of the Norwegian Lutheran Church.

The Norwegian Lutheran Church established its colleges, seminaries and Bible schools to carry out a programme of education that was true to the character of the church, to provide leaders and workers for the total ministry and to prepare its youth in general to be positive Christian witnesses in all sectors of society. To this end the church endeavoured to safeguard her schools and to maintain their Christian identity and character over the years.

In 1937, Lars W. Boe, President of St. Olaf College, made an extensive trip in the interest of higher Christian education. The burden of his message was that "our day is in danger of losing its soul in the midst of the many things that engross our attention." In his report to the General Convention of the Church, of which Canada District was a part, he wrote:

> We need vital Christianity. We need a reconsecration to the revealed Word of God, the foundation, and our Lutheran Confessions. We need good men and women who will witness and testify, whether it be in pulpit or pew. It is from the colleges of the Christian Church that we shall get the workers who will stand by without fail, a salt against corruption and a light in the midst of darkness. . . .[10]

By 1948, the Evangelical Lutheran Church in convention established a Commission on Christian Higher Education to "study the policy, aims and objectives of Christian Higher Education in our Church and to report to the Convention of the Church in 1950."[11] By this time there were many "danger signals definitely in evidence in many Lutheran colleges." Several of the colleges were hiring more and more non-Lutheran faculty and the percentage of Lutheran students enrolled was dropping to new lows. In some cases the ties to the church were weakening and some colleges were pursuing goals and activities contrary to the historic purposes as established by the church.

After two years of exhaustive study in consultation with the colleges, the Commission on Higher Education reported to the General Convention of the Church representative of both Canda and the United States. The traditional Christian objectives were reaffirmed and the colleges of the church were encouraged to remain "in all phases of their classroom and campus activities distinctly and positively Christian" and to emphasize a college training which would develop "positive Christian leaders in Church and State." Colleges were admonished to give preference to applicants from Lutheran congregations and to give more consideration to "religious and moral qualifications of applicants." The Convention endorsed "the policy of the Church to preserve carefully the principle of ownership and with it that authority, in relation to its colleges, so that it shall always retain the unquestioned right to administer these institutions in such ways as it may deem best." The report also stated that "no member of the faculty or administrative staff shall be engaged or retained whose witness in word or deed or whose personal influence inside or outside the classroom is evidently contrary to the principles and objectives of the Church in maintaining its colleges."[12]

The Commission gave special emphasis and importance to setting forth "the Christian Character of our Colleges." In doing so, the Commission declared that it was not passing advance judgment upon what had been or was, but rather was "affirming the principles upon which these institutions were founded." Section VII declared:

This day of popular secularism and compromise in religion and morals calls strongly for basic reaffirmations. Therefore, BE IT RESOLVED:

(a) That the Church charges the Board of Education, the presidents and faculties, and the local boards of the colleges with the responsibility under God of insuring that the colleges become increasingly and in every phase of their classroom and campus activities positively and aggressively Christian, not merely in a broadly cultural sense, but in the distinctly evangelical sense of seeking to win for Christ those who do not know Him and challenging to unreserved consecration those who belong to Him.

(b) That, consistent with such Christian aggressiveness, it shall be the definite purpose by means of the Word of God and prayer to make the daily chapel service the outstanding experience of the day for the college family.

(c) That, for the purpose of bringing all faculty members and students under the daily influence of the Word, and because it is essential to its ministry at the Christian college, the Church expects every student who has registered to attend chapel regularly, and instructs the college administrations to make known through their catalogs and bulletins that this is an essential part of the ministry of the Church at its colleges.

(d) That there shall be a college pastor on each senior college campus, whose primary responsibility shall be to minister as a pastor to the spiritual needs of the individual student. The college presidents in consultation with the Board of Education shall put into effect the provisions of this resolution.

(e) That a minimum of twelve semester hours in Christianity shall be required of all students regardless of church affiliation.[13]

A concluding statement of the report was very specific on several matters that had become controversial for some of the colleges. It stated in the closing sections that:

. . . the Church looks to its colleges to be significant strongholds of Christian truth and witness against the false and disintegrating philosophies of the day and therefore declares it to be essential to its ministry at the Christian college, that all courses in all departments be taught in such a way that the subject matter, particularly at significant points of contact, be correlated with the truth of the Word of God, and that local boards, college administrations, and faculties continue to emphasize their disapproval of worldly amusements and social customs such as gambling, drinking, and dancing, which weaken and destroy the positive Christian life and witness on the campus.[14]

When the report of the Commission was formally presented to the convention, St. Olaf College endeavoured to delay action on the report by moving referral to various groups within the church for "continued study."[15] This action did not surprise the convention, for it was well known that this college, under the recent leadership of its president, Dr. C.M. Granskou, had caused many sections of the church real concern because of "lax and liberal attitudes."[16]

The strategy of the St. Olaf College delegation failed and on the following Monday the Convention adopted the Report of the Commission on Higher Education with only minor changes in wording relative to certain administrative procedures. The convention fully accepted the statement on General Policy, Enrolment Policies and the Christian Character of the Colleges. All the colleges of the church including those in Canada were fully informed on this affirmation of historic and traditional guidelines for its colleges.[17]

To this cosmopolitan and more indulgent generation, these actions by the General Convention in relatively recent times may seem strange. The current generation is often intolerant of those who are unique by choice or conscience. It is particularly disconcerting when theologians label separation from worldliness as legalism and fail to distinguish between sanctification and Christian liberty. One authority endeavoured to set these problems in historic perspective when he wrote:

> Notwithstanding a considerable amount of indulgence in liquor among the early Norwegian immigrants and the retention of many time-flavored amusements and festivities from the old country, there was a deeply rooted Puritan spirit among them, particularly among those who shared the Haugean religious viewpoint. This spirit expressed itself not only in the movement for temperance reform but also in severe disapproval of dancing, the theater, card playing, display in dress, and other practices and customs that for one reason or another were considered worldly and sinful. Alongside this Puritanism ran a more tolerant attitude which sprang from traditional ways in the old country that had not been bent by the Haugean philosophy.[18]

In this generation radical departures in policy and practice have taken place in many of the colleges of the church. However, significant changes did not occur at Camrose Lutheran College in Alberta until after 1966 under the interim presidency of C.M. Granskou, former president of St. Olaf College of Northfield, Minnesota.

Against the general background, it is now possible to turn to more particular aspects of the Lutheran Church among the Norwegians in Canada. It should be remembered that the Canada District did not achieve autonomy until 1967, and was therefore an integral part of the continental Lutheran Church until then.

THE NORWEGIAN LUTHERAN CHURCH IN CANADA

So far this study has revealed that the early Norwegian settlement in Canada resulted from an overflow of earlier settlements in the midwestern American states. Usually these were people who had already established roots in the various synods of the Norwegian Lutheran Church in America. In many ways the Lutheran Church followed them into Canada with a far greater sense of responsibility and concern for the Norwegian people than the Church of Norway had ever shown. The Home Mission work of the United Norwegian Lutheran Church of America was particularly aggressive and did the most to supply pastors and aid to the early scattered congrations of the Prairie West. The larger church anchored in the United States reached out to establish the Lutheran Church among the pioneers in Alberta, Saskatchewan, Manitoba and British Columbia even before the first two became provinces.[19] With this kind of encouragement, it was possible to establish many congregations and preaching places. For example, in Saskatchewan the Norwegian Lutherans established 224 congregations and 98 preaching places in the period from 1903 to 1916, largely the work of an intensive Home Mission programme. The count was almost as large in the Province of Alberta.

In 1914 the United Norwegian Lutheran Church of America alone had a Home Mission budget of $65,000. In all this provided support for 116 congregations across the continent. Of this total there were 27 congregations in Canada, distributed as follows: Alberta 11, Saskatchewan 15, Manitoba and Ontario 1. As early as 1906, this synod had helped to establish 12 pastors in Canada. In retrospect, N.C. Brun reported: "After 1900, there was a great dispersion from those older settlements and our people were spread throughout the great prairies and the northwest of Canada."[20] Because the church thought of these dispersed ones as their own, they followed them with the ministry of the church.

One of the antecedent groups of the United Norwegian Lutheran Church was the Norwegian Augustana Synod. Pastor Abraham Jacobson came from this group to work among the immigrants in 1862 for a few months. In 1876 Pastor Nils Ellestad reached out from Portland, Maine, to serve a congregation of 62 souls at Bury, Quebec. Other pastors like K.G. Faegre, S.N. Garmoe, Y.A. Preus and O.O. Klevjord of the United Norwegian Synod reached into eastern Quebec from bases in the United States to serve the early colonies. M.P. Ruh organized a congregation at Jarlsberg, Ontario, in the Parry Sound area, followed by another congregation at Gravenhurst in 1880 served by pastors living in Michigan or Wisconsin. As noted earlier, the colonies in Quebec soon faded, but the work in Ontario continued until the third decade of the twentieth century. With sporadic services by pastors from distant places, it was impossible to build a work that endured. Some of these early American pastors were responsible for considerable movement of the early colonists into the United States.[21]

Of the early Norwegian emigrants to Western Canada, it can be generally said that they were a religious people of the Lutheran faith. Some were devout Christians, many would not deny the need for the church, others were indifferent, and a few were scoffers. Wherever Norwegians established a settlement they would soon establish a Lutheran congregation in their midst. They felt that the community was incomplete without a church. Children should be baptized into covenant relationship with God, marriages should be solemnized by the Word of God declared by a pastor, in sickness and in death there was need for a minister and a suitable burial ground. The church was often found in their homes, for here the Bible was shared, devotional books were read with the family and songs and prayers rendered from believing hearts.

As shown in the following table, there were seven early congregations established in British Columbia and Alberta. It should also be mentioned that the Norwegian Synod began work in the Icelandic settlement at Gimli, Manitoba, where a settlement of Icelanders had been established in 1876. Pastor P. Thorlakson was the first Icelander to be ordained in America by the Norwegian Synod.

The story of Bersvend Anderson has been told by his granddaughter, Mrs. Magda Hendrickson in the book *Pioneer Days in Bardo, Alberta*. He came to the Red River Valley in Minnesota in 1876 with his wife and eight children. Driven by great missionary zeal he sought out the lonely, unchurched homesteaders on the prairies of Minnesota and North Dakota over a period of 18 years. Then in the year 1894, already 73 years old, he came with relatives and friends to be a part of the Bardo settlement in central Alberta. For the next 20 years, he travelled far and wide in Alberta preaching the Word of God to the Norwegian settlers. He and his horse "Sam" were familiar figures even in the long winters that otherwise isolated the settlements. When he was almost ninety-three, then the oldest Norse pastor in America, he preached at a special service at Camrose Lutheran College. This beloved pastor died in 1917 at the age of ninety-six. He was instrumental in organizing several influential congregations of the Hauge Synod in central Alberta.[22]

As has been previously noted, most of the Norwegians settled on homesteads in the prairie West. In general, the Government of Canada was opposed to solid blocks of one ethnic group in any township. Only the even numbered sections could be claimed for homesteading and of this the HBC claimed sections 8 and most of 26. The rest belonged to the CPR with sections 11 and 29 designated as school lands. Because of these settlement patterns, the Norwegians were, on the whole, widely scattered. The so-called settlements of Norwegians in Canada would be in-

Gudbrand Berge (Gilbert Berg) first came to Calgary from Eau Claire, Wisconsin, in 1886. (Courtesy S. Lillian Loken)

Marit Anderson and daughters Emma and Magda in 1914 by the original 1894 Bardo home. (Courtesy Magda Hendrickson)

Pre-1896

Pioneers of Camrose area in 1908. (Courtesy Mrs. S. Bosman and Glenbow-Alberta Institute)

Gathering of Norwegians at John Spokkeli home, Camrose, in 1912. (Glenbow-Alberta Institute)

Mossing threshing outfit at Viceroy, Saskatchewan, in 1912. (Courtesy Oscar E. Mossing)

View of Eau Claire mills, piles of lumber, and Prince's Island, at Calgary in 1893. (Glenbow-Alberta Institute)

Norwegian farmers from Morrin, Alberta, building the railroad bed near Blackfalds, Alberta, in 1910. (Courtesy Pete Notland)

Camrose Lutheran College Choir directed by C.A. Ronning in 1933.
(Courtesy S. Lillian Loken)

Seven former presidents of Camrose Lutheran College taken in 1964. Chester
A. Ronning, Canadian Ambassador and China expert, is second from left in
back row. (Courtesy Lyseng Studios)

John H. Lingjerde General Store at Byemoor in 1924. (Courtesy S. Lillian Loken)

Gilbert Berg's pioneer store in Edmonton, Northwest Territories. (Courtesy Provincial Archives, Alberta)

FRAM SKI CLUB TOURNAMENT.
CAMROSE. FEB.17 ~ 1912.

Ski club tournament at Camrose, 1912. (Glenbow-Alberta Institute)

Henry Larsen's R.C.M.P. boat, St. Roch, held fast in Arctic ice in 1942. (Glenbow-Alberta Institute)

⌃*Una Bond at Viceroy, Saskatchewan, in 1922. (Courtesy Oscar E. Mossing)*

❬ *Amateur orchestra at Bergen, Alberta, in 1918. (Glenbow-Alberta Institute)*

Sabrine Jacobson and Josephine Solberg, lady homesteaders at Square Deal, c. 1912. (Glenbow-Alberta Institute)

Celebration of Norway's Independence Day at Moland Lutheran Church, Camrose, 1911. (Camrose Museum Society)

Part of the crowd at a rally of Norwegians in Camrose, 1926. (Camrose Museum Society)

TABLE 3

Early Norwegian Lutheran Congregations in Canada

Place	Date	Pastor	Synod
Vancouver	Nov. 15, 1890	S.R. Tollefson	United Norwegian
New Westminster	Oct. 8, 1892	S.R. Tollefson	United Norwegian
Tofield (Bardo)	May 23, 1895	Bersvend Anderson	Hauge Lutheran
Bella Coola	January, 1895	Christian S. Saugstad	Lutheran Free Church
Wetaskiwin (Vang)	May 18, 1899	H.C. Wik	United Norwegian
Calgary	*May 28, 1900	H.C. Wik	United Norwegian
Camrose	*Sept. 39, 1901	H.C. Wik	United Norwegian

*Services were conducted before these official organizational dates.

Source: See footnote 21.

tersected with a variety of nationalities, many of whom were in a position to buy land from the various land companies.

The Norwegian immigrants were almost exclusively Lutherans, but their synodical backgrounds varied greatly because of their particular affiliations on the American frontier where many had first pioneered. There were Norwegians of the following synods of American origin: Norwegian Synod, Hauge Synod, United Norwegian Lutheran Church, the Lutheran Free Church and the Lutheran Brethren Church. Those who later came directly from Norway belonged to the State Church of Norway. Consequently, Norwegians were split into six different Lutheran groupings or synods. There were many difficulties for the Lutheran churches in Canada in that the people were so widely scattered and fragmented into so many synodical backgrounds. Fortunately, they had much in common – the Norwegian language, faith in God's Word, adherence to basic Lutheran confessional articles, *Landstad's Salmebog* (hymnbook), and Luther's small catechism. Many found one another, but for others the controversies over various emphases in church practices and social customs led to sustained separations and controversies. Then there were the recognized and established churches in Canada that regarded the Lutheran groupings as foreign churches. Faced with such labelling, some capitulated and joined the Anglicans or Presbyterians or Methodists. When the United Church of Canada came into being, there were new pressures to join a group that promoted itself as the national church for all Canadians. Also, sectarian splinter groups attacked the Lutherans for their formal approaches to worship and their practice of infant baptism.

The great shortage of pastors, the separated settlements scattered over vast areas and the slow and difficult transportation hindered an effective outreach ministry to the Norwegian pioneers. Nevertheless, the first

137

pastors, functioning as circuit riders, endeavoured to reach as many as possible. Pastors were required to submit an annual statistical report to church headquarters. One such pioneer simply wrote boldly on the otherwise uncompleted report form, "I spend most of my time hunting up Norwegians." For many, this would be a laconic analysis of the role of the early Lutheran pastors sent into Western Canada.[23]

The general history of the Norwegian Lutheran Church in Canada may be analyzed under the following five periods: Planting and Growth, 1890 to 1916; Consolidation Efforts, 1917 to 1929; Dislocation and Transition, 1930 to 1939; Major Progress and Advancement, 1940 to 1959; and Lutheran Mergers and Canadian Autonomy, 1960 to 1979.

Planting and Growth, 1890-1916
During the pioneering period, the five different synods reached out to plant and nurture the Lutheran Church among the Norwegians in Canada. In spite of the many pioneering difficulties and some overlapping of efforts, this was a time of enthusiastic response and much optimism. Hence, it was an era of expansion and outreach.

The establishment and development of the Norwegian Lutheran Church in the early Eau Claire settlement is indicative of some of the pioneering problems. Although the settlement was established in 1886, the Lutheran Church did not reach it until 1899. In these many years there was considerable loss to other groups. Several families became associated with the early Methodist Church in Calgary. Others attended services held by the Salvation Army, familiar to them because of its work in the cities of Norway.

There has been some disagreement concerning the actual year in which the congregation at Calgary was established, as has been the case for several of the early congregations in Canada. On January 11, 1924, *The Calgary Daily Herald* reported that this local Norwegian Lutheran Church was organized in 1899. Pastor H.C. Wik left a record in his daily register, now stored at Messiah Lutheran at Camrose, indicating that the church was formally organized by him on May 28, 1900. In any event, the present Trinity Lutheran Church at Calgary was one of the first to be organized in the prairie West.

Halvor C. Wik was born in 1844 in Norway, became an immigrant to the United States in 1880 and was ordained in 1887. After a brief ministry in Wisconsin, the Home Mission Board of the United Norwegian Lutheran Church of American sent him to the District of Alberta in 1899. However, Bersvend Anderson, a pioneer pastor of the Hauge Synod, had already established the first Lutheran group, the Bardo congregation near Tofield as early as May 23, 1895, and Vang congregation near Wetaskiwin had been organized on May 18, 1899, by the Home Mission Superintendent of the United Norwegian Lutheran Church of America.

Pastor H.C. Wik reached out far and wide to such points as Calgary,

Edberg, New Norway and any other places where Norwegian Lutheran settlers could be found. Because he also was from Wisconsin, he soon made ready contact with the Eau Claire people in Calgary where he held intermittent services from 1899 to 1901. Unfortunately, there are no congregational records of the work at Calgary from 1899 to 1910. One can only conclude that it was limited and sporadic.

The next pastor to reach Calgary was C.M. Nodvedt, who was stationed at Edberg from 1902-1908. To begin with this pastor served a scattered empire of eight congregations, but this proved to be too much. He managed to reach Calgary occasionally in 1902 and 1903. From 1904 to 1906, the new pastor at Wetaskiwin, Ole I. Saetre, assumed responsibility for Calgary. When Moses B. Anderson became the pastor at Claresholm, he also served the Calgary congregation from 1906-1910. Thus, for the first 10 years of congregational life there was no resident pastor at Trinity and only intermittent services. The period 1910-1926 can be described as a time of building.

Pastor Carl O.B. Ness was the first resident pastor to serve Trinity. When he arrived in Calgary on June 30, 1910, there was no one to meet him in spite of advance notice. As yet there was no church or parsonage but the Swedish church was rented for meetings. A basement structure had been started but was not yet completed. Ness spent the first days searching for potential church members but had little success. In a letter written in 1965, he reported that at the first service he had to install himself because there was no district president in those days and the nearest pastor was about 100 miles away. He wrote:

> I had an audience of 13 and some of them were Swedes. And I had been told that there was a congregation of 26 families and that they were *so anxious* to get a pastor. Yeah! Most pastors (young ones) would have bought a return ticket the next day and left. I didn't expect much and had made up my mind to stay three years.[24]

More and more people came to Calgary during a real estate boom. By fall the new basement was ready for services. It was a happy day on October 23, 1910, when J.R. Lavik, pastor at Claresholm, dedicated the basement facilities. That same year the name of the congregation was changed to the Norwegian Lutheran Church because the congregation was made up of Norwegians living at Calgary who now had little connection with Eau Claire, Wisconsin. Early in 1914, the decision was made to build the present parsonage. In the fall of that same year Sunday school was started. In 1914 Pastor A.H. Thorsen, a recent graduate from the seminary arrived, but he returned to the United States in 1916.

In the pioneering period instruction of the young was often committed to parochial school teachers who usually taught their classes in Norwegian. Iver Olson, who later became a pastor and a seminary professor, has recalled the work of his Norwegian parochial school teacher, Odin Jacobsen. In 1893 Odin Jacobsen had left Norway, where he was a teacher, to homestead in Polk County in Minnesota. Because there was insufficient land for his family of ten children and two stepsons he came to Canada in the spring of 1903. By 1905 he was established in what is now the Loreburn district of Saskatchewan. Here he became both a farmer and a parochial school teacher. In May and June of 1912, Iver Olson has recorded that in the morning before recess they studied the Catechism and the Explanation. After the first recess in which they had a play period, Iver had this recollection of the events that followed:

> But the Gospel came also. That was after the first recess; every day we read a chapter from one of the Gospels in this period. We sat in rapt attention when our teacher explained. But the real "gospel meeting" came right after dinner when we had Bible History. I believe this was Odin Jacobsen's specialty. He always started out with yesterday's lesson, and before recess came in the afternoon he had given us a preview of tomorrow's assignment. We listened with our whole bodies, and the period went by far too fast. The assignment might be the one about Joseph and Potiphar, Daniel in the lions' den, Moses in Midian, or the pair of liars – Ananias and Saphira. The lesson was always the same: God is on the side of those who fear the Lord. As we listened we were assured that God would take care of us, too, and above all forgive us; that's what our teacher said, and that's what he believed.
>
> Thirdly, he taught us to appreciate good songs. Landstad's "Salmebok" and "Fredsbasunen" were his books. The last half hour of each day was given to singing and the rudiments of music. It was fortunate that he could sing well; we tried our best to follow. Most of us were neither Carusos nor Jenny Linds; but at least the doors were opened to us into the treasures of psalmody.[25]

From 1890 to 1916 there was rapid growth in the number of congregations and preaching places in the Canadian West. By 1905, British Columbia had at least three Norwegian Lutheran churches; by 1916, 15 were organized. In Alberta, there were 20 congregations in 1905, and 159 organized churches and 20 preaching places by 1916. Similarly, the Lutheran churches among Norwegians in Saskatchewan grew from 10 in 1905 to 231 congregations and 89 preaching places in 1916. Manitoba started with two congregations in 1905 and had 23 by 1916. In total for the Canadian West there were 35 established congregations by 1905 and after a decade or so this number had expanded to 413 congregations and 119 additional preaching places.[26] The spectacular growth was a response to the great influx of Norwegians to Western Canada from both the United States and Canada. Also in this time of much organization and building, Camrose Lutheran College was founded in 1911 and Outlook College in 1915. Much support for both church and college came from the Lutheran synods already well established in the United States. Thus the period from 1890 to 1916 was an era of expansion of the larger

Lutheran Church into Canada – a time of probing, planting and providing especially by the United Norwegian Lutheran Church of America.
The Hauge Synod was most active in central Alberta. Many of the congregations that were established in this rapid growth era were small and
in isolated rural communities. Many were short-lived. By 1917, the mortality rate had reduced the number of congregations and preaching places
to 340.

Consolidation Efforts, 1917-1930

The year 1917 was especially significant to the fledgling Norwegian
church in Canada because of the merger of the United Norwegian
Lutheran Church, the Norwegian and Hauge synods into the Norwegian
Lutheran Church of America. The years from 1917 to 1930 became a
time of consolidation and adjustment as the larger synods found it expedient to work together.

At the time of the union there were 49 pastors serving Norwegian
Lutherans in the Prairie Provinces: 37 from the United synod, 6 from the
Norwegian synod, five from the Hauge, and one Lutheran Free Church
pastor who served an independent congregation that affiliated with the
newly formed synod.[27] In addition, there were a few pastors serving
several congregations in the Province of British Columbia. The total
membership was around 13,000 persons, and about two-thirds of the
parishes were receiving at least some home mission support.

The Norwegian Lutheran Church of Canada was established June 12,
1917, with Pastor J.R. Lavik as its first president. The new district was
divided into ten circuits: Manitoba, one; Saskatchewan, five; Alberta,
four. The congregations in British Columbia, separated by the mountains from the prairies, were assigned to the Pacific district. Steps were
taken to incorporate the Canada District as a Canadian legal entity but
functioning also as an integral part of the larger Norwegian Lutheran
Church of America. On June 1, 1922, the Secretary of State granted the
Norwegian Lutheran Church of Canada its Charter of Incorporation. It
had taken five years to clear all the legal hurdles and to secure approval
from the Mother Church and the Parliament of Canada.[28]

The union of the three synods enabled many congregational mergers
and parish realignments for more efficient operation. However, there
were many setbacks and problems in the period from 1917 to 1930.
World War I decreased the available supply of pastors. The young men
from the congregations became a part of the military forces; many never
returned. Then came the devastating influenza epidemic from 1917 to
1919 which claimed more lives than did the war. Regular church worship
was disrupted. It was also a period of crop failures in many areas of the
West, with a large scale severe drought in 1919 and a bitter winter in
1919-1920. In many places it was deemed necessary to combine two or
three mission parishes under one pastor because of the shortage of both
money and manpower. This was a tragic mistake in the emerging church,

for it led to "a decreasing ministry, a declining membership and a church that generally lost much ground."[29] The decline started after 1923. Similar short-sighted policies were pursued at the colleges of the church. Here both boards and administrators sought to hire those American teachers who would come for the least money. Hence, the quality of instruction deteriorated so that enrolments fell to perilous levels in the 1920s. Another problem that hindered growth in this decade was the determination of various Lutheran groups to preserve both their foreign label and their language.

The Norwegian Lutheran Church met for its first district convention in 1919. One of the issues brought to the convention was that consideration be given to changing its ethnic name. A resolution from the Prince Albert circuit condemned the idea of dropping "Norsk." This resolution was accepted without debate and carried with only three dissenting votes. One can judge the mood of the church at this time by what happened next. The convention rose to its feet and sang "Norsk Mand in Hus og Hytte Tak Din Store Gud" [Norwegians in House and Hut Now Thank Almighty God]. To counter this ethnic audacity, the president requested that "God save the King" be sung.[30]

The question of changing the name of the church again came under consideration when the following resolution was passed: "It is with grief that we, in this part of the country note that the question of change of name is again being discussed and that it may be a subject for consideration at the Convention in St. Paul. In this matter, Canada District assembled in extraordinary session at Moose Jaw, Saskatchewan from May 31 to June 3, 1933 pleads that our church body will not make any change of name. Grant us that we may work in our Church."[31]

There was a fierce determination to retain the Norwegian language for both services and instruction of the young. Thus the Lutheran Church not only failed to reach out but lost many of its own. Evenson has pointed out:

> Another factor that hindered the growth of our churches was the nationalistic spirit that dominated the various groups. As a result of this emphasis local Lutheran churches were until recently known to non-members as the German church, the Swedish church, the Norwegian church . . . it is tragic that the emphasis on nationality and language continued to the point that English speaking descendants of immigrants left the church of their fathers, and that it erected an effective "language wall' that kept out many who otherwise would gladly have identified with a Lutheran congregation. Examples of this undue emphasis on national background culture and language are easy to find.[32]

Such ultra-Norwegian sentiment in Canada gave this district the reputation of being a "Norwegian Church" and it drew pastors from the

United States who were devoted to the Norwegian language. Many pastors who could not speak English fluently came to Canada. Many of them were older men who had very nationalistic and narrow concepts of the church and often isolated the new Canadian generation by insisting that instruction of the young be in Norwegian. As late as 1928, Canada remained the most Norwegian district of all with 69% of services conducted in Norwegian as contrasted with an average of only 40% for the entire Norwegian Lutheran Church of America.[33]

Many of the pastors who came from the United States were not in Canada to stay. Pastorates of two or three years were all too common. They did not stay long enough to become familiar with Canadian problems and opportunities. This transient ministry hindered the work of consolidating the merged synods.

From 1925 until 1929 the economy prospered because of good crop years and the material abundance of the 1920s. The new prosperity seemed to engender less interest in the church but jubilation in the great nationalistic rallies held at Winnipeg, Camrose, Viking and Outlook to celebrate the centennial of Norwegians first coming to New York in 1825. The note of materialism, secularism, outward show and worldiness was becoming evident among the communities to the great concern of many of their spiritual leaders. The large numbers who came directly from Norway in the late 1920s generally showed little interest in the church.[34]

However, the period from 1917 to 1930 was not without some significant developments. The total membership rose only slightly from 13,035 to 14,108 persons. Canada began to be represented on foreign mission fields. For example, in 1921 Palmer and Adelia Anderson and Chester and Inga Ronning went to China as missionaries. In 1924 Peter and Ragna Stolee and Constance Stolee left for Madagascar. Often missionaries were supported by strong Young People's Luther Leagues that began to expand into regional associations which sponsored large well-attended conventions usually held biennially. For example, the Saskatchewan and Manitoba *Ungdomsforbund* or Young People's League was organized at Outlook in 1918.[35]

As a protest against the emerging drinking problems in many of the settlements, numerous *Avholdsforening* or Temperance Societies were organized. Saskatchewan alone had 15 such organizations anchored in congregations and promoting the crusade for total abstinence from the use of alcoholic beverages.

In 1919 the women of the church formed a district-wide auxiliary which became known eventually as the Canada District Women's Missionary Federation. The first president was Mrs. J.R. Lavik. By 1929 there were over 3,000 women on the membership rolls of this organization. One of their first projects was to lend major support to Bethany Old Folks' Home at Bawlf, Alberta, which had been opened October, 1, 1922.[36]

Dislocation and Transition, 1930-1939
The decade from 1930 to 1939 was an era of transition and dislocation, largely due to the Depression. Church members in the impoverished sections of the prairies were in many cases forced to move out or were unable to support the programme of the church as before. Total membership dropped from 14,108 persons in 1929 to 10,930 in 1939, and income for benevolences fell to the pitifully low level of $7,657. Local expenses fell to $47,009 for the 222 congregations in the Prairie Provinces.[37] As described in the previous chapter, not only whole communities but also churches were in disarray. Poverty-stricken families were forced to leave lands and buildings, load their wagons with what they could salvage, and head for the primitive north to become a part of extremely scattered and mixed settlements. Financial woes and low enrolments almost ruined the colleges of the church. Outlook College closed in 1936. Pastors and teachers barely survived. No one starved but there was little or no money to maintain the standard established in the 1920s.

Under stress and strain and having lost material prosperity, the Norwegian people in Canada turned to help beyond themselves. Many communities such as those in central Alberta and southern Saskatchewan experienced a time of extensive spiritual awakening. Both young and old came together to study the Scriptures and to have fellowship in prayer and worship. In spite of the hard times, the Canadian Lutheran Bible Institute at Camrose came into being with a large enrolment. Outlook College re-opened in the fall of 1939 as the Saskatchewan Lutheran Bible Institute. Luther Theological Seminary was organized and began its first school year on September 26, 1939. Also indicative of the spiritual interest and concern that developed was the district-wide establishment of Bible camps for youth across the Canada District and in the various circuits. So extensive and rewarding was this summer programme that the district Young People's Luther League elected a Bible Camp Coordinator to promote the programme and share ideas. It was a programme that came out of the Depression, but it represented a return to the spiritual heritage of lay activities, Bible study and free expression of the Christian life in testimony, song and virtuous living. From 1930 to 1945, about 10 Lutheran Bible camps were established among the Norwegians. The Bible camp movement became a "feeder" for both the Bible schools and the seminary. In spite of the severe reversals of the Depression there were therefore many evidences of revitalization of the spiritual life of the Lutheran Church.

Major Progress and Advancement, 1940-1959
The period from 1940 to 1959 was a particularly successful time for the Norwegian Lutheran Church in Canada. Membership increased from 15,792 persons in 1949 to 27,699 in 1959. There were frequent showers of

rain so that the fields produced abundantly and numerous showers of spiritual blessings that prospered the church in its several activities, as Engen has reported:

> The language transition was completed, and the youth were encouraged to take an active part in an English speaking church. The rise of the Bible Camp movement and the establishment of Bible Schools, the increased activity of Camrose Lutheran College, and the High School which had re-opened at Outlook, all began to bear fruit. Then the increase in the native ministry through the work of Luther Seminary at Saskatoon meant much to the Church. All these facts were blessings under God, allowing the Church to advance.[38]

John Precht was Canada's first graduate at the seminary at Saskatoon – the first of many – that followed beginning in 1941. The colleges and Bible schools were filled with disciplined young people of firm purpose and strong convictions. Many of them became leaders in the church and community. While some of the older generation seemed to lose their sense of direction during the Depression, the youth from many families had a revulsion against wantonness and permissiveness. The Depression had at least produced one crop that prevailed.

During this era the church also took some brave steps. In 1944 the Norwegian Lutheran Church of America voted to remove its foreign label. In 1946 it became the Evangelical Lutheran Church. Because federal legislation was required the Canada District did not officially become the Evangelical Lutheran Church of Canada until 1951. With enthusiastic leadership and committed purposes, the church had new appeal and made great progress. Its institutions and services were expanded and strengthened. It was a time of great advances on all fronts. The Home Mission programme of the church reached out to all people rather than just Norwegians. Giving to benevolences increased from $7,657 in 1939 to $149,211 in 1959. Congregational properties were worth $360,055 in 1939 but $4,149,555 in 1959. Local church expenses increased from $47,009 to $854,575 in the 20-year period.[39] In 1959, there were 191 congregations, 81 parishes, 77 parish pastors and 13 serving in the institutions of the church, 42 enrolled at Luther Seminary and 390 enrolled in the colleges and Bible Schools. Dr. Mars Dale, the District President, reported that in the year 1959 alone there had been 26 dedications of new facilities including the Administration and Classroom Building at Camrose Lutheran College.[40]

Lutheran Mergers and Canadian Autonomy, 1960-1975
For many years the Lutheran Church on this continent had been fragmented because of national backgrounds, unique concerns and practices, but above all because of language barriers. Because they all had a common confession of faith anchored in the Bible, the Augsburg Con-

145

fession and Luther's small catechism, it was logical that doctrinal unity would promote organic unity once the ethnic distinctions became less sharply defined. Thus after long and systematic discussion the Evangelical Lutheran Church of Canada of Norwegian background, the United Evangelical Lutheran Church of Danish background and the American Lutheran Church of German background formally constituted themselves as the American Lutheran Church in 1960. Because the new name was not acceptable to Canadians, the Canada District grouping chose the name of the former Norwegian group.

The period from 1960 to the present is a new era of co-operation, but not without many stresses and strains. The Lutheran Free Church joined the larger union in 1963. Then in 1967 the Canada District of the American Lutheran Church became the *autonomous* Evangelical Lutheran Church of Canada. Merger discussions are continuing and now it is proposed that all the major Lutheran synods in Canada unite in the 1980s.

Because of continued growth and the significant merger of 1960, the Evangelical Lutheran Church of Canada had 318 congregations, 182 pastors and a membership of 82,045 persons as of December 31, 1975.[41] From 1960 on the Canadian church was under the presidency of two Canadians, Karl Holfeld and S.T. Jacobson.

The ministry of the church as a whole is manifest through its major divisions which currently are: Congregational Life, Canadian Missions, World Missions, Communications, Social Services and Education. In all of these the greatest evidences of institutionalized ethnicity are to be found in the various colleges of the church. Normally, these are deemed to be servants of the church as well as bastions of the cultural heritage of the ethnic group. Each of these will now be examined in perspective.

CAMROSE LUTHERAN COLLEGE

The initial suggestion of building a church school in Alberta came from the Home Mission Committee of the United Norwegian Lutheran Church of America. In 1909, after consultation with leaders in Alberta, Superintendent Glasoe reported:

> The Home Mission Committee requested me on my tour through Canada to explore the possibilities of organizing and building an academy there. This I have done and find the conditions favorable.[42]

As a result of this report, the following resolution was adopted at the annual meeting of the church body:

> The annual meeting sanctions the preliminary steps taken by the Home Mission Committee together with the Superintendent for establishing an academy in Canada, and authorizes the Home Mission Committee to secure a site and to continue its work in this matter.[43]

In the spring of 1910, Professor T.P. Tandberg was sent to Alberta to do the organizational work. He had immigrated from Norway in 1868 and later graduated from the St. Olaf College at Northfield and the seminary. He had taught for four years in church colleges, served as an academic head for two years and been in the real estate business from 1903 to 1911. With this background, T.P. Tandberg was to become the first president of Camrose Lutheran College from 1911 to 1913.

An organizational meeting of delegates from local United Lutheran churches was held in Camrose on June 29, 1910, where the young town had made an offer of a suitable site for a college. Another meeting on July 29 decided to extend an invitation to the Lutheran churches belonging to the Hauge Synod to co-operate in this school venture. On August 9 and 10 delegates from both Lutheran synods organized under the name of The Alberta Norwegian Lutheran College Association.

As soon as the basic organization was completed, the gathering of funds began. The foundation was completed in the spring of 1911 and the cornerstone formally laid on July 1 of that same year. The erection of the building proper was delayed until the summer of 1912 because of a shortage of funds. College supporters wanted the school to open as soon as possible. On October 2, 1911, the school was officially opened with 71 young people enrolled, taught by a staff of five. Temporary quarters for dormitory and dining were secured by renting the Heather Brae House, a hotel building. Classroom space was secured in the two churches and an old schoolhouse.

The early minutes of the Board reveal that O. Molstad from Bawlf was the foreman for the construction of the building. He was hired at 70¢ per hour. The wage for first-class carpenters was set at 40¢ per hour. Hoyme and Aanstad were given the plastering contract at 9¢ per square yard. These examples explain why the cost of the total project including furnishings, plumbing and steam heating was just slightly over $28,000. This 48 x 72 building, complete with basement and standing four and one-half stories high, was for over 35 years the sole building on the spacious campus. It still stands proudly, having been declared an historic building by the Government of Alberta in 1977.

By October 21, 1912, the new building was ready enough to be used and the second school year began with an initial enrolment of 108 students. In 1913, Dr. J.R. Lavik negotiated a loan of $15,000 for the College from the United Norwegian Lutheran Church. Later in 1917 and again through the work of Lavik, this amount was donated to the school plus a further gift of about $1600. Thus at the annual meeting of the Association held July 14, 1917, Dr. Lavik could announce that lease of mortgage had been received. A letter of appreciation was sent to Edmund Thompson of Kingman "for the service he had rendered the school by providing his valuable credit at the time the debt was most pressing."[44]

One of the motivating forces promoting the establishment of Camrose

Lutheran College was J.R. Lavik, who initially served as Chairman of the Board. At the official opening of the College on December 9, 1912, the local paper reported some of his remarks:

> Mr. Lavik dwelt strongly on the religious convictions of the Norwegian people which led to the establishment of a school where Christian principles might be instilled in the hearts of the young. He said that while they were Norwegians, they wished also to be Canadians, and to be familiar with the English language. But they did not forget that the fear of God was the beginning of all education and that without this ideal there was little reason for the founding of the school.[45]

On March 25, 1913, a special act of the Legislative Assembly of Alberta incorporated the Alberta Norwegian Lutheran College Association. Thereby, each affiliated Lutheran congregation was entitled to send two delegates and its pastor to annual or special meetings of the corporation. Thus control was vested in local Lutheran congregations until 1957, when enlarging needs and greater opportunities caused the Association to yield its control to the Evangelical Lutheran Church of Canada. Here the necessary legislative enactment became effective on April 1, 1958.

Aims and Objectives, 1912-1966

The aim of the College was stated from the very beginning:

> Camrose Lutheran College is enlisted in the cause of Christian education. Its founders were actuated by the conviction that only that educational training which is secured under the refining and regenerating influence of the Christian religion can be complete or adequate for the purposes of life. The general aim of our College, therefore, is to give young men and women a higher education based on the Christian faith and to foster, encourage and guard the Christian life of our students. The College will endeavor to give its students an efficient training in the various courses outlined and at the same time seek to transmit to them in as large a measure as possible religious and cultural treasures.[46]

This lucid statement of aims remained the same in all college calendars for some 25 years.

A briefer statement of the Christian aims of the school is found in the 1965-66 calendar:

> Camrose Lutheran College is dedicated to the pursuit of excellence in the Christian context. The motto of the school is Luke 2:52. The program of the school offers unique opportunities for Christian fellowship, positive teaching, disciplined study and worthwhile activities. It is desired that learning might lead to wisdom (Col. 2:3).[47]

The college was established not as a free and independent institution but as an instrument of the church with specific aims spelled out in constitution, by-laws and annual calendars. The college was organized "to give young men and women a higher education based on the Christian faith as taught in our Evangelical Lutheran Church and to foster, encourage, and guard the Christian life of our students."

When the constitution and by-laws for Camrose Lutheran College were formally revised and adopted June 22, 1957, the following article was included on "Student Life":

> In recognition of the Christian principles that have motivated the establishment and that govern the maintenance of Camrose Lutheran College, all students are required to be present at the devotional exercises of the school. They will also be expected to attend worship service regularly at the church of their own choice.[48]

In setting forth the courses in both the high school and the junior college, the by-laws stipulated that "all students will be required to take the regular religious instruction prescribed in their course."[49]

A careful reading of the calendars over the first five decades provides evidence of rules designed to promote a disciplined environment with abstinence from that which was judged to be wordly or questionable. For example:

> All students are required to keep their rooms clean and tidy and to abstain from the use of tobacco in any form within or about the building. . . . The participation in dancing or card playing, visiting gambling houses or other places of questionable nature, and the use of intoxicating liquors, are strictly forbidden.[50]

The general regulations in the 1943-44 calendar are introduced in part as follows:

> The most potent factor determining the conduct of students is the atmosphere, or as we more often term it, the spirit of the school. Discipline is an important factor in the creation of atmosphere and cannot be excluded from school life. To eliminate discipline in the supposed interest of free development of the individual would be to deprive growing young people of the benefits to be derived from the experience of previous generations. Intelligent discipline generates self-discipline which is an indispensable condition for freedom.
>
> It is the policy at Camrose College to let discipline remain in the inconspicuous background of school life. Attention is diverted to it only when absolutely necessary. The aim is to make discipline as automatic as possible. . . .[51]

The page of general regulations concludes with a quote from Samuel Johnson "where law ends, tyranny begins."

After 1966, several subtle changes appear in the aims of the school, its general regulations and the constitution. These will be discussed in the chapter which analyzes the impact of the new land upon Norwegian in-

149

stitutions. However, for some 55 years there was commitment and consistency to the avowed purposes of Camrose Lutheran College.

PIONEERING ERA, 1912-1926

The curricular history of the college can be grouped into distinct eras. In the first decade the staff was composed entirely of American teachers who had been educated in church colleges in the United States. The academic courses offered by the college were perhaps chiefly designed to prepare students for American institutions of higher learning. The courses offered were grouped under the headings of academic, parochial normal course, pre-seminary, preparatory, and business including stenography. During this era, the presidents were all Norwegian-American pastors: J.P. Tandberg (1911-13); J.R. Lavik (1913-17); H.G. Fatland (1917-18); and A.H. Solheim (1918-27).

CANADIAN TRANSITION, 1927-1939

By 1927 the staff of the college was composed entirely of Canadian teachers with Canadian training and education. The courses for preparing parochial teachers had been dropped as had the preparatory programmes for those lacking completed common school education. No longer was there a focus on preparing students for American colleges.

The offerings of the Academic Department were now in conformity with the requirements of the Department of Education and the University of Alberta. The Commercial Department was reorganized to meet the standards of the Department of Education. College graduates could now be freely admitted to Normal Schools and the University of Alberta.

During this second curriculum period which lasted from 1927 to 1939, two interesting innovations were attempted. A course for new Canadians was again offered because of the heavy influx of immigrants from Norway. The influx began in 1926 and ended in 1930. The course for newcomers was dropped in 1933. In 1936, a new department offered folk school courses during the winter months. These courses were modelled after the programme of the folk high schools of Norway. With the major revision of the Alberta high school programme in 1939 and its heavy demands upon the resources of the college, the folk school courses had to be dropped.

Revisions and Experiments, 1939-1959

The third curriculum period began in 1939 and extended to 1959. In 1939 a new pre-seminary course was organized in co-operation with Luther Theological Seminary in Saskatoon. However, Canadian universities would not recognize the courses in this programme. Then with the outbreak of war, there were new problems. It was in this era that careful planning was undertaken to establish college courses which would meet

150

the stringent requirements of the University of Alberta. During this 20-year period, the major effort focused on the two departments, Academic and Commercial, in conformity with the expanded Alberta curriculums. The presidents during this time were: C.A. Ronning (1927-45); G. Moi (1945-49); K. Bergsagel (1949-54); and, G.O. Evenson (1954-57). These men were all Canadians but all had been born outside of Canada. During this period a large war surplus building bought at a cost of $28,300 was added as a temporary unit in 1947 and a girls' dormitory was built in 1952 at a cost of $138,680.

Junior College Beginnings, 1959-1966

In the period from 1959 to 1966 Camrose Lutheran College became the third college in Alberta to be affiliated with the University of Alberta. Mount Royal College, a school of the United Church of Canada, had been affiliated since 1931, and Lethbridge Junior College since its opening in 1957. Recognition by the University of Alberta fulfilled a hope clearly articulated as early as 1939 by Dr. C.A. Ronning when he wrote:

It is the intention of the College to broaden out this course (the preseminary course) to a general junior college course that will be recognized by the University of Alberta. There is an increasing demand from young people who do not intend to enter the Seminary for junior college courses. The College Board is definitely planning to meet this demand as soon as possible.[52]

But the war effort at home and abroad and the short tenures of a series of college presidents who succeeded Ronning were important factors in postponing the realization of this important goal for some 20 years.[53]

In the early 1950s concrete planning was undertaken to achieve junior college status. In 1955, under the presidency of G.O. Evenson, a specific study relative to implementation was carried out. In 1956 a Fulfilment Fund Campaign was launched whereby funds were raised to build a large classroom-library structure at a cost of $240,000. This was completed in 1959 under the presidency of C.E. Lund. Then in the 47th academic year of the college a first-year university programme was inaugurated, offering approved courses in Arts, Science and Education. All credits were transferable to the University of Alberta. In the whole process of negotiation, the Government of Alberta and the President of the University of Alberta had been most helpful and encouraging. In the first year there were only nine students in the junior college programme but by 1965-66 this had risen to 76 full-time and 50 part-time students.[54]

In 1959 that the Board of Regents established a committee to implement a special programme for the Golden Anniversary year of the College, to begin October, 1960, and to conclude October, 1961. Also a Long-Range Development Program was to be implemented, as authorized by the Evangelical Lutheran Church of Canada in 1959. A Development Council was established in 1960 by the Board of Regents of the col-

151

lege. Soon eight important committees were working hard to plan a proper celebration of the 60th anniversary of the college and to raise funds under an Associate Program for the erection of a new gymnasium-auditorium building to be called Convocation Centre.

The College celebrated its Golden Anniversary in the fall of 1961 with a special weekend of activities. Enrolments had reached new levels. Under the leadership of C.E. Lund as President and with the work of the Development Council, the significance of the event registered positively with a receptive constituency. Dr. J.R. Lavik was the guest speaker. He warned that during the past 50 years a departure from conscience towards a spirit of permissiveness and lawlessness had developed. He stated that it was necessary to be awake in our consciences, for it is inner sensitivity that makes one a dynamic worker for God. An upsurge of spiritual power can only come to this generation as we are sensitive to the Law and the Gospel.[55]

In January, 1962, G. Loken, who was serving as the Principal of the High School Department, became the tenth president of Camrose Lutheran College, and was installed for a six-year term by Dr. K. Holfeld. During his administration a Director of Development was added to the staff, the campus enlarged by ten acres, and the educational facilities expanded from a declared value of $465,442 to $1,400,000. On July 18, 1963, President G. Loken and President W.J. Collett of Mount Royal College at Calgary presented briefs to the Cabinet of the Government of Alberta. These joint briefs were favourably received and on April 15, 1964, the Legislature passed an Act which authorized major support of $630 for each approved student enrolled in an affiliated junior college in Alberta. By 1967, this amount was increased to $900 per student.

On Sunday, October 18, seven of the 10 presidents who had served the College over the years from 1911 to 1964 were present for the dedication of Convocation Centre and the new Junior College dormitory.[56] Dr. J.R. Lavik, the oldest surviving president present and one who had been instrumental in founding the college, wrote:

> Three things especially gave me a real lift. First, the outward progress of Camrose Lutheran College. I cannot too highly commend the administration for the vision, courage and determination which are evidenced by the results so far. Secondly, and even more important, from various conversations I felt assured of what I had not doubted, you are as a school holding firmly to the Christian ideals and objectives of the founding fathers. Thirdly, it was a real joy to meet again old friends, some of them quite old in years, with whom in past years I have shared a wonderful Christian fellowship. . . .[57]

The period from 1961 to 1966 was a time of rapid expansion and growth for Camrose Lutheran College as shown in Table 4.

Table 5 sets forth the enrolments at Camrose Lutheran College for

TABLE 4

Growth at Camrose Lutheran College 1961-1966

Category	1961-62 Figures	1965-66 Budget	Approximate Increase
Student Enrolment	194	309	59%
University Teachers	9	15	66%
Student Fees	$ 45,593	$ 99,000	117%
Government Grants	7,679	52,866	588%
Church Appropriation	26,365	33,950	29%
Operational Income	143,499	345,000	140%
Forward Phase Funds	4,220	30,000	611%
Development Program	17,099	30,000	76%

Sources: College Bulletin, Vol. III, No. 2.

selected years from the beginning to 1975. In the last decade, expansion of the junior college department has led to considerable curtailment of the high school programme. At the present time only Grade 12 is offered in the senior high school programme. There has also been a drastic drop in the percentage of Lutheran students, from 60% in 1959-60 to some 30% at the present time.

In the decade from 1966 to 1976 a major effort was directed into expanding university courses to the second year level in selected faculties. This fact plus a generous scholarship programme has led to increased enrolments. Increased and retroactive operational and special grants from the Government of Alberta have enabled the college to overcome severe problems of financing.[58]

OUTLOOK COLLEGE

There was snow on the ground and frost in the air, but Nary school near Outlook was packed with congregational delegates on November 22, 1911. They had come to deal with the important matter of a Lutheran church school for Saskatchewan. The chill of winter could not dim their faith, for their hearts were filled with the optimistic spirit of the West. Under God they were determined to have a Christian school for their youth.

Already at four previous meetings there had been much discussion and planning. In fact, as early as May 14, 1909 (even before Outlook was on the map), at the second meeting of Saskatoon circuit, the idea of a church school in Saskatchewan had been officially proposed by Pastor N.C. Brun. Later, the general president of the church, T.H. Dahl, had encouraged their hopes. But now in 1911, the delegates had met to make some big decisions: the location of the school, a constitution for the

153

TABLE 5

Enrolments at Camrose Lutheran College for Selected Years from 1912 to 1975

Academic Year	High School	Special[1] Enrolment	University Level[2]	Total Full-Time	Per Cent Lutheran
1912-13	23	90		113	98
1914-15	27	68		95	89
1919-20	42	66		108	82
1924-25	21	27		48	83
1929-30	54	48		102	90
1934-35	74	29		103	65
1939-40	92	18	2	112	47
1944-45	101	17		118	59
1949-50	90	17		107	72
1954-55	142	12		154	65
1959-60	193		9(3)	202	60
1964-65	201		78(16)	279	52
1969-70	89		234(92)	323	30
1974-75	58		261(78)	319	32

1. Special includes such categories as parochial, preparatory, pre-seminary, newcomer's class and commercial.

2. Part-time university enrolment shown in brackets.

Source: Ronning Thesis and Annual Reports.

association, and officers for the new organization. Hanley, Outlook and Watrous had strong delegations to present their bids for the school. There was much discussion and oratory. Finally, as darkness began to settle over the rural school house, the vote was taken. The decision went in favour of Outlook by a margin of three votes over Watrous. The tension was broken, and all were encouraged to unite in building the school in Outlook and to support it with their prayers and their means.

The following day the delegates assembled again to adopt a constitution for the Saskatchewan Norwegian Lutheran College Association. Not long after they hitched up their teams and drove over winding trails to bring a full report back to each congregation. Four years later, on a beautiful day in November, 1915, the main building was dedicated to the glory of God. This sturdy building still stands, sound and strong – a monument to the vision and faith of the pioneer founders. Several had mortgaged their farms to secure the required cash. Old Main complete with furnishings had cost $42,500.

Official opening of the school was on January 16, 1916, with a student body of 28. The first full-time teachers were Pastor H.O. Gronlid as principal and Mrs. Laura Brun as both teacher and Dean of Women. The first student to register was Alexandra Mossing from Viceroy, Saskatchewan.

Because Outlook College was founded after Camrose Lutheran College, and established also by the United Norwegian Lutheran Church of America, both schools had very parallel approaches and aims in the early years. The Saskatchewan Norwegian Lutheran College Association consisted of the congregations in Saskatchewan which approved of the constitution and whose application for membership was approved. Representation at annual meetings consisted of the pastors and two delegates from each of the congregations. No drive for funds was made but the need for support for the college was made widely known. The response was good and by the end of 1913 a sum of $15,000 had been subscribed. The town of Outlook offered $15,000 and donated 40 acres. The major brick building was dedicated in July, 1916, with Pastor N.C. Brun, one of the early Gaspe colonists, as a special guest.

In the second year the attendance had increased to such an extent that further building was urgent. It was decided that a dormitory for boys should be built. This brick structure was erected in the summer and fall of 1917 and opened for use in the winter term of 1918 when it was also pressed into service as a hospital for influenza patients.

Aims and Objectives

The first school catalog issued in 1916 stated these aims and objectives:

> The College stands for Christian education. As its name implies, it is a school primarily for the Norwegian Lutherans in Saskatchewan. As members of the Lutheran Church, its founders have sought to meet the growing demand among the Norwegian Lutherans of our province for higher education combined with positive Christian teaching. We believe that an institution where the religion of Jesus Christ is made a subject of study and His Word forms the basis for discipline and conduct, has a place in the educational system of our land.
>
> The aim of the College is to provide a general education which shall include as a distinctive and important element, the development of Christian character. While this College is founded and maintained by the Norwegian Lutherans of Saskatchewan, its doors are open not only to Lutherans of other nationalities, but also to members of other denominations. All such students will be required to attend the services of their respective churches and identify themselves with that work that these are doing.[59]

In 1917, O.B. Grimley, who was both professor and treasurer, wrote the following in a document submitted to O.M. Norlie, a Norwegian-American historian:

> The main aims of Outlook College are to build up true Christian characters, preserve our mother tongue and mould true Canadian

citizens. . . . We also believe that this citizenship will be sounder and truer if we preserve our Norwegian language as long as possible. Furthermore, we aim to lend a helping hand to those of our young people who came into new settlements where there were no schools and therefore grew up without securing even an elementary education. But at the same time we want to blend this instruction with Christian teaching. . . .[60]

After the school reopened as the Saskatchewan Lutheran Bible Institute in 1939 this statement was usually printed in the school calendars:

Our motto, "We would see Jesus," expresses the aim and goal of all our school activities. To the extent that our students see Jesus and become more like Him, and then in turn hold forth the Word of Life in word and deed, to that extent our work is successful. To that end we seek God's blessing for "except the Lord build the house, they labor in vain to build it."[61]

When the school name was changed by the Board in 1953 to Lutheran Collegiate Bible Institute to reflect the existence of the two departments, Bible and High School, the aims remained the same. All through the years the school at Outlook declared its definite Christian emphasis. However, the nationalistic emphasis found in the earlier years disappeared. As a school of the Lutheran Church it has given priority to serving its own Lutheran young people and recognized that special responsibility because of the financial support provided by the church. Consistently, the school has maintained a very high percentage of Lutheran enrolment.

To further the programme of the school, each class day begins with a chapel worship period. Evening vespers are held twice a week and the private devotional life of the student is stressed. The pattern of conduct emphasized for the lives of staff members and students is stated to be:

(1) The establishment of high moral standards and spiritual ideals as a life characteristic.
(2) The promotion of an environment most favorable to scholastic success.
(3) The maintenance of such standards as will reflect credit to a Christian schools.[62]

Pioneering Era, 1916-1927

In the first years the courses provided were College Preparatory, Normal, English, Parochial, Music and Commercial. Elementary English was also taught for those newly arrived in Saskatchewan.

By special act of the Legislature in Saskatchewan and with the approval of the church in 1923, the Articles of Incorporation were amended in 1926 to make the corporation identical with the Norwegian Lutheran

Church of Canada. Since the corporation name was cumbersome, the Board of Directors authorized the name Outlook College.

Pastor H.O. Gronlid served as president of the school from its beginning until 1922. During the school year 1923-24 Pastor C.N. Sandager was president. In 1924, Knute Bergsagel was selected, and the school debt was liquidated in the early years of his administration. The first two leaders were born and educated in the United States while K. Bergsagel came from Norway in 1910 and received his degree from St. Olaf College in 1917. Prior to coming to Outlook, he was a teacher at Camrose Lutheran College from 1918 to 1923.

Junior College Programme, 1928-1936

In 1927, the Norwegian Lutheran Church of Canada voted to make Outlook College a junior college affiliated with the University of Saskatchewan. This programme became effective in the fall of 1928 and received endorsation by the University of Saskatchewan from the beginning. The faculty and the constituency were enthusiastic and optimistic.

The total enrolment in the high school and junior college departments reached 127 persons in 1929-30. In the second year of the Depression enrolment dropped to 111 and then plunged to 35 students in 1931-32. By 1935-36 the college had only 22 enrolled, and was in serious financial trouble, able to pay only part of the salaries already drastically reduced. In the summer of 1936, the painful decision to close the school for at least a year was made. The Great Depression had crushed another prairie dream. Suddenly, Grimley's enthusiasm which overflowed in his 1917 report seemed unreal, for then he had written:

> . . . to the one who has travelled over our wide prairies with their fine farms or seen the smiling parklike landscape of the central part, Saskatchewan has become a land of promise – a land with a live present and a splendid future. He has found that our summers have plenty of God's sunshine – rewarding in full measure the efforts of the thrifty. He has found in our winters a healthy invigorating air, and in our beautiful winter moonlight a worthy rival of the charms of southern skies. To this great province have come thousands of Norwegians during the past years . . . between 35,000 and 40,000. . . .[63]

But now the campus was full of Russian thistles caught in the maples and elms planted by enthusiastic pioneers who drove in with horses to cultivate these rows of trees – and the dormitories and classrooms covered with a fine choking dust. Grasshoppers swarmed over the foundations of the solid brick buildings to soak up more of the burning sun. Marauders stripped the buildings of some of the fixtures and chopped down the native elms for firewood. An even more stunning blow struck the faithful builders of Outlook College when the Committee on

Higher Education presented its report to the District Convention in 1937. They recommended "that Outlook College be consolidated with Camrose College, and that we seek to make Camrose College a first-class junior college by, among other things, providing for it the necessary subsidy from the Church."[64]

This committee also recommended "that it shall be the purpose of the District to maintain its junior college as a distinctly Lutheran institution, not only with respect to the work of instruction, but also in regard to student attendance, by making such modifications in policy as might in certain circumstances be necessary to maintain a predominantly Lutheran student body." But the final suggestion really created a stir. It recommended that the buildings be placed at the disposal of the Board of Charities so that the college with better buildings than at Camrose would become an old people's home.

The 1937 Canada District convention was held in the hot days of early July in Saskatoon. But speeches from delegates and delegations pertaining to the issue of permanently closing Outlook College were even hotter. There were those who revived the argument that the college should have been built in Saskatoon on the 10 acres freely offered by Fred Engen in 1909 – that it was a mistake to have built at Outlook in the first place. After all the speeches, the voting began. The delegates rejected the proposal to merge the two colleges and voted to delete the recommendation of turning Outlook College into an old people's home. The convention also carried a motion – "Be it further resolved that it is the purpose of the Canada District to reopen Outlook College and make it the Junior College."[66]

Unfortunately, the drought and depression persisted and the college remained closed from 1936 to 1939. K. Bergsagel accepted a parish at Kyle and G. Moi and E.F. Marken moved to Camrose Lutheran College to teach there. The convention of 1937 led to prolonged controversy between the Alberta and Saskatchewan school constituencies.

In the 20-year period from 1916 to 1936, Outlook College had a total of 307 graduates distributed as follows: Junior Matriculation, 117; Senior Matriculation, 83; Commercial Course, 51; and, Junior College, 56. Of the 307 graduates, 225 were Lutheran.[67]

Renewal and Outreach, 1939-1951

When the Canada District convention was held in Edmonton in 1939, two significant motions carried "that a Bible School be begun at Outlook College this fall" and that "a committee be elected to investigate the possibility of opening a high school at Outlook College in the near future and that this committee make definite recommendations to the 1940 district meetings concerning this matter."[68] Here, the District President, Dr. Iver Iversen, provided strategic leadership. Pastor G.O. Evenson, serving at Moose Jaw, was asked to divide his time between his parish and the new school. Miss Gladys Gurholt was called as full-time Bible teacher and Dean of Women. Ten other pastors of the area taught short courses during the year. The school opened on October 19, 1939, with only 8 students in attendance, but after Christmas there were 30. The next year there were 74 and in the third year 76. However, in the fourth year enrolment dropped to 27.

The Board of Directors decided that the time had come to re-open the High School Department. A call was issued to G. Loken to head the high school with Miss Tryphena Sylte as the second teacher. In all there were 58 high school students in Grades 10, 11 and 12 and 25 in the Bible Department. In the second year Miss Mildred Joel joined the high school staff. Total school enrolment climbed to 107.

After three years of operation, the high school principal reported that out of 65 high school graduates, 10 had entered the seminary programme at Saskatoon. Many of the graduates from the Bible Department became parish workers or went on to seminary training. It soon became evident to the church that the programme of Christian college education was providing a steady stream of congregational workers and men for the ministry.[69]

The period from 1939 to 1951 was not only a time of recovery for the school at Outlook but a time of building. In 1948 a large war surplus building was moved to the campus and transformed into a kitchen and dining hall. In 1950, the gymnasium-auditorium was added to the campus. On a lower level these buildings also provided more room for the growing student body which peaked at 138 in 1948. In this era, the percentage pass on the departmental examinations averaged 90 per cent. The staff gave freely of their talents in establishing a bookstore, a film library, Sunday School by mail in co-operation with a Board of Parish Education, audio-visual services to the congregations, regular radio broadcasts in co-operation with Luther seminary and much outreach to congregations and Bible camps. The school choir began to reach out on its tours. During these years the school operated under the name Saskatchewan Lutheran Bible Institute. From 1939 to 1951 there were 29 graduates from the Bible Department and 212 from the High School Department. Pastor G.O. Evenson served as the school president for these 12 years and then returned to the parish ministry. Under his leadership the school made a remarkable recovery marked by bold faith, growing enrolment, substantial building and restored confidence and support in both the church and constituency.

Consolidation and More Expansion, 1952-1978

In the 25 years from 1952 to 1978, the college at Outlook reached its first peak enrolment of 156 students in 1961 with 141 in the High School Department and 15 in the Bible Department.[70] During this period there was a major effort to consolidate and improve the campus facilities.

In 1954 a library extension was added and the major buildings were connected by tunnels which provided shelter from harsh winter winds.

Then in 1960 a new brick building providing classrooms for the Bible Department, extra office space, a bookstore, more dormitory space and a large suite was added at a cost of over $80,000. Major funds were raised by the alumni of the school and by a church-wide College Advance. Then, in 1965 the Norman Salte Memorial Library was added to the Bible Building erected in 1960. In 1968 a president's residence was added to the campus facilities. In 1976 a major men's dormitory was dedicated and designated as the diamond jubilee project. In 1978, at a cost of over $450,000, a major gymnasium-auditorium was added replacing the small gymn built in 1948.

Thus in the past 25 years major facilities have been added to the campus. Essentially it has remained a small school with a dedicated staff that has remained remarkably constant. In 1954 A.N. Solheim was appointed as business manager. E.J. Anderson became the high school principal in 1961. Pastors Norman Salte, Edward Hedlin and David Kaiser have served as deans of the Bible Department. Pastor K.G. Grundahl was president from 1952 to 1955; J.B. Stolee from 1956 to 1968; J.F. Haugen from 1968 to 1972; Paul Nostbakken from 1972 to 1977; and Gordon Hoeflicher from 1977 to the present. The last five presidents have all been graduates of the college.

In 1965, a very negative report was made on the school by two Americans, C.M. Granskou and N. Fintell, appointed by the Board of College Education at Minneapolis. On the basis of American experience, they submitted that the school was too small to be economical. They proposed that the high school be merged with Luther College at Regina. They criticized the location of the school in the small town of Outlook. Finally, they revealed their anti-Bible school stance when they wrote: "Furthermore, the new church might find it expedient to underwrite the Bible School at a new location and to guarantee the quality and the spirit of its program as long as there remained a demand for such an institution."[71]

There has remained in Saskatchewan a demand for "the quality and the spirit of its program." The school continues to be recognized as a school that serves the purposes of the church. The school has always had a sound and enviable scholastic record as well as providing a unique programme for the spiritual growth of its students. It has been a major source of workers for the church in Canada. It has consistently maintained a very high Lutheran enrolment: in 1974-75, 86% of its students were Lutherans. In 1968, the Canadian Board of Education made the following statement about the school:

> Though the smallest of our schools and often derided by officialdom and clergy and laity as not worthy of a place under the sun, the astounding record of this school has yet to be challenged by many schools of greater stature in name and finance and prestige and general net worth, when it comes to a consideration of those

TABLE 6

Full Time Enrolments at Outlook College and Lutheran Collegiate Bible Institute for Selected Years from 1916-1979

Academic Year	Per Cent Lutheran	High School And Special*	Bible School	University Level	Grand Total
1916		28			28
1919-20		103			103
1924-25		78			78
1929-30		112		15	127
1934-35		27		20	47
1939-40		0	30		30
1944-45		69	38		107
1949-50		97	36		135
1954-55	77	131	18		149
1959-60	81	132	20		152
1964-65	77	140	17		157
1969-70		100	13		113
1974-75	85	100	8		108
1978-79	81	127	17		144

*Special includes pioneering era categories and commercial.
Source: College Records and Church Reports

purposes and reasons for the existence of a church college interested in Christian education that furthers the Kingdom of God.[72]

During the agricultural recession in the late 1960s there was some retrenchment of services at the school with the closing of the bookstore and film library and the cancellation of its bi-weekly radio programme of the Evangelical Lutheran Hour. The consolidation of the Office of President and Bible Dean was also a backward step. Since then, the Board has taken steps to restore staff, improve salaries, increase services and develop facilities.

Table 6 sets forth enrolment data for selected years. Since the school reopened in 1939, it has sent forth almost 1500 graduates, many of whom have entered the church professions.

CANADIAN LUTHERAN BIBLE INSTITUTE

The concept of Bible courses in a school setting has a long history in the Camrose area. The minutes of the Camrose Lutheran College for October 30, 1916, record that the Executive Committee of the College

Association "unanimously agreed that a Bible Course of four months be offered about December 1st, 1916." On February 13, 1917, a joint meeting was held between the Board of Directors of the Alberta Norwegian Lutheran College Association and the Central Alberta Norwegian Innermission Society. The latter society had been formed in Alberta as early as 1905 and represented a strong Hauge movement of lay people directly involved in Christian meetings of sharing and edification.

When Pastor J.R. Lavik was elected president of Canada District in 1917, having worked at the college from the beginning, he reported to the district convention in 1918 that there was a need for a Bible school. He also urged the colleges at Camrose and Outlook to add Bible departments to operate alongside their academic departments. It was many years before these far-sighted suggestions were implemented.

The concept of Bible schools was not new to the people from Norway. In 1893, the first of the Christian Youth Schools called *ungdomsskoler* was established at Hoibo in Heddal. The second was built at Framnes in Hardanger in 1897. Many more followed. These schools have their roots in the Christian revival that swept Norway at the beginning of the nineteenth century, started by Hans Nielsen Hauge. Today in Norway there are some 30 of these Christian Youth schools owned and promoted by various Christian organizations such as the Inner Mission and Missionary societies. These schools encourage the expression of the Christian life both on the campus and the community and provide training for Christian workers. In modern Norway these schools are considered to be an important part of some 75 folk high schools and are eligible for government support.[73]

The Lutheran Bible School movement began on the North American continent in 1919 when a school was founded in Minneapolis. From here the concept was extended to many other cities. In 1932, a group of concerned pastors and laymen decided that the time had come to organize such a school at Camrose. They were largely leaders within the Innermission Society involved with their annual conference known as "Camrose Week." On September 19 in a meeting at Edmonton a Board of Trustees was elected with membership from the United Danish Evangelical Church, the Swedish Augustana Synod and the Norwegian Lutheran Church of Canada. Membership in the Association was open only to members of Lutheran congregations. Thus from the beginning the school was inter-synodical but anchored in local congregations. Its first officers were Pastor Amund Tveit as president and A.G. Lewis as treasurer.

Classes began November 14, 1932, in a rented cottage school in Camrose with Pastor Paul C. Nyholm as the first dean. The other teachers were pastors G.M. Trygstad and A.E. Erickson. Each of the teachers came from a different Lutheran synod. In the first year there were 61 students registered in the fall term and 83 after Christmas. Predominantly, they were young converts to the Christian faith from the various recent revivals in central Alberta. Pastor G.M. Trygstad served as dean from 1933 to 1939.

The goals and objectives of the school are to establish, conduct and maintain a Bible Institute specializing in systematic, intensive and devotional study of the Bible; motivate individual students to be witnesses to Jesus Christ in their daily lives and regular occupations; prepare students for service in the home congregation, develop useful skills for service in specialized ministries of the church at home and abroad; and provide facilities and resources for the attainment of its objectives.[74] Thus its programme is anchored in Biblical studies oriented toward Christian witness and service. The purposes of the school are further amplified in the annual calendar.[75]

The Bible school is neither a seminary nor a liberal arts college but a Christian youth leadership school. The central core of its curriculum is studies in the Bible. The school year is divided into fall, winter and spring quarters in a two-year programme. There are courses in the Old and New Testament, doctrinal studies, historical courses and practical studies. Practical studies include missions, evangelism, Christian Education, Christian Life and Christian Ministries, such as the Parish Workers' Course.

The first building was erected in 1939 on a block of land donated by the City of Camrose. Here Pastor C.A. Bernhardson served as dean from 1939 to 1946. During the headship of Pastor A.M. Vinge from 1946 to 1957, a large girls' dormitory was added to the campus in 1953. Pastor C.R. Pearson headed the school from 1957 to 1962. Since 1962 Pastor A.B.H. Hagen has provided the leadership for the school. In 1974 a major classroom and administration building was dedicated. By 1978, capital assets had reached $1,400,000, including recent purchases of more lots and houses.

The school regularly publishes a brochure entitled "Bible Tidings" and sponsors groups of singers who travel to churches across Canada and the northern United States. There is a full-time faculty of six and several part-time teachers. The school sponsors an annual Fellowship Week and works in close co-operation with other Lutheran Bible schools, Lutheran Evangelistic Movement, Lutheran Youth Alive, Lutheran Youth Encounter and World Mission Prayer League. These are all inter-Lutheran organizations predominantly operating on a free independent basis but in full co-operation with synods and churches.

Students and support come from primarily within the Province of Alberta but the school is attracting both national and international enrolees. Ninety per cent or more of the students are from the various Lutheran churches. Most of the current students have completed high school prior to registration but this is not a requirement. Table 7 indicates selected enrolments over the years.

Bible schools are not unique to the Lutheran Church. Since the 1880s

TABLE 7

Enrolments at Canadian Lutheran
Bible Institute for Selected
Years from 1932-1975

Academic Year	Full Time Enrolment[1]
1932-33	61
1934-35	48
1939-40	40
1944-45	30
1949-50	45
1954-55	71
1959-60	43
1964-65	38
1969-70	41
1974-75	115

[1]Exclusive of correspondence courses and other part-time enrolments.

there have been nearly 200 Bible schools founded in Canada. In the Province of Alberta, since 1920, some 25 Bible schools have been founded of which 14 still operate. Many have been closed due to mergers and relocations.[76]

LUTHER THEOLOGICAL SEMINARY

During the first 50 years of the work of the various Norwegian Lutheran Churches in Canada, up to 1941, all of the pastors were trained in seminaries in the United States. The need for a Canadian seminary was stated by P.B. Stolee in 1935:

One of the first things which comes to mind when considering the situation in Canada from the outside or inside is that Western Canada should have a theological seminary of her own. There are many considerations which seem to favor this. Many of the Canadian men who have attended the seminaries in the United States have not gone back to work in Canada, or have done so only for a short period. The feeling has naturally arisen that this condition can only be remedied by getting Canadian men trained in Canadian institutions for the ministry in Canada.[77]

He also pointed out the "grave difficulty of starting a Lutheran seminary in the immediate future is not only that funds are scarce, but that nationalistic and ecclesiastical loyalties are still too strong in the various groups." He also underlined the dangers of establishing a small seminary, for these "often tended to make of all the graduates weak duplicates or caricatures of the favorite professor with his mannerisms, pet expressions, and slogans."[78]

In the convention of 1936, the Canada District of the Norwegian Lutheran Church of America enlarged its Committee of Higher Education and gave it a special mandate to study the school problems of the district and to submit a report to the district convention in 1937. The appointed chairman was J.R. Lavik and the secretary J.B. Stolee. The other members were C.A. Ronning, K. Bergsagel, I.V. Saugen and B.O. Lokensgaard.

This committee agreed that the principal objective of higher education in the church is the training of pastors and missionaries. The church must educate and train such workers for the simple reason that no one else will do so. The committee came unanimously to the conclusion that it was essential for the future progress of church work in the district that a theological seminary be established in Western Canada. In summarizing the rationale for such a recommendation the committee reported:

> Experience has amply proven that our Church in Canada cannot depend upon our Church in the States to provide the necessary supply of well qualified and permanent pastors. . . . But there are also differences and barriers which separate. This is proven by the very tangible restrictions embodied in immigration and customs laws . . . and these restrictions may at any time become practically prohibitive. The difficulties we have had up to this time are a sufficient warning of what may happen in the future. But even greater differences and barriers which separate these countries are the rather intangible but powerful restraints of national feeling and family ties, which make it difficult to get well qualified young men from our Seminary in the States to come to Canada, and still more difficult to keep them here for a number of years. . . .[79]

The committee also indicated that the language transition was much further advanced in the United States than in Canada and that the seminary in St. Paul was graduating few men who were proficient in both English and Norwegian. Thus it was argued that any theological seminary for the Canada District would have to stress instruction in Norwegian sufficiently to meet this special need in Canada.

The convention accepted the resolutions bearing upon the seminary and resolved that "this convention strongly recommend to the Norwegian Lutheran Church of America that a theological seminary be established within the District as soon as possible." The responsibility for implementation was placed upon the Committee of Higher Education, but the convention resolved that the most desirable location for such a seminary was Saskatoon, Saskatchewan, because of an amenable university.

By March, 1938, the Mother Church had approved the proposal for a Canadian seminary and provided an appropriation from the Board of Home Missions. The 1938 convention of the NLCA approved the plan also, but recommended that an agreement be worked out in conjunction with the Lutheran College and Seminary at Saskatoon of the United Lutheran Church of America. In due course this was accomplished.[80] In 1939 the Canada District convention elected Dr. J.R. Lavik as president of the new seminary at Saskatoon and requested its District President, Dr. Iver Iversen, to assume part-time teaching there. On September 26, 1939, Luther Theological Seminary began its first year of work with seven students registered: Sigmund Bue, Erik and Josef Haave, Lars Knudson, Adolph and Marvin Odland, and John Precht.

The purpose of the new institution was clearly enunciated by Dr. Lavik in his address at his installation service:

> The missionary motive must actuate all our teaching and studying. This involves the principle that the students must not only increase in theoretical knowledge and in the formal skills required, but that they must simultaneously grow in the grace and in the knowledge of our Lord Jesus Christ. We recognize that what the Church wants in its ministry is, not walking encyclopedias, but consecrated personalities.[81]

Dr. Lavik served the seminary with distinction for 15 years until his retirement in 1953. By that time the effects of the severe economic depression were over. In 1946 the church at large had provided funds from its Centennial Appeal enabling the building of a major seminary building on a block of land adjacent to the university campus. Dr. Lavik was succeeded by Dr. O.K. Storaasli who served from 1953 to 1959 and by Dr. G.O. Evenson, who had previously served as president of the colleges at Outlook and Camrose, from 1959 to 1965.

Throughout the years much cautious negotiation over merger went on among the various Lutheran synods of Norwegian, Danish, Swedish and German backgrounds. Agreements were usually tentative and exploratory as the synods sought understanding and co-operation with one another, but there were many tensions, as Evenson has recorded:

> While both were theologically conservative and loyal to the Lutheran confessions, the heritage of the two groups was different, for Lutheranism had developed dissimilarly in Germany and Norway. As historic pietism came to Norway a century after it arose in Germany, it had greater influence in Canada on Norwegian Lutherans than on German Lutherans. Also, in this country the language barrier had isolated and insulated the two groups from each other to a large extent.
>
> Different heritages meant different practices at the two seminaries. Only formal worship by one, but also informal worship,

including group prayer sessions, by the other. Approval of the dance and the use in moderation of alcoholic beverages by one, disapproval by the other. Stress by one on the objective doctrines of the Christian faith, stress by the other on the subjective experience of faith. . . . In the circumstances it was easy for each group to be more concerned about *maintaining* its heritage than about sharing it.[82]

For example, while the Norwegian group recognized the emphasis on basic Lutheran confessions and loyalty to their church by the Germans, they had difficulty reconciling strong doctrine and strong beer. While the German group envied the large enrolments at Luther Theological Seminary, most of them considered the Norwegian group to be legalistic and too independent. This and other differences continued for years and led to the two campuses operating apart for many years.

However, mergers of major Lutheran synods by 1960 and continued negotiations led to new levels of co-operation and enterprise resulting in a unified Lutheran seminary in Western Canada called Lutheran Theological Seminary. The new agreement between the merged Evangelical Lutheran Church of Canada and the western synods of the Lutheran Church of America came into effect September 1, 1965. The Board of Governors consisted of nine members from the ELCC and six from the LCA based on the relative sizes of the church bodies.

In a daring departure from tradition, in 1965 the seminary called a former United Church minister to be its president. Dr. William Horden was the first Canadian-born president of the seminary. He joined the Lutheran Church during his years of post-graduate study. Thus as has been pointed out "he came to his assignment with both the advantages and the disadvantages of non-involvement in the histories of the prior institutions and the heritage of the participating churches."[83] Recently, the seminary has given evidence of considerable departures from the conservative heritage and the long tradition of the Norwegian Lutheran Church by promoting both humanistic positions and social practices that have caused considerable controversy.

ETHNIC PRESS

As evidenced in this study, there has been a close relationship between Canada and the United States in the beginnings of Norwegian settlement in Canada and in the Lutheran Church that encompassed Norwegians in both countries. A similar situation prevailed in respect to the ethnic press which in the early years was primarily based in the United States but reached out to Norwegians in Canada in a significant way.

On July 29, 1847, the first issue of the pioneer Norwegian paper in America appeared in print. *Nordlyset (The Northern Light)* was printed in a log cabin at Muskego, Wisconsin, on a press purchased in

Philadelphia. Its declared purpose was to enlighten the Norwegian immigrants, who could not yet readily read the American newspapers, concerning the history and government of the new land, to present general news, to purvey information about happenings in Norway and to do "everything else that may be appropriate and useful toward the enlightenment and entertainment of our readers."[84] *Nordlyset* after a few years was replaced by *Democraten,* a paper with a political stance. This pattern was to become almost typical for Norwegian periodicals in that from 1847 to 1925 some 500 papers began to publish but less than one-fourth of these survived, due mostly to limited circulation. Nevertheless, in spite of many Norwegian papers falling by the wayside, a large number persisted to attain a position of expanding power and influence in both the United States and Canada.

In a special study of the Norwegian ethnic press which was funded by the Carnegie foundation, the circulation of Norwegian papers in 1918 was reported as follows: North Dakota, 120,000; Wisconsin, 85,000; Iowa, 40,000; South Dakota, 35,000; Illinois, 30,000; Washington, 30,000; New York, 10,000; California, 10,000; Michigan, 5,000; and Canada, 15,000. The circulation in all other states was 50,000, bringing the grand total to 615,000. Not only was the circulation widespread but significantly there were 15,000 subscribers to some Norwegian papers in Canada in 1918.[85]

This study also reported that 89% of the papers started were printed in Norwegian only. It tabulated the more popular papers in circulation. *Decorah-Posten* led with 42,478; *Minneapolis Tidende* had 33,505; *Lutherameren,* 32,193; *Washington Posten,* 11,600; *Normanden,* 8,375; *Skandinaven,* 17,000; *Barnevennen,* 28,000; *Sonner av Norge,* 12,250; *Ungdommens Ven,* 13,000; *Luthersk Borneblad,* 19,000; and *Visergutten,* 13,000.[86]

Most of these papers had large circulations in Canada, especially *Decorah-Posten,* which had been established in 1874 at Decorah, Iowa, and *Minneapolis Tidende,* formed in 1872 by the absorption of several smaller papers. In 1935 *Decorah-Posten* absorbed *Minneapolis Tidende* and has long continued to be a widely read and influential paper among Norwegians in Canada and the United States. The several Norwegian church papers were also widely read in Canada as long as they existed.

This ethnic press gave the Norwegians in the new land a sense of solidarity and provided an international bridge to maintaining culture and language. Many of the papers provided not only insight into problems and issues of the day but also light-hearted entertainment – an ameliorating influence in the hard circumstances of the frontier. Not only did the immigrant press supply news from Norway, but newspapers in Norway often reprinted articles and news items from the pioneer publications. This served to promote more interest in both Canada and the United States in Norway.

Many sections of the press were under partisan editors who espoused particular causes related to political parties, temperance movements, immigrant transition issues, controversial philosophies, religious controversies and land settlement problems to mention a few. The battles between editors of various papers were often bitter and rabid. When a Chicago paper finally expired after a stormy era, a rival editor in another state caustically wrote that it died of a "stroke after periodic attacks of insanity."[87] The Norwegian press was also a clearing house for immigrant thought as well as a round-robin letter providing reports and letters from various Norwegian settlements scattered across the continent. The numerous letters printed by Norwegian papers provide a remarkable record of migration and frontier experience.

In his study of the press and immigrant life, Blegen has provided an excellent perspective:

> The leaders of the pioneer press were, in general, men of considerable competence, who naturally represented a somewhat higher level of training, experience, and cultural outlook than that of the ordinary immigrant. The newspapers were therefore leaders along many lines, especially in the transition of the Norwegian settlers, new and old, who were adjusting themselves to American ways. As reporters, purveyors of literature, debaters on problems of church and state, and fathers of a regional Norwegian-American family, the newspapers gave direction and solidarity to immigrant life. They helped to shape and to make articulate a Norwegian America that has lasted, notwithstanding time and new circumstance, to the present day. They added to that life an imponderable element of interest. Viewed in the full range of their services, therefore, the pioneer Norwegian newspaper constituted a basic social and cultural immigrant institution.[88]

A feeling for the human factor in the settlement of the Prairie Provinces may be discovered in the hundreds of letters written by immigrants to the Norwegian newspapers of the American Middle West. In this way the dispersed settlers maintained contact with the older settlements that they had left. Often the correspondents justified their move to Canada by expounding the benefits of the Canadian West, but there were many evidences of new problems to be reported, such as early frosts, higher prices for machinery, prairie fires, mosquitoes, grasshoppers, swamp fever that killed their horses, drought and winter cold. The limited social life, especially for lonesome bachelors, and the fact that Norwegians in Canada formed a minority group in most settlements was also recorded, plus the fact of irregular church services since the pastor served an empire of congregations and preaching places. Others complained that the Anglo-Saxons felt that they were born to rule and that the English and the Scotch held all the cards in Canada as well as all the political posts and appointments.[89]

However, many of the Norwegian Canadians were keenly aware that

169

they were regarded almost as traitors by a considerable section of the English-language press in the United States. In support, the following article is quoted:

A settler in a solidly Norwegian community in central Alberta, calling himself "Max McOle," gave vent to his irritation at a statement frequently made in American newspapers – that the immigrants would have to submit to an "English tyranny" in the Canadian Northwest. People, he argued, tended to identify all that was most desirable with their own institutions and were blind to the good qualities of others. Nothing, it was now being said, could compare with the United States, especially in matters having to do with government – not even in the countries of Europe that, after centuries of struggle, had brought into being the world of 1905. He, too, loved the republic to the south, having lived there for many years; perhaps he loved even more his native Norway. But Max McOle had become a British subject, and it was his moral duty to be loyal to a new flag and government. In culture and in political institutions, Britain was second to none - certainly not in the area of personal freedom. He would like, he said, to see "complete understanding with one another, whether we live on Alberta's or on Dakota's prairies." It might be agreeable to some people if Canada were to become a part of a larger American Union, "but this situation will never come about. Anyone who has travelled a bit in the Dominion and has had a chance to observe and study its situation knows that it has three choices: complete independence, annexation to the United States, or autonomy within the British Empire. Canada long ago made its decision – in favor of the last." Except among some newly arrived Americans, there was no real sentiment either for annexation or for absolute political independence.[90]

Canada also had its own Norwegian papers. Foremost among these was *Nørrona*, founded at Winnipeg in the spring of 1910. Over the years the paper has had subscribers over the whole continent of North America as well as in Norway. The aim of this paper has been to keep members of the ethnic group together, to serve as a connecting link between the immigrants and the Old Country and to provide a clearing house for contributions from the readers. In 1976, it is Canada's only Norwegian-language newspaper still publishing. The news coverage in this unique paper is estimated as follows: Norway 65%, international 5%; ethnic organization 15%; church 5%, literary 5%; and sports 5%. About 30% of the space is alloted to advertising.

In 1970 Norwegian-Canadians were in danger of losing *Nørrona*. Then Gunnar Warolin appeared on the scene. Warolin was a native of Oslo who emigrated to Canada in 1955 at the age of 25. He was living in Delta, B.C., was the owner of a Scandinavian food store, and served as a *Nørrona* correspondent for 12 years. A former steelworker, millworker and insurance man, he liked to write for a hobby. His life had been filled with variety because he "likes to jump into things." But there is one constant, his love of Norway and its heritage. It was that love that influenced his decision to purchase *Nørrona*. All he received in the transaction was the list of subscribers and 60 years of back issues. He later had to purchase typesetting and other equipment.

Nørrona's circulation of about 4,000 has held steady for the past four years, but the future is not bright. The number of older persons who speak the language is dwindling, and while the younger generations have some interest in their Norwegian heritage, a much smaller number know the language.

Nørrona's editorial policy includes "everything from birth to death," Warolin says. To give news from Norway he clips from Norwegian newspapers. He gets "heavy" input from the Prairie Provinces, and takes care of the B.C. news himself. Regular columnists include Hadrew Gilstein, originally from Romsdal, .Norway, now living in Victoria, who writes a historical column. The Winnipeg correspondent is Mrs. Thingelstad, originally from Tonsberg. Paul Jacobsen and Asgerd Lein, formerly of Oslo, do fishing and gardening columns. History of Scandinavians in B.C. is the expertise offered by Jorgen Dahlie, a professor at the University of British Columbia. *Nørrona* also features sports coverage from Norway. Most of the advertising support comes from Scandinavian businesses and the Canadian government.

Warolin lives in an area where two communities, Surrey and Delta, are heavily populated with Norsemen. The primary occupation is fishing, and the sons are staying with the trade. He is currently President of the Norwegian Club in Vancouver and has been active in Sons of Norway since coming to Canada. Though his bi-monthly paper is not self-supporting, he plans to continue to publish indefinitely and to work at whatever enables him to fill out the family budget.[91]

The other significant Norwegian paper in Canada was *Hyrden (Shepherd)* first published in October, 1924, as an organ of the Norwegian Lutheran Church. The first editor, Pastor Lokensgard, declared "the upbuilding of the Lutheran Church in Canada on the foundation of God's Word is our program." The first issue had eight pages, six in Norwegian and two in English. Over the years it has been published in a variety of formats.[92]

The thrust of this paper, widely read among the Norwegians of Canada, can be seen in the editor's report in 1937:

> For 13 years the messenger, "Hyrden," has come to many homes in Canada District and also in the United States. This last year the number of subscribers increased several hundred . . . I am convinced that "Hyrden" has gained the love and appreciation of its readers more and more as the years go by. It becomes thus an instrument whereby the confidence of our people can be

strengthened. . . . The need to foster and strengthen such confidence, some will say, can best be done by our church official publications, "Lutheraneren" and "Lutheran Herald." Far be it from me to underestimate the value of these in that respect. I think we all agree that it would be a great blessing and strength in our work, as a Lutheran Church in Canada, if one or the other of these papers was found in every home of our people. However, those of us that have tried to get those papers into the homes have found it very hard to do so. Not because they do not like the papers but rather on account of the amount of subscription and more so because very little is found pertaining especially to the work in our own District. "Hyrden," first and foremost, deals with the work within the District. Many homes at least have "Hyrden" that otherwise would have no church paper. The need of such a paper is, no doubt, apparent to all well-wishers of our Church in Canada.

Publishing the paper bi-monthly has met with great satisfaction and proved to be a step in the right direction. Another forward step should now be taken if ways and means can be found to do so. May I in the way of suggestion recommend that the convention consider the enlarging of the paper from 4 to 8 pages, published bi-monthly as now. Further, that 3 pages be used for Norse and 5 pages for the English language. It has also been mentioned that the name should be changed. It is to be hoped that due consideration will be given these suggestions.[93]

By 1936, the second half of the paper, printed in English, was given its own heading, *Shepherd*. As the language transition continued in Canada, by 1942 the English section became the front of the paper. Thereafter, there was less and less space devoted to the Norwegian section. Finally, in 1949 the heading *Hyrden* disappeared and the *Shepherd* was an all-English paper. Canada had some short-lived local Norwegian newspapers printed at Outlook, Saskatchewan, and Vancouver, British Columbia, but the competition from the larger American-based papers soon proved to be overwhelming.

In the general field of communication, an ethnic radio programme was established in 1952 by CKUA, the University of Alberta station. Every Sunday afternoon for nine years the station aired the Scandinavian programme alternating among the Danes, Swedes and Norwegians. Since 1961 the programme has been broadcasted every second Sunday. The programme, under the general direction of Erik Pedersen, features news and ethnic music and has survived over the years while other ethnic radio programmes have come and gone.

ETHNIC ASSOCIATIONS

The earlier Norwegian settlers considered themselves in transition from one nation to another. There was concern among them that any rapid transition to the new country would mean cultural losses so that the bridges of understanding between parents and children would be in danger. Thus there were many organizations that sprang into being to conserve the Norwegian heritage and identity.

This effort to preserve cultural solidarity with the past was particularly evident in the *bygdelag* or district societies that were popular for many years prior to the Depression. In Norway it was usual to refer to a particular settlement of people in some mountain valley or living by some fjord or inlet or by some river or lake as a *bygd*. The term *lag* can be either singular or plural in reference to a society or societies. The word *bygdelag* means a district society which embodies a unified body of customs, traditions and costumes. This regionalism often asserted itself in the propagation of unique dialects explained by the extreme isolation of many communities or *bygder* in the rugged land of Norway. Groups of people sharing the same fjord or valley formed a cohesive unit with unique characteristics that were proudly promoted as marks of the clan.

Bygdelag

The regional culture of Norway carried over to the new country. On the American continent close to 50 national *bygdelag* societies were formed, representing the district culture of the homeland. Their objectives were to restore the acquaintanceship of former neighbours from Norway, to preserve and cultivate traditions in song and folk dances and fiddle playing, to perpetuate memories of the home district in Norway, to promote the pious religious heritage, and collect and publish records relating to their own groups. At the height of *bygdelag* activity before World War I, and again in the 1920s, some 75,000 persons came together annually to confirm the epics of a district folklore in Norway to the new settlements in America.

As this study has underlined, Norwegian immigrant settlement in Canada began as an extension of the American frontier. In the beginning of the exodus to Canada, many members living close to the border would attend *bygdelag* meetings in the United States. However, as the Norwegian settlements became larger and more flourishing, these unique societies were organized in the four western provinces of Canada in the 1920s. A characteristic of the Canadian movement was the custom of arranging for large joint conventions or festivals. This procedure followed in Canada resulted from the sparse and widespread settlement of Norwegians. There were too few members of any one district to conduct a large inspiring reunion.

Because Norwegians regard the arrival of the *Restauration* in 1825 at New York as the Norwegian *Mayflower,* the centennial year of 1925 became a year of many rallies. The first of these national Norwegian celebrations in Canada, and in some respects the most significant, was held in Outlook, Saskatchewan, July 11-13, 1925. People streamed onto the Outlook College campus, some arriving by train but most by Ford touring cars. In addition to the dormitory and dining facilities of the college, a large tent was raised to seat the crowd for the general sessions.

The event had been arranged by the local Norwegian society at Outlook. It was at this convention that a number of *bygdelag* local to Canada were organized. Several small groups had already existed. A *Hallinglag* had been organized at Govan, Saskatchewan, in 1916. A *Nordfjordlag* organized in 1922 centered on the town of Herbert, Saskatchewan, and a *Valdreslag* came into being at Crooked Lake, Alberta.[94]

The president of Outlook College was closely involved in all the arrangements. Knute Bergsagel has written about the historic celebration in Outlook in 1925:

> The evening of the first day was banquet night. About five hundred were expected, nearly seven hundred came and were served. How, I do not know, but it was done with precision and expertise. Mina Brein was in charge and she had too much experience to be upset by an extra hundred or two. Besides the usual banquet fare a great assortment of Norwegian national dishes were served.
>
> With good food went good entertainment. There was staged a "bønde bryllup" correct in all details with the participants in "bunud" (national costume). Recently I met the bridal couple of that "wedding" at the airport in Saskatoon as they waited to board a plane to Oslo. They have evidently lived happily ever after.
>
> There was also a full length play, "Til Seters" staged with a most talented cast. The writer can still see the three students, Harald Larson, Chester Larson, and Haftor Hagerup, as they arrived at the "seter." Space will not permit me to name the singing by groups and individuals. What moved me most was the heartiness whereby everybody joined in the singing of the songs of their homeland.
>
> Several noteworthy addresses were given and much time was given for discussion. Mr. O.B. Grimley, former teacher at Outlook College, received an ovation as he presented his address on building bridges between Norwegians abroad and the home land.
>
> Wilhelm Morgenstierne, for many years Norway's ambassador to the United States, represented Nordmanns-Forbundet. Mr. Morgenstierne had attended the Centennial in Minneapolis, had met with the Canadian delegation who took the initiative in planning the Outlook meeting and had promised to attend. He was the chief resource person during the deliberation and his address contributed much to the program.[95]

After the feasting, fellowship and fun, the Norwegians started to deal with the serious purposes of the gathering. The Norwegians in Canada expressed a desire to have an organization of their own that would be in more direct rapport with their homeland than was possible through Norwegian-American organizations. After much discussion, there was general agreement on two major resolutions:

1. That a national conference be formed consisting of *bygdelag* and other Norwegian societies and individuals for the promotion of Norwegian culture.
2. That this national conference be affiliated with *Nordmanns-Forbundet* (League of Norsemen), a world organization.[96]

The above resolutions represented a compromise, for in the convention one group favoured a federation of *bygdelag* while the other desired a Canadian league of Norsemen.

Bergsagel has also reported:

There was another resolution passed at the convention which is pertinent today. It was the unanimous opinion of the convention that the University of Saskatchewan ought to offer Norwegian as a foreign language option, and as the writer was the president of Outlook College he seemed to be the most logical person to approach the University with the convention resolution. President Walter Murray and the University Council acceded to this request as well as several others from Outlook College when accreditation was sought for a junior college. Today, nearly fifty years later, Norwegian is still on the curriculum and is being taught at the University of Saskatchewan.[97]

In 1926, thousands of Norwegian Canadians from all parts of the Dominion assembled in the small prairie town of Camrose, Alberta, for a three-day festival, July 4-6. The Canadian *bygelag* conducted individual *stevner* as well as a large joint meeting on the first day of the festivities. Here the presidents of the different *lag* were introduced, and "they came upon the platform one by one, robust and stately farmers from Norway's valleys and mountains, who have devoted themselves to cultivating Canada's soil." The second day there were religious services. On July 6, the last day of the festival, the League of Norsemen in Canada (*Nordmanns-Forbundet i Canada*) was organized as an independent nationwide association closely affiliated with the international federation of Norwegians based in Oslo, Norway. Members of the Canadian League would automatically also be members of the international Norsemen's Federation. In 1927, a joint *bygdelag* convention took place at Watrous, Saskatchewan, on July 9-11. A committee appointed at that time planned the large festival to be held on July 13-16 the next year at Saskatoon, Saskatchewan. At the 1928 gathering, as many as 3,000 people assembled – a significant achievement in the history of the Canadian movement. At that time, *Bygdelagenes i Canada Faellesraad* (The Council of Bygdelags in Canada) was formed in order to better coordinate and encourage the activities of member *lag*. It adopted, with minor alterations, the constitution of its counterpart in the Middle West.[98]

By 1930, thirteen societies were represented in the Canadian Council. These included *Nordfjordlaget, Gudbrandsdalslaget, Telemarkslaget,*

175

Tronderlaget, Hallinglaget, Oslolaget, Nordlandslaget, Stavangerlaget, Vestfoldlaget, Vestmannalaget, Valdreslaget, Osterdalslaget and Morelaget. The last society was a merger of *Sunnmorslaget* and *Romsdalslaget,* both formed in 1925 at Outlook.

The Saskatchewan meeting in 1928 revealed a splitting of the Norwegian forces in Canada; the convention conflicted with the efforts to arrange a large Norwegian festival at Winnipeg, Manitoba, on July 5-11. The Canadian League of Norsemen headed the gathering in Winnipeg and extended invitations to all *bygdelag* – those in Canada and those in the United States – to conduct their annual *stevner* during the festival. The Canadian *lag* largely ignored the occasion and concentrated on their own meeting the following week. The site of the Winnipeg convention was inconvenient because the heaviest concentration of Norwegians was farther west. The basis for the disagreement was also in part a struggle between the League and the Council of Bygdelag over who would direct Norwegian-Canadian activities. This situation lasted for some time, and *Decorah-Posten* deplored it, stating: "And it shrieks of quarrels up there about who is to blame for the splitting and separation. But it's Norwegian, this also, unfortunately."

The Winnipeg festival was intended to show the force of the Norwegian spirit in Canada. The week-long event had been directly influenced by the Centennial activities in the Twin Cities, which a large number of Canadians had attended. A varied programme by choirs and singing societies was presented; as at the larger celebration in the Middle West, there was also a special *bygdelag* day. *Nordlandslaget* of America was actually the only society to conduct its annual *stevne* at that time. A number of other groups, however, sent representatives and arranged small meetings, where fellow *bygd* folk from Canada also met. No Canadian *lag* was represented, and efforts to organize local Winnipeg groups were largely unsuccessful. The committee on arrangements had set up about the largest attendance with 200 present; *Setesdalslaget* was honoured for the best programme. The committee on arrangements had set up about 20 tents for *bygdelag* gatherings, but these were not used a great deal. A large number of people, however, were present. Local Winnipeg papers estimated a total attendance of about 10,000 – a miniature Centennial. Official Canadian representation made the occasion a significant event in the Norwegian-Canadian experience. This joint celebration, as some claimed, demonstrated that the center for Norwegian activity on the continent was shifting northward.

The Canadian *bygdelag* continued their joint activities under the auspices of the Council, but local *stevner* were also held by individual societies. *Syvde og Vanylvslaget* of Canada was formed in 1928 at Meadows, Manitoba, and met regularly for a number of years. The joint meeting of all *lag* for 1929 was held at Swift Current, Saskatchewan. On such occasions, official Norway was represented. This Old Country support contributed to bridge-building efforts, promoted the formation of new societies, and generally emphasized a Norwegian-Canadian identity. There was no joint *stevne* in 1930 because of plans for a national celebration by the League of Norsemen and because of collective *lag* tours to Norway on the occasion of that country's 900 years as a Christian nation. The next year, however, a meeting of the *bygdelag* was convened at Moose Jaw, Saskatchewan. In 1935, the societies met at Round Lake and the following year at Prince Albert, both in Saskatchewan.

From that time on, activity almost ceased. As in the American organizations, there was a strong connection between the movement and the church. The organized *bygdelag,* during their short independent existence, worked closely with Canadian-Norwegian Lutheranism. Representatives of the Established Church met with the *bygdelag* council and participated in the joint festivities. As time passed, the emphasis on one specific locale in Norway became a serious liability to the growth and success of the *lag.* It limited their appeal and did not attract persons of the second generation. If the movement was to have any future, it needed to find a new reason for being. There was little evidence that this would come about. One reporter, who attended the 1926 *Tronderstevne* in Duluth, unkindly characterized the meetings as "an old folks' coffee party." *Normanden* editorially commented that unfortunately this judgment was gradually becoming an accurate one. The "Norwegian self," with its dialects and tradition, was dying out with the passing of the original immigrants.

Syver Morck has recorded a bit of history about the Norse Society organized in 1920 at Torquay, Saskatchewan, under the championship of a zealous promoter of all things Norwegian, Pastor Hendrick Vodal. He wrote:

> The program was conducted in the Norwegian language. The meetings were held in the Lutheran Church in Torquay in the winter time and in the summer they were held on the farms in the congregations.
>
> The 17th of May, Norwegian Independence Day used to be a very enjoyable day. Some come from a distance of 60 miles. The 17th of May marks the climax of a long and fascinating history. After several hundred years under Danish rule Norway was yielded to Sweden in 1814. This day was a memorable day for those who came from Norway. The church was filled to capacity with afternoon and evening meetings. Several were dressed in native costumes. National songs were sung; among them were "saterjentens Sondag" and "Kan du glemme gamle Norge. . . ." The 17th of May buttons were also sold which many of the old Norwegians were proud of. A delicious lunch was served by the local members consisting of Norwegian food as: Lefsa, rommegraut, kromkakar, etc.
>
> During the depression years in the 1930s the Norwegian Society discontinued for lack of support of the Norwegian language. Some

of the Old Timers moved away; others were placed to rest at the Cemetery.[99]

The Great Depression of the 1930s affected the *bygdelag* most adversely, as it did many other Norwegian social organizations including the church. The slump in farm prices, mass unemployment, the crippling effect of extensive relief and general deterioration of the economy allowed little surplus energy or money for attending these district societies. At the same time, the membership of Norwegian-born people was decreasing and many *lag* appealed only to a small and widely-spread immigrant body. For example, the membership list of *Gudbrandsdalslaget* in Canada consisted of 168 members scattered all over Western Canada from Bella Coola to Winnipeg, but with the majority centered in central Saskatchewan. In 1928, the president was C.T. Haug, Outlook; vice-president, Hans Anderson, Outlook; secretary, Hans M. Hansen from Naicam; and treasurer, Martin Lier from Wingello, Saskatchewan. In addition there were three directors from the outlying districts of Saskatchewan.[100] Vast numbers of Norwegians had roots in the Gudbrandsdal valley of Norway extending from Lesja in the north to Lake Mjosa in the south terminating near Eidsvold. Norwegian romanticists made it the centre of a national cult, the valley of valleys in Norway and the producer of true ethnic genius. But even this *bygdelag* did not survive after the depression in the West.

Sons of Norway

The Sons of Norway organization was first formed in 1895 at Minneapolis, Minnesota, by 18 young Norwegian immigrants who leagued themselves together for mutual aid and fraternal benefits. The idea spread so that by 1940 there were over 300 lodges in 17 American states, Canada and Alaska, all integrated into a compact organization. On the material side, the organization provides millions of dollars of insurance among its membership and on the cultural side expresses active interest in all things Norwegian. Every month it issues a magazine that contains much information about Norway and on the Norwegians in the United States and Canada. Today it is the largest organization of Norwegian Americans and Norwegian Canadians working together. The total membership exceeds 80,000 persons.

Sons of Norway lodges are divided into seven districts. District Four consists of people from Alberta, Saskatchewan and the states of North Dakota and Montana and thus is a distinct international district. For example, Alberta has five lodges: Calgary, Claresholm, Camrose, Edmonton and Grande Prairie. In 1974, the Alberta lodges hosted the 43rd International Convention at Banff Springs Hotel, Banff, Alberta, from August 21 to 24. The Banff Centre provided space and a programme for 150 delegates from various youth groups within the international organization.[101]

While the *bygdelag* promoted regionalism and particular aspects of the Norwegian identity, the Sons of Norway were more fraternal, universal and socially oriented. From the beginning there was tension between the *bygdelag* and Sons of Norway. For many, the Sons of Norway were too secular, and for some, their ceremonies linked them to the secret orders. Others distained the *bygdelag* because they felt that they had degenerated into mutual admiration societies. While many of the clergy had little objection to the *bygdelag,* there were many who were deeply suspicious of this new fraternal order. However, the Sons of Norway continued to appeal to many Norwegians from all sectors of Norway and from various settlements across the face of the United States and Canada.

The supreme convention of 1974 in Banff featured displays of Norwegian handicrafts, jewelry, costumes and other examples of the cultural heritage. The day sessions were set aside for business and major addresses. The evening sessions consisted of a western barbecue the first night, a medieval Viking supper the next evening and a wind-up banquet and dance on the final evening.

In February of 1974, the various lodges of Alberta met at Camrose for business, socializing and a curling championship bonspiel in which 22 teams competed. Ski competitions were held at the Camrose Ski Hill. This convention ended on Saturday night with a dinner and dance at the local Elks hall.[102]

In Vancouver, the Sons of Norway were instrumental in building an "imaginative 15-storey complex" called "Norway House."[103] It is essentially an office building catering to Scandinavian business interests such as the Marine Insurance Company but includes a large restaurant catering to weddings, banquets and other functions. The second floor is set aside for Sons of Norway activities with a part set aside for use of the Evangelical Lutheran Church in ministering to the many Lutherans that live in high-rise apartments in downtown Vancouver. The part used by the church includes a chapel and offices for counselling and other pastoral services. There is also a common reading room. The project is unique because it involves the co-operation of three diverse groups: an insurance company largely operated by Scandinavians, a Sons of Norway local lodge and a church synod. Thus Norway House is a new centre in the heart of Vancouver providing a unique approach to cultural and spiritual heritage. In Victoria, the lodge there has established a social centre known as "Little Norway."

In recent years, several organizations of Norwegians have tended to merge with Swedes and/or Danes to form Scandinavian centres. Such an organization was established in Edmonton. Here a busy schedule of activities is carried on from a large comfortable social centre. To celebrate Norwegian Independence Day on May 17, 1976, the Norwegians staged a parade down Jasper Avenue to City Hall where the proclamation of Norwegian independence from Sweden was read and the Norwegian flag raised for the day. The celebrations concluded with a dinner and dance at the Scandinavian Centre.[104]

In Calgary, there has developed a co-operative society involving the Swedish Vasa Lodge, Club Finlandia, the Icelandic Club and the Sons of Norway. The building which was purchased is now known as the Scandinavian Centre. There are about 300 members. Membership is through sale of shares at $50 per share. The Department of Culture, Youth and Recreation has assisted with a grant. This society endeavours to promote Nordic culture and a greater awareness of the heritage and history of the Scandinavian countries. Language classes are sponsored for the five participating groups – Danish, Finnish, Icelandic, Norwegian and Swedish. Groups sponsoring handicrafts, folk dancing and drama are promoted. A library of several hundred books from the various embassies at Ottawa and from private sources has been set up in the Saga Room, which is the library room in the centre.[105]

SPECIAL HOMES AND HOSPITALS

An example from Norway emulated in the new land was to provide special homes for the elderly when their health or circumstances made it impossible for them to live alone or with relatives. The Norwegian Lutheran Church opened Bethany Old Folks' Home at Bawlf on October 1, 1922, in a former hospital building. The first manager was Pastor N.R.T. Braa. After some 25 years of service at Bawlf, this home was moved to Camrose. When Sister Marie Weiks retired in 1955, Mrs. Tilda Bergh became superintendent. The home added a 50-bed auxiliary hospital in 1957. In 1964, Bethany Home and Hospital added a nursing home. In 1965 Pastor O.H. Haugen became administrator. He had previously served as chaplain. Currently this home, hospital and nursing home has 190 beds and a full-time equivalent staff of 98 with plans for further expansion.

A similar institution opened as late as 1955 in Saskatoon. This was named the Lutheran Sunset Home. Pastor K. Bergsagel was the first superintendent. In all it serves about 135 people but a new tower is under way estimated to cost over five million dollars.

Also in more recent times, Lutherans have established care centres for the elderly and disabled which have incorporated as societies under provincial statutes. Outstanding examples are the Good Samaritan Society in Edmonton and the Lutheran Welfare Society in Calgary. Today these are recognized as outstanding Scandinavian contributions to hospital care. Because these homes maintain the highest standards, they are eligible for both federal and provincial subsidies and support. The importance of these institutions has grown as more and more of the pioneers have reached the sunset years. In these homes they have found loving care and a ministry that meets the needs of both body, mind and soul. In the area of social ministry and service, these institutions have established a unique identity which is now generally recognized by society.

In the early years these institutions served only the ethnic groups they represented. Today under a programme of government support, the pioneers of every nationality, colour and creed are welcomed.

In Retrospect: 1825-1975

Ever since the first boatload arrived in New York in 1825 and now for over 150 years, the Norwegians have been an identifiable ethnic group on the American continent. Their presence in Canada cannot be isolated from that on the American frontier because of the initial overflow from the United States to the western provinces of Canada. Further, they were held together in a Lutheran Church and various other ethnic organizations that transcended the 49th parallel and generally existed as international institutions until very recently. Initially, the churches, the colleges, the seminary and to some extent the ethnic press were founded and nurtured as extensions of basic goals that embraced so many of the Norwegians in the New World. The Norwegian heritage was common to both the United States and Canada. Norwegians in Canada profited from the American example and their initial support. It is only in this last generation that nationalism has exerted itself to the point where several Norwegian institutions in Canada have sought and obtained Canadian autonomy. However, several of the ethnic associations still maintain bonds and relationships with both the United States and Norway. Meanwhile, a new identity is emerging for Norwegians in Canada.

Predominantly, Norwegians have maintained their religious identity in the Lutheran Church but are increasingly aware of how much they have in common with other Christian denominations in Canada.

NOTES

1. W. Burton Hurd, *Ethnic Origin and Nativity of the Canadian People* (Ottawa: Queen's Printer), pp. 250-251.
2. Nicholas Tevuchis, *Pastors and Immigrants* (The Hague), pp. 10-11.
3. J. Magnus Rohne, *Norwegian American Lutheranism up to 1872* (New York: Macmillan, 1926), p. 5.
4. I Peter 2:9.
5. O.M. Norlie, *History of the Norwegian People* (Minneapolis: Augsburg, 1921), p. 189.
6. *Ibid.,* p. 222.
7. *Ibid.,* pp. 269-270.
8. *Ibid.,* p. 375.

9. *Ibid.*, p. 381-383.
10. *1937 Annual Report of the Norwegian Lutheran Church of America,* p. 100.
11. *Annual Report 1950 of the Evangelical Lutheran Church,* p. 48.
12. *Ibid.*, pp. 49-50.
13. *Ibid.*, pp. 50-51.
14. *Ibid.*, p. 51.
15. *Ibid.*, pp. 485-486.
16. K. Olaus Finseth, Supplement to the Pamphlet "The Problem for the Betterment of the College St. Olaf," February 1950, p. 3. He also advocated that the term of the incumbent President should not be renewed. For example, he reported that a member of the graduating class had criticized the chapel exercises as being more secular and historical than religious, whereupon the President, in a rare display of firmness with students, placed this student on probation.
17. *Annual Report 1950,* pp. 529-530.
18. Theodore C. Blegen, *Grass Roots History* (Minneapolis: University of Minnesota Press, 1947), p. 92.
19. See Ingrid Semmingsen, *Veien Mot Vest* (Oslo: Aschehoug, 1950), p. 404. and also O.M. Norlie, *History of the Norwegian People in America* (Minneapolis: Augsburg, 1925), pp. 324-326.
20. N.C. Brun, *Fra Ungdomsaar* (Minneapolis: Augsburg, 1915), p. 203.
21. For more details on these early beginnings see Harold Engen, *A History of the Evangelical Lutheran Church of Canada* (Saskatoon: Luther Theological Seminary, 1955), pp. 8-9; G.O. Evenson, *Adventuring for Christ: The Story of the Evangelical Lutheran Church of Canada* (Calgary: Foothills Lutheran Press, 1974), pp. 1-2; and O.M. Norlie, *Norsk Lutherske Menigheter i America 1843-1916* (Minneapolis, 1918), Vol. II, pp. 400-405.
22. See Ragna Steen and Magda Hendrickson, *Pioneer Days in Bardo, Alberta* (Tofield, Alberta: The Historical Society of Beaver Hills Lake, 1944), pp. 101-111. Also see Appendix for a sermon by Bersvend Anderson.
23. See G. Loken, *A History of Trinity Lutheran Church* (Calgary: University Printing, 1975), pp. 1-12; and C.M. Cherland, *The Lutheran Legacy* (Calgary: Century Calgary Publications, 1975), p. 9.
24. Letter in congregational files.
25. M.V. Joel, *Who is Who Among the Jacobsens* (a 1955 family history).
26. Harold Engen, *op. cit.*, p. 86.
27. *Ibid.*, p. 87.
28. Evenson, *op. cit.*, p. 88-89.
29. Engen, *op. cit.*, p. 96.
30. P.B. Stolee thesis, *The Norwegian Lutheran Church in Canada,* p. 26.
31. *Ibid.*, p. 28.
32. Evenson, *op. cit.*, p. 91.
33. *Lutheran Church Herald,* May 20, 1930.

34. Engen, *op. cit.*, p. 101 reports that of the thousands who came only 500 were claimed for the Norwegian Lutheran Church.
35. See Evenson, *op. cit.*, p. 100-101.
36. For more detailed information on encouraging aspects see Evenson, *op. cit.*, pp. 98-108.
37. Evenson, p. 169.
38. Engen, *op. cit.*, p. 110.
39. Evenson, *op. cit.*, p. 169.
40. From Annual Report of the Evangelical Lutheran Church.
41. *1976 Pre-Convention Report to the Fifth General Convention of the Evangelical Lutheran Church of Canada,* p. 39.
42. N.C. Brun, *Fra Ungdomsaar* (Article written by J.R. Lavik, Minneapolis: Augsburg, 1915), pp. 192-196.
43. *Ibid.*, p. 192.
44. From official college minutes translated by J.B. Stolee.
45. *The Camrose Canadian*, December 12, 1912.
46. *Camrose Lutheran College Calendar*, 1939-40.
47. *Ibid.*, 1965-66.
48. Constitution and By-Laws of Camrose Lutheran College, Section VIII (1957).
49. *Ibid.*, Article III, Section 2.
50. *Camrose Lutheran College Calendar,* 1939-40.
51. *Ibid.*, 1943-44.
52. Ronning thesis, *A Study of an Alberta Protestant Private School, The Camrose Lutheran College*, p. 51.
53. Based on Board minutes and documents of Camrose Lutheran College and the *Report and Findings of the Camrose College Committee of Inquiry*, August 4, 1966, which placed much blame on the Board when it reported:
    The Board has largely failed to understand its role in the governance of an educational institution and one could be so unkind as to say that, in some instances, the Board looked upon the institution as an almost private fief. The existence of a strong Board Executive located in or near Camrose, which expressly existed to help the president administer the College, could only cause difficulties, no matter the personal feelings or strength of the president. The minutes of the Executive show this only too well.
54. See "An Analysis of the Junior College in Alberta: Progress, Program and Prospect," Unpublished Masters Thesis, University of Alberta, 1965, p. 42ff.
55. See 1962 E.L.C.C. Annual Report, p. 60.
56. Present were J.R. Lavik, C.A. Ronning, Georg Moi, K. Bergsagel, G.O. Evenson, C.E. Lund and G. Loken. Deceased former presidents were: J.P. Tandberg, H.G. Fatland and A.H. Solheim.
57. Letter to the president, October 24, 1944 quoted in President's Report to the Board of Regents, November 9, 1944.

183

58. By special warrant, the Government of Alberta provided $200,000 extra in 1973 and $406,908 extra in 1974 above the regular per student enrolment grants.
59. 1916 Calendar of Saskatchewan Norwegian Lutheran College Association.
60. From O.M. Norlie collection in archives of the Norwegian-American Historical Asssociation at Northfield, Minnesota.
61. 1946 Catalog of the Saskatchewan Lutheran Bible Institute.
62. *Ibid.*, 1953-54.
63. Grimley, *op. cit.*, p. 1.
64. *1937 NLCA report,* p. 79.
65. *Ibid.,* p. 81.
66. *Ibid.,* p. 381.
67. *Analysis and Self-Study Report, 1965.*
68. See 1939 NLCA Report.
69. Report of the High School Department, March, 1947.
70. 1961 Report of the High School Department.
71. *Board of College Education of The American Lutheran Church: Canada Study – A Report and Evaluation,* pp. 92-94.
72. *1969-70 Yearbook and First Convention Report of the ELCC,* p. 54.
73. G. Loken, "A Study of the Government of the Folk High Schools of Norway," Unpublished Ph.D. Thesis, University of Alberta, 1968, p. 111.
74. Article III of CLBI constitution.
75. 1977-78 CLBI Catalogue, p. 2.
76. Report of Academic Dean to Task Force on church-related schools, p. 1.
77. P.B. Stolee thesis, *op. cit.,* p. 95.
78. *Ibid.,* p. 99-100.
79. *1937 Report of the Norwegian Lutheran Church of America,* p. 77.
80. For details see G.O. Evenson, p. 133-135.
81. *The Shepherd,* February 1940.
82. Evenson, *op. cit.,* p. 188.
83. *Ibid.,* p. 231.
84. *Nordlyset,* July 29, 1847.
85. Norlie, *op. cit.,* pp. 399-400.
86. *Ibid.,* p. 401.
87. Theodore C. Blegen, *Norwegian Migration to America,* pp. 304-305.
88. *Ibid.,* p. 330.
89. See Kenneth O. Bjork, "Scandinavian Migration to the Canadian Prairie Provinces, 1893-1914" in *Norwegian American Studies,* Vol. 26, 1974, pp. 22-28.
90. *Decorah-Posten,* July 7, 1905, quoted by Bjork.
91. From *Ny Verd* by James L. Peterson
92. Evenson, *op. cit.,* pp. 104-105.

93. See Report by H.L. Urness to Canada District Convention in *NLCA 1937 Report*, pp. 393-394.

94. See Sverre Lovall, *The Bygdelag in America* (Norwegian-American Historical Association, 1975), pp. 178-179.

95. *The Lur*, Summer 1972, p. 3.

96. *The Lur*, Summer, 1972, p. 3.

97. *Ibid.*

98. Lovall, *op. cit.*, p. 179ff. The author is indebted to Lovall for this and the ensuing paragraphs on the *bygdelad*. Lovall also wrote a doctoral thesis on this subject.

99. From the Fiftieth Anniversary Booklet of Trinity Lutheran Church, 1966, p. 24.

100. See *Gudbrandsdalslaget i Canada* (Gundlov og Medlemsliste, 1928), pp. 15-20.

101. *The Lur,* May-June 1974.

102. *The Camrose Canadian,* February 27, 1974.

103. *The Lur,* June, 1970.

104. *Ibid.,* May-June, 1976.

105. *Ibid.,* Article by Alice Jean Smistad.

SIX

Impact and Legacy of the First Century

Except for a few glaring exceptions, such as the Hutterites and our native peoples, Canada in not considered to be a land of ethnic stratification. In the early years there were people who were treated as second-class citizens and consequently suffered considerable discrimination. In recent times, the diminished status of the Anglo-Saxon Protestants has provided the opportunity for members of various ethnic groups to move into positions of power and influence in the political and economic life of the country. For Norwegians in Canada, there has been little economic or social discrimination since World War II.

Currently, cultural distinctiveness is not only tolerated but regarded as something desirable and worth preserving. Today all cultures have assumed new importance and the pressures to conform to the Anglo-Saxon entity have diminished. For many Norwegians this new climate comes too late. Propelled by a desire for upward social mobility in a society earlier dominated by Anglo-Saxons, they burnt their bridges behind them and adjusted to the host society as quickly as possible. Others retained their heritage and in the process made and are still making their unique contribution to the Canadian panorama.

This chapter examines some of the major factors promoting assimilation of the Norwegians in Canada over the past century. Assimilation was promoted by the numerical superiority and dominance of Anglo Saxons, the vast influence of the public school system, the readiness of Norwegians to speak English and to marry into other groups, their propensity to naturalization and Canadian citizenship, and their above-average educational status which opened doors to advancement in the new society. Where Norwegians settled in urbanized areas, assimilation was most rapid. It is only in more recent times that pervasive American influences have altered the uniqueness of several important Norwegian ethnic institutions in Canada.

In spite of the fact that Norwegians have assimilated rather readily in the new land, they have made important contributions to Canada in the first century. Aspects of this legacy over the years are traced in the section entitled "Northern Lights."

PURVIEW OF ETHNIC SURVIVAL

An ethnic minority is identified chiefly by distinctive cultural practices and unique values that govern the lifestyle of its members. The early Norwegians who came to Canada had their own language but soon learned to speak some English even if it was with their own distinct accent. They soon built their Lutheran congregations and colleges, and formed their ethnic societies. Here they were helped to survive by their religious and educational leaders. They came with their own folkways, manners and customs. They had their Norwegian attitudes towards the everyday life of hard work, their food habits and their ideas of play and recreation. Here most of them were anchored by the fact that they accepted Christianity as a basis for living. Often this was in common with other European ethnic groups in the new land.

In spite of all that was unique, the Norwegian settlers in Canada were readily accepted into Canadian society with its British precedents. They were hailed as most desirable citizens. Their cultural practices were not generally offensive to other groups. Nevertheless, the dominant group of Anglo Saxons promoted ways and means whereby the minority group was moved towards incorporation. The dominant group tended to regulate its relationships to minorities in ways which led to varying degrees of segregation, assimilation of the variation, or pluralism.

Segregation is the separation of minorities by law, choice, custom or environment. This can lead to territorial separation. For example, the various Indian treaties set these people apart on their reservations. Also Canada's early land settlement policies tended to scatter the lands that were open for free homesteading. This hindered solid settlements by any one ethnic group. However, these policies were not always successful because early homesteaders were eventually able to purchase lands first reserved for such corporations as the CPR and the HBC.

Assimilation occurs when the dominant group absorbs members of a minority to the extent that the minority no longer exists as a distinct group. Here the minority group generally alters its way of life so as to adapt to or even adopt the culture of the dominant group. The minority group does not necessarily adopt the ways of the new land completely, for it may retain some of its old customs or modify some of the new customs in the process of adopting them. To a large extent many Norwegians have been assimilated into much of the Canadian way of life. However, most of them still open their presents on Christmas Eve rather than on Christmas morning. There well may be *lutefisk* and *lefse* on Christmas Eve but likely Canadian turkey on Christmas day. On the

187

whole, Norwegians do not feel that they belong to a less-favoured group any longer, nor is there a sense of isolation or discrimination. Their Nordic traits are shared and respected.

Pluralism is a compromise approach to the extremes of segregation and assimilation. It does not deny ethnicity and may even encourage the minority group to retain much of its cultural baggage as long as it does not threaten dominant group practices that are considered necessary and desirable to the well-being of the total society. Thus Canadian society may permit Doukhobor colonies but will punish those who parade in the nude. Obviously, Canada has followed pluralistic policies in permitting religious freedom for its many different groups. Then, Canada's relatively recent efforts in the area of multiculturalism indicate a growing acceptance of concepts of pluralism. However, these policies came so late that many ethnic groups had already been conditioned by Canadian patterns and policies. And strangely, when the French group began to be given concessions all across Canada, the Province of Quebec suddenly pressed unilingual and unicultural policies and proposed separatism as the ultimate solution.

The major processes of segregation, assimilation and variation are not distinctly separated in actual practice but elements of each may affect an ethnic group. Interaction among diverse cultures normally results in some levelling in most groups over time.

Norwegians have not resisted acculturation in many areas. By them there has been little withdrawal even though most of them were segregated on the rural front in the Canadian West. On the whole, Norwegians have accepted the common elements of Canadian cultural, political and social mores but many still preserve their own cultural awareness and values in customs, traditions and principles, anchored in the home, endorsed in their colleges and propagated in their ethnic societies. Under pluralism, even of this type, Canada remains a collection of groups living side by side more ready than ever to share their special heritage encouraged by the new emphasis on multiculturalism.

FACTORS PROMOTING ASSIMILATION

For the Norwegians in Canada, the era of most rapid transition took place in the years from 1930 to 1945. Therefore this section focuses attention on developments and data related to this transitional period, and also examines major factors promoting assimilation.

Dominance by Elite Groups

By the time that most Norwegians arrived in the West, nearly all positions of power and influence in government – federally, provincially and at the municipal level – were controlled by the dominant and numerous Anglo-Celtic peoples. High places of business and corporate enterprises were likewise controlled mainly by the English or the Scotch. They knew the language from birth and were well versed in the practices, the patterns and the laws deemed to be right for Canada. Further, they felt they were the special representatives of the King to have and to hold the new country for the British Empire. The new immigrants from other lands were under considerable pressure to conform to the British patterns and to master English as quickly as possible. In the nineteenth century a Canadian nationalism was also developing, influencing Norwegians to become Canadians.

There are many examples of Anglo-Saxon dominance. Many Norwegian settlements tried in vain to choose names for their post offices and villages that reflected their choice and their ethnic backgrounds. During the early pioneering days, the Norwegian homesteaders in one area of Central Alberta named their post office "Eidsvold." To them this place name had much meaning, for in Norway this was the centre where the Norwegian constitution has been formulated and adopted in 1814 as Norway's declaration of independence. With the coming of the Canadian Northern Railway to this area, pressures arose for a new name. In 1911 a petition signed by 113 people was presented for the retention of the name "Eidsvold" for this village in the centre of a large Norwegian settlement. However, the Board of Trade included several active members who strongly opposed the Norwegian-sounding name for the village. Finally the name selected by the pioneers was rejected in favour of the name "Donalda," after Donald A. Mann who built the railway through the village.[1]

Olaus Molstad was not only the first postmaster in the Bawlf area, but also a skilful carpenter and contractor who built many major buildings in the district including Old Main at Camrose Lutheran College, the pioneer hospital at Bawlf and church furniture for many Lutheran congregations. When the railroad came in 1906, the Molstad Post Office name was officially changed to Bawlf. The new name was in honour of W.R. Bawlf, the President of the Winnipeg Grain Exchange. In a few short years after that, the Norwegian farmers around Bawlf came to rue the very existence of the Winnipeg Grain Exchange and worked hard to supplant it with their own co-operative agency for marketing their wheat.

Not all areas accepted such changes without a struggle. A history of Viking recalls the determined effort of the Norwegians in that area in the matter of naming the town:

> Before the coming of the railroad in 1908, people arrived, some as early as 1902 and settled as close as possible to the area through which they thought the railway might go. There was some speculation that the railroad would follow the old Battleford Trail. . . . Little did anyone dream that the railway would be surveyed through the low lying, slough filled land in between [the two hamlets of Viking and Harland]. When this occurred, apparently because the more level land created fewer difficulties for loading railway cars, the

189

railroad engineers staked out a new village site and gave it the name, "Meighen."

"Meighen" was named after a high railway official but proved unpopular among the residents because of the similarity in pronunciation of "mean."

Immediately the competition for a new name became a serious bone of contention. The name, Viking, suggested by Gilbert Sorenson, was favored by many, especially those of Scandinavian extraction and "Harland" named after Basil Hilliker's son, was the choice of others.

Wily Ben Gray who was on the board at that time favored "Viking" and was not to be outdone when it came to a vote. When he saw that things might go against him, he brought in several Norwegian ladies whom he had standing by, to cast their votes – which was all that was required to win the majority. This caught the opposition by surprise as women, though at that time were entitled to the franchise, rarely exercised their voting privileges.

Apparently, several names had been forwarded to the government but the name, Viking, was given final approval.[2]

The Nordic pioneers were able to promote and retain the names of Bardo, Edberg and New Norway in recognition of the pioneers who settled this vast parkland so thickly that it was often said, "Beside every major bluff of trees you will find a Norwegian on his homestead."

More autonomy was possible for the Nordic settlers in determining the name of their local school districts. In example, the first school in the Armena district was named Thordenskjold School after the great Norwegian seaman. Near Donalda, Norwegians named their rural school "Norbo" and near Bawlf they named one of their rural schools "Scandia."

Greater tolerance was evident in later years. For example, the Norwegians who settled in the Eagle Hills district north and west of Calgary, named their villages Bergen and Sundre. One of their pioneer school districts was named Eidswold. The dedicated pioneers who moved from Bardo to the Grande Prairie area named their village "Valhalla" which in ancient Norwegian mythology was the dwelling place of the gods.

A cursory examination soon provides similar evidence for other provinces. There are centres named Gruenfeld, Hagen, Gronlid, Stenen, Erickson, Engen, Nelson, Norway House and Norland, but a much greater number of school districts named after Norwegian leaders, places and pioneers. Thus near Buchanan, Saskatchewan, there still is in existence Norway School District No. 1469 and near Lake Lenore there was a school district named Norwegian Grove School District No. 2630. In one area of southern Saskatchewan surrounding the town of Torquay there were several school districts named after Norwegian pioneers: Flaeta, Gilbertsen, Hagen, Solheim and Tenold.

The failure of the Anglo-Saxon elite to accept the names the Norwegians preferred for their villages and towns often led to bitterness and misunderstanding. The choice of names associated with railway management, corporation leadership and political office holders was particularly rankling to the egalitarian Norwegians. Many came to the conclusion that "the only way to beat them was to join them."

Segregation

Assimilation of immigrant people is dependent in considerable measure on the extent to which the constituent elements of our population are distributed over the inhabited parts of Canada and are in a position to intermingle with one another. The influence of the media cannot supersede that of actual physical contact in promoting mutual understanding and appreciation among the ethnic groups making up the total population.

Segregation, whether rural or urban, voluntary or involuntary, constitutes one of the greatest obstacles to those personal and social contacts which alone can break down the barriers between peoples of different races and ethnic origins. In any study dealing with the aptitude of different peoples for acquiring Canadian customs and ideals and for fitting into the social, political, and economic life of the nation, an adequate measure of evenness of spread, or its converse, segregation, is of first importance.

Clearly, the more evenly spread the ethnic group is, the greater is the opportunity and probably also the necessity for intermarriage with other peoples of the country. This is notably the case with single males migrating to or living in a district where no females of their own country are to be found. Such conditions which promote intermarriage are usually coupled with stress on the official language and the influence of dominating educational and social standards. Hence the building of a homogenous population is speeded up. The scattered ethnic minority is readily absorbed.

If a given group is distributed throughout the census divisions in the same proportions as in the total population, it is evident that the proportion which the groups formed of the total population would be the same for all areas. Variations in the ratios of group to total population for the various areas would indicate absence of uniform distribution of the group and therefore a certain degree of segregation. Differences in degree of segregation for different groups can be measured in terms of the dispersions found to exist in these ratios. The Census data for 1931 and 1941 were subjected to these approaches and thereby indices of segregation for the ethnic origin groups were published as shown in the table below.[3]

The indices in Table 8 show that the distribution of the British races was the most general and uniform of all. The Swedes and Norwegians

TABLE 8

Indices of Segregation for Selected Ethnic Origins in Canada, 1931 and 1941

Ethnic Origin	1931	1941	Size of Group 1941
Irish	59	48	1,267,702
Scottish	50	53	1,403,974
English	45	59	2,968,402
Danish	85	79	37,439
Polish	93	91	167,485
German	101	95	464,682
Swedish	100	98	85,396
Ukrainian	108	103	305,929
Norwegian	100	106	100,718
Finnish	107	109	41,683
Italian	119	123	112,625
Icelandic	158	135	21,050
Jewish	129	137	170,241
Japanese	196	180	23,149

Sources: W. Burton Hurd, *Ethnic Origin and Nativity of the Canadian People,* 1941 Census, Table XLIV, p. 94.

were largely on the rural front and were fairly evenly settled over wide areas of the country. However, the Norwegians were heavily concentrated in the Prairie Provinces and their index of 106 was higher than the average of 100 calculated for the 1941 Census year. As Table 8 indicates, the Norwegians were much more segregated than the Danes.

Public School Influence

In the early decades the dominant Anglo-Saxon population in the Dominion of Canada believed that the British possessed the best language, culture, traditions and institutions ever devised by man. This precious legacy had to be cherished, preserved and enhanced at all cost. Therefore, it was important to compel minorities to adopt the cultural norms based on Anglo-Protestant values.

The elifes, for whom cultural homogeneity and national unity were synonymous, considered the public school to be the ideal instrument to transform the various ethnic minorities into responsible British and Canadian citizens. Curriculum planners aimed to minimize pluralism and to promote assimilation so that the new Canadians might be welded into one harmonious whole, loyal to the Empire, anchored in basic British values and common citizenship, and all speaking one common language. Generally, instruction in French was outlawed in the provinces of the West. Senior students could study French as a subject but Latin was the more commonly available course. Only after a hard and bitter battle did the Ukrainians win the right to have their language approved as an elective. The Norwegians never did win this right for their language. In short, planned assimilation was the order of the day in the early decades of Canadian education. Several decades of discriminatory provincial legislation against the use of "foreign" languages in school instruction succeeded only too well. The mother tongue disappeared at school, then at home, and finally altogether. The restoration of language rights came too late to be really useful or supportive of the richness of other languages and traditions.

Most of the children from the Norwegian homes attending Scandia S.D. No. 2913 could not speak English when they arrived at school. Patiently and faithfully, the teacher taught them the English language. Most teachers strictly forbade the pupils to use the Norwegian language at recess or in the noon hour. Under the threat of punishment, they soon learned to speak the approved language and eventually taught it to their parents at home. The negativism at school towards Norwegian had future implications as Laura Derdall has written:

> I didn't have much trouble learning to speak English, or adapting to this country. My husband had more difficulty. He learned his English working in a sawmill in the States. It seems that the Norwegian traditions have been difficult to carry on. I have kept up my Norwegian baking. I feel it is too bad that the young people show no interest in learning to speak Norwegian or in carrying on the traditions.[4]

Camrose College had been founded to give young men and women a higher education based on the Christian faith and to preserve the Norse culture. As time went on, it became increasingly difficult to teach the Norwegian language and culture. Ronning has recorded some of his problems in implementing the desired curriculum back in the 1930s and 1940s:

> But Camrose College, like other high schools, was soon chiefly engaged in the work of preparing students for the normal school, the university and the theological seminary. The Department of Education or the University fixed entrance requirements. Other courses were crowded out. Many students, whether or not they were preparing to enter the seminary, normal school or university, took such prerequisites as trigonometry and Latin. . . . Courses became rigid. Camrose College was no exception to the rule. It fell into line . . . The curriculum was failing to meet the needs of a large section of high school students who would never go beyond high school. The folk school principle – that education is a matter of giving vision and filling youth with purpose rather than a process of stuffing the mind with facts – was being forgotten.[5]

193

In those years there were many Norwegians who earnestly desired to study the language of their forefathers, but the Department of Education regulations were so unbending that it had to be Latin, French or German instead. The prescribed matriculation programme was so heavy that there was little time to study other courses in extra classes. However, in spite of all of these demands, Camrose Lutheran College did attempt to offer several folk high school-type courses and to provide related extra-curricular activites.

Language Issues and Trends

The public schools in their monopoly over education and the colleges under close prescription from the Department of Education legally prevented the use of Norwegian in schools and colleges. As has been pointed out earlier, the Norwegian Lutheran Church in Canada was reluctant to give up the Norwegian language.

This became a real issue in Bawlf Lutheran Church in the early 1930s. When the new minister, Peder Lerseth, arrived he saw the need for at least some English services to reach the younger people who could not speak Norwegian and to reach out to a larger constituency of people than just the Norwegians. His arguments prevailed, and it was agreed to have one monthly service in the English language. But when he proposed that every other service be English this was too much. At a properly-called business meeting conducted in Norwegian, one officer rose from his chair in anger to tell the pastor that "all you have done since you came to our town has been to undermine the Norwegian." With that he dashed out slamming the door of the church most violently. Several bachelors who had donated a bell for the belfry, threatened to have the bell taken down if there was any more English in the church. In spite of all the pro-testation, the motion carried to alternate Norwegian and English ser-vices. Some years later, there were three services per month in English and one in Norwegian. Before the decade was over all services were in English with special services only in Norwegian.

However, many parents insisted on having their young people con-firmed in Norwegian rather than English during this decade because to them the catechism and the explanation had more richness and meaning in Norwegian than in English. By the middle of the decade Pastor Lerseth was conducting his large confirmation classes in both English and Norwegian to the same group at the same time on Saturday morn-ings. The whole group benefited from both the Norwegian and the English instruction.

In 1937, the President of the Norwegian Lutheran Church of Canada reported as follows to the Canada District convention:

> However, it should be clearly stated here that our responsibility is not limited to our own Norwegian people. It is true, they are our first responsibility. No one can so effectively bring them the gospel

message as can our Norwegian Lutheran Church, if it is faithful to its high calling. The influences of the language of the heart, a common cultural heritage and racial characteristics are very important elements in the work of bringing a people under the saving influence of the gospel of Jesus Christ. While we should recognize these factors and take advantage of them, we should not over-emphasize them, or because of them ignore other important factors. The time has come – it came long ago in some communities – when we must frankly accept the responsibility of bringing the gospel also to people of other racial stocks. This follows inevitably from the fact that we are living in a land of many nationalities. In the communities where we work the people of other national origins are not only neighbors to our people, but they intermarry with our young men and young women. Under these circumstances we must broaden the scope of our work in most, if not all, of our fields, not only because God "would have all men to be saved and come unto the knowledge of the truth," but because, if we are to keep our own, we must also win others. The other alternative involves a definite shirking of responsibility, and points to an inevitable fading out of our Church as a positive and permanent force in the building of the kingdom of God in this land. The "open door," which God has set before us as a Church, is wider than many seem to realize.[6]

The language transition gained momentum during the 1930s, but not without numerous and often bitter controversies. By 1940 only about 30% of the services of the Church in Canada were still in Norwegian, and almost all the Sunday Schools were conducted in the English language. In this period, many urban churches changed their names. For example, the Norwegian Lutheran Church in Edmonton became Central Lutheran, but not without a prolonged debate and a vote which was far from unanimous.[7]

By 1945, 107 churches reported that they had all English services; 64 reported more than half English, five reported half Norwegian and half English, six reported all Norwegian and eight more than half non-English. Obviously, the transition to English was almost complete in Canada by the end of World War II. Thus it was that the Norwegian Lutheran Church voted to change its name to the Evangelical Lutheran Church in 1944. Because this was a constitutional change, it could not be ratified until the 1946 convention.

The prolonged controversy over language issues is interesting because as early as the 1931 Census only 3.1% of Norwegians in Canada could not speak English. This low percentage was exceeded only by 2.9% for the Swedish group. On the other hand 29.8% of the Japanese and the Chinese could not speak English in 1931.[8]

Based on official Census reports, in 1941 there were 60,084 people in Canada with Norwegian as the mother tongue. By 1951 this figure had dropped to 43,831 and in 1961 to 40,054. In 1971 the total was only 27,405. The 1971 total was distributed across Canada as follows: Newfoundland 35; Prince Edward Island 10; Nova Scotia 220; New Brunswick 65; Quebec 580; Ontario 2,525; Manitoba 1,285; Saskatchewan 6,850; Alberta 6,880; British Columbia 8,860; Yukon 65; and North West Territories, 35.[9] In relation to total population, it is only the three most westerly provinces of Canada that have any significant numbers who report Norwegian as their mother tongue. Even in these provinces the numbers are small in relation to the total number of people of Norwegian origin. For example, in 1971, of 36,150 people of Norwegian ethnic origin in Saskatchewan only 6,850, or 18.9%, had Norwegian as their mother tongue. In the 1971 Census, only 2,160 of 179,290 Norwegians in Canada reported that Norwegian was the language most commonly spoken at home. Projections for the future indicate that linguistic assimilation of the Norwegian language in Canada seems inevitable.

There are many processes that promote the disappearance of the mother tongue among Norwegians in Canada. There is widespread intermarriage between Norwegians and other ethnic groups. For decades there has been a planned policy of using the public schools as assimilatory agents to ensure conformity to the dominant use of English. From the beginning Norwegians have been scattered across the land both by land settlement policies and the uprooting caused by the Great Depression. It was never possible to establish ethnically homogenous communities. Further, when Norwegians after considerable struggle adopted English in their Lutheran worship services in order to serve the larger community, another of the last opportunities to preserve the language disappeared. The large-scale movement of people from rural communities to urban centres promoted less use of Norwegian. The use of Norwegian in rural homes is also disappearing rapidly. Finally, it is unlikely that there will be any major increase in the present small numbers of Norwegians immigrating to Canada.[10]

The issue of language preservation in Canada was put in humorous perspective in the following paper read at at Norwegian literary society in 1921:

> . . . I'm not putting all the blaim on the yong people born in contery for not to understand our language the Norwegian so good as they could, but it depends on the parents altso, if they have some interest in learn theyr chuldern to speek Norwegian, becaus, I tink it is the parents that in manny caus are responsibel for not to have learn theyr chuldern to speek our language. I know it are manny coming from old contery that will not speek theyr own language after they have been in thus contery a chjort time. I have a azempel from one I come to Canada togeder whit I was working whit him the first wunter I was in thus contery and he said, when I gett marerid I don't

TABLE 9

**Percentage of Selected Foreign-Born Naturalized
Classified According to Birthplace 1921, 1931 and 1941**

Birthplace	1921	1931	1941
Sweden	67.4	59.8	77.3
Norway	71.7	56.5	76.1
Germany	65.9	47.1	71.4
France	55.2	66.1	70.9
Denmark	56.3	31.2	66.2
United States	63.3	72.4	51.7
Japan	33.5	37.3	33.6
China	4.8	7.0	7.8

Sources: W. Burton Hurd, *Ethnic Origin and Nativity of the Canadian People,* 1941 Census, Table LV, p. 117.

tink I will learn min chuldern to speek Norwegian. I asked him if he was asjemd of his own language. No he said, it was not that. Then you must be a beeg fool I said. I'm not blaiming annyone for speeking the Engelish when they wanted to, but when peopel having chulderen purposely avoid to learn them the Norwegian language somting meost be wrong.[11]

Marriage Patterns

Marriage has always been a crucial factor in the assimilation process. The main characteristic of a closed group is that it has few social contacts with the surrounding culture and practically no intermarriage. Intermarriage is at once an index and a method of assimilation.

Of the linguistic groups, the Scandinavians have married out to the greatest extent – approximately 54% for the men and 52% for the women according to the 1931 Census. More specifically for the Norwegians, there is a marked propensity for this people to intermarry with Anglo-Saxons. For example, based on the 1931 Census 30.3% of Norwegian males were married to Anglo-Saxon wives, and 31.3% of Norwegian females were married to Anglo-Saxon husbands. Studies by Hurd indicate that Norwegians in Canada tend to marry more with geographically, linguistically and religiously allied people. There is also religious compatibility between British and Norwegian people.[12]

The fact that so many Norwegians in Canada have married out and in particular married into the dominant Anglo-Saxon group has been a powerful factor in promoting assimilation into the predominant group. The marked tendency to marry outside of the group was aided in 1941 by the fact that the percentage of Norwegian males exceeded Norwegian females by 156% as late as 1941.[13]

TABLE 10

Percentage Reporting Less Than Five Years of Schooling for the 1941 Population Ten Years and Over

| | Percentage Reporting Less Than Five Years of Schooling | | | |
| | Rural | | Urban | |
Birthplace	Males	Females	Males	Females
Canada	17.58	14.48	9.89	8.29
British Isles	4.69	2.88	2.84	2.52
United States	12.56	7.78	6.81	4.70
Denmark	3.14	2.37	1.98	1.97
Germany	8.48	9.52	5.30	7.19
Norway	5.32	5.56	4.21	3.43
Russia	40.45	41.48	32.41	38.29
Sweden	11.38	11.48	7.24	6.60
Asia	45.21	25.88	40.93	34.38

Sources: W. Burton Hurd, *Ethnic Origin and Nativity of the Canadian People,* 1941 Census, Table LXIV, p. 137.

Naturalization

Naturalization signifies the intention of the immigrant to make a more or less permanent home in Canada and his readiness to participate in the political destiny of Canada by accepting the full rights and responsibilities of citizenship. Naturalization may normally be taken as an indication that the assimilative process has proceeded to a moderate extent at least. As shown in the following table, the percentage of Norwegians naturalized was very high compared to selected groups in the critical years of 1921, 1931 and 1941. This has continued to rise in each ensuing census year. For example, in 1961 there were only 4,084 people in Canada who claimed Norwegian citizenship out of 148,681 people of Norwegian ethnic origin.[14]

Educational Status

There were marked differences in educational status reported by the several ethnic groups in the 1941 Census of Canada. Formal education favours the propensity to thrive in the new land. Norwegians ranked very low in the percentage reporting less than five years of schooling for the population 10 years of age and over. Educational status opens doors to urban employment and variety in occupational choice and tends to promote assimilation in the urban setting.

198

TABLE 11

Percentages of Specified Ethnic Origins in Cities of 30,000 and Over in Canada, 1921, 1931 and 1941

Ethnic Origin	1921	1931	1941
Jewish	86.34	87.88	87.55
Chinese	48.10	57.22	52.58
British	30.56	33.30	33.69
French	25.37	29.12	29.12
Danish	19.32	23.22	22.83
Swedish	11.52	16.14	17.42
German	13.95	17.79	17.22
Norwegian	7.44	10.99	13.36
Indian	1.06	1.17	1.49

Sources: W. Burton Hurd, *Ethnic Origin and Nativity of the Canadian People*, 1941 Census, Table XXV, p. 62.

Urbanization

In studying assimilation it is important to know which ethnic groups tend to concentrate in rural districts and which congregate in urban parts. Rural isolation tended to delay the assimilation of the immigrant. In the years 1921, 1931 and 1941 Norwegians were the lowest of all immigrant groups in cities of 30,000 and over. Only the native Indians surpassed them. This situation has changed rapidly in the last 30 years.

In no province of Canada is the assimilating effect of urbanization more amply demonstrated than in Ontario. While in 1921 there were only 3,416 people of Norwegian ethnic origin in Ontario, by 1951 there were 10,938. By 1961, the number had risen to 15,444, and by 1971 to 20,590. In relation to total population, the number of Norwegians in Ontario has been much below the percentages registered in the four western provinces. Overall, the Norwegians who came primarily to southern Ontario were incorporated readily into the industrial settings. Individually, they were quickly assimilated to the extent that ethnic identity in the collective, institutional or associative sense is not readily apparent or visible today. This same process of assimilation of the minority group in the urban setting has also been evident in the large cities of British Columbia to which many immigrants from Norway have been attracted especially since World War II.

Norwegians were enabled to retain their ethnicity by the considerable segregation in the rural setting especially in the Canadian West. It was in the West that they were numerically strong enough to build enduring Lutheran congregations and their own colleges. However, in many instances the Great Depression had a most unsettling effect and thousands were driven into new settings that hastened loss of ethnic identity because of the uprooting that took place.

Perspectives on Recent Influences Promoting Conformity

The Norwegians in Canada are greatly indebted to their kinsmen in the United States. From early colonial attempts in Quebec in the 1860s and for the next century, there were many bonds of interaction, common ethnic institutions and associations. Dedicated leadership and generous support often came from across the line. The ethnic identity manifested itself in ways whereby the Norwegians in both countries were in many respects recognizable as a particular and peculiar people. This was especially true in those organizations which demonstrated ethnic solidarity and focus.

The major factors promoting assimilation and integration of the immigrants have been operative for a longer period of time in the United States than in Canada. There most people of Norwegian background no longer think of themselves as an ethnic people but as proud American citizens dedicated to an American way of life. Here their ethnic organizations have been subjected to the levelling influence of Americanization. In the current generation many American leaders have come to view the Norwegian heritage in Canada in these terms. This has been especially true in regard to the Canadian Lutheran Church and its colleges which recently have been judged by some Americans to be "parochial, puritanical and pietistic." How did this variation come about?

Over the past two decades or more, dramatic changes have taken place in the American Lutheran Church. This church too has become representative of an American way of life that appeals most readily to the large middle class. In this situation the church tends to reflect the North American culture of conformity where the values of organization, planning, manipulation, achievement, salesmanship, consumption, gratification and efficiency are emphasized. Here one's existence is compartmentalized, standardized and programmed. The environment has become yet another area to be exploited in accordance with the principle of immediacy. Relationships with people are structured according to anticipated roles but subject to the processes of upward mobility. The pursuit of immediate happiness is the ultimate goal for many.

Such societal values have produced mass conformity and centralized regimentation even in the worship services of most churches. Linda Johnson has analysed this development thus:

> A minister, trained in an institution of higher learning, wears his vestments on Sunday morning; he leads participants through a prescribed ritual, printed out for them in a church bulletin or prayer book. Here believers gather for one hour's worship – no more, no less. Eleven o'clock on Sunday morning is probably the most isolated, regimented hour in American society. The service is

calculated, structured, predictable and efficient. So much time is allotted for the sermon, so much for the collective confession of sin, so much for the collective prayers, and so much for the taking up of the offering. Participants sit, stand and respond on cue. . . .[15]

These structured and smooth approaches to worship tend to produce "the comfortable pew" and a false sense of security. Formalized religion denies creativity and spontaneity and often fails to challenge. In the end it spawns ceremonialism and thoughtless repetition – a form of godliness devoid of power. Over time it professionalizes religion and thus denies the doctrine of the royal priesthood of believers. These ritualistic approaches have failed to excite the current generation of young Canadians who desire alternatives.

American leadership prevailed for the Norwegian Lutherans in Canada until 1967. However, it was not until 1947 that the Canada District under new American leadership was subjected to real pressures to establish uniformity in worship based on the prescribed rituals of *The Lutheran Hymnary*. Many in Canada felt that this was a contradiction of the Augsburg Confession which declared "And to the true unity of the Church, it is enough to agree concerning the doctrine of the Gospel and the administration of the sacraments. Nor is it necessary that human traditions, rites or ceremonies, instituted by men, should be everywhere alike."[16]

The pressures towards ritualistic conformity were particularly unacceptable to those fostered in the Norwegian tradition of Hauge who had promoted lay witnessing and testimony, sharing of the Word, prayer fellowship and simplicity in worship. The declared purpose of the Central Alberta Norwegian Lutheran Inner Mission was "to help bring about a richer and fuller measure of the preaching of the Word of God according to our Evangelical Lutheran Confession of faith." This purpose was reached by calling and sending out qualified and gifted men as evangelists, by seeking to help the Christians to come into deeper insight in the Word of God, by letting all the gifts of grace in the congregation be put to their rightful use; by supporting as much as possible the spiritual activity as carried on by the Lutherans, and by supporting and assisting in all works of charity and mercy that promote the welfare and happiness of our people, such as Christian schools and similar institutions.[17]

By tradition, many Lutheran congregations in Canada favoured low-church practices and promoted variety in the types of services held in the church. Some stipulated in their constitutions certain restrictions that barred high church approaches to worship. For example, "The pastor shall not chant, or use a gown in conducting divine ceremonies."[18]

Now the freedom to be different was ridiculed. Ministers were encouraged to wear not only one gown but two plus other liturgically correct accoutrements. Choirs were not to be seen but only heard, preferably from a rear balcony. Participation by laymen was confined largely to Laymen's Sunday in October or to membership on the local church council. The evangelical and Biblical activities of the Young People's Luther League were scuttled. In their place came an emphasis on "programs and problems; on personality and pep." A new Luther League book emphasized "Doctrines in the Flesh" and Luther Leaguers were reminded in a new programme guide that they were "called to be human." In these new programmes, they explored themselves and their society but lost sight of the Way.

The congregations in central Alberta were slow to respond to the new emphases and soon came to be criticized by various American church leaders. The ultimate in this criticism was demonstrated by an all-American committee which spent two days in Canada in 1966 investigating Camrose Lutheran College and then wrote the following:

> Related and somewhat antithetical is the feeling of the Committee that the over arching issue in the present as well as future development of Camrose Lutheran College is the theological orientation of the College. It is doubtful to many that a strict legalistic, fundamentalistic spiritual context can or will result in a top-ranking College. That time will be necessary to educate the immediate constituency of the College is granted, but *the College leadership will have to take a foremost position in providing the education rather than to foster the extension of and perpetuation of the present religious atmosphere and environment in which Camrose Lutheran College is placed.*[19]

The American Lutheran Church was in a position to exercise much influence and direction of the church colleges in Canada. Late in 1963, a new acting executive director of higher education came on the scene. He and a former American college president were appointed to study the colleges in Canada prior to the anticipated autonomy of the Evangelical Lutheran Church of Canada. One of the recommendations made directly to the board of Camrose Lutheran College was that social dancing should be introduced. In 1965 this was rejected by the board. Whereupon, the director wrote to the board members quoting from the book, *Pre-Seminary Education* to stress the importance of secular cultivation:

> . . . Again looking at its peculiar functional significance in the educational process, the undergraduate college has a unique role in *secularizing* its students. *It is not primarily concerned with perpetuating the religious nurture of the home, nor in preserving the intimate "family" ethos in other respects. Its task is to introduce its students to the world.* . . . For the future minister this secularization is peculiarly essential. . . .[20]

For the colleges in Canada such advice from influential American leaders created controversy. Not all could accept the thesis that the church college should be a place of "liberal" learning ever leading man into a deeper understanding of himself through the competing disciplines of the natural and social sciences, philosophy, comparative religion, history and other humanities. They felt that there were real weaknesses in taking the approach of humanism anchored in secularism as has been identified:

> The attempt of liberal learning to preserve an attentuated God as the cohesive center of academic study collapsed a generation ago into a pantheon of competing gods; the substitution of a hierarchy of moral values in turn emptied into a value-vacuum. The current fashion is to escalate the secular into the totality of human concerns and to exclude the transcendent supernatural. It espouses the culture-dependence of religion, philosophy, and morals, and enthrones individual creativity, seeking somehow to correlate this with ethical duties to others. Its undergirding premises are the absolute autonomy of man, the comprehensive contingency and total temporality of the real world, and the radical relativity of all beliefs and commitments. Here is no basis for moving confidently into an assured future but rather a way of eroding confidence in the truths and values of the past and in the worth and meaning of life in the present.[21]

So determined was the Board of College Education at Minneapolis to change the course and direction of Camrose Lutheran College that a retired American college president was sent to Canada for the year preceding Canadian autonomy. Upon his arrival in June, 1966, he announced to the former president, now designated as his interim adviser, and to the school principal, that his priority objectives were to introduce social dancing and make chapel attendance optional. However, the latter could only be accomplished legally by a constitutional change which would require at least two years.

In the summer of 1968 a new constitution was framed and approved for Camrose Lutheran College which deleted all specific clauses related to chapel and courses in Christianity. Because the former constitution was not presented to the church delegates in parallel to the new, most voters were unaware of the basic changes taking place with their approval.

The 1975-76 calendar of the college stated that "It was established in the hope that the dynamic faith of the church might be a live option on the College campus . . . Camrose Lutheran College seeks to provide a liberating experience for its students."[22]

The changes have resulted in a very limited attendance at the chapel periods, which are now being held less frequently. As one of its last acts prior to defeat in the election of 1971, the Social Credit Government of Alberta reduced the drinking age to 18. This change in provincial legislation coupled with the more permissive trends in recent times has created problems for the college in the use of alcohol by its students and weakened the stance of many concerned parents. To many it seems that both principle and precept are now lacking.

Currently, it is still compulsory for each student to take a half course in religion from the fields of ethics, death and dying, religious awareness, theology, history of the Old or New Testament or a number of other approved courses. "This is not religious indoctrination," says the Associate Dean and Registrar. "It is part of a liberal education. The idea of a college education is to experience and study a variety of subjects." The principal of the high school and awards officer agrees. "I don't want to indoctrinate anybody. I just want them to explore themselves."[23]

Changes in direction and attitude at the College did not happen all at once. In the decade of the 1960s it was difficult to secure qualified Canadians for either college or university positions. In this decade, the college solicited many American faculty members. Because their qualifications were rarely fully approved by either the University of Alberta or the Department of Education, many were refused or hired on an interim basis and then released after a year or two. Some of these lacked understanding of the academic setting or standards in Canada and the unique Christian objectives of the college. A few were privately abetted by local leaders and American pastors in lobbying for early modification of the aims and charter of the college.[24] In particular, most of the American faculty members worked to delete the ten-month high school programme and concentrate on the eight-month college programme. Because social dancing was not permitted under the regulations of the college, several of the faculty members in collusion with some of the students hired the local Anglican hall and staged a private dance in defiance of college regulations.

These recent influences on the Camrose Lutheran College have met with considerable populist support but much community concern. However, such influence and example have not been limited to the college. In recent years there has been a doctrinal drift in most Lutheran seminaries but most strongly in the United States. Canada has been short of Lutheran pastors but during the Viet Nam war a surplus developed in the United States. In this situation many American Lutheran pastors found their way to Canadian parishes, especially to large town and city calls in which about 20% of the pulpits are currently filled with Americans of other than Norwegian descent. Some Canadian leaders have resented the domination of a few pastors in pressing for changes based on an American way of life without real regard for regional mores and norms in the Canadian situation.

However, the controversy is not limited to Western Canada. Many Americans are concerned about the drift of contemporary society and the changes in church institutions on the American continent. Elton Trueblood, a prominent Christian educator, is particularly concerned about the swing in the church colleges. He has recently written:

... Though a few institutions have maintained the integrity of the vision in both theory and practice, these now constitute a minority. In the majority, the major features are today conspicuously absent. The chapel, far from being central in fact as well as architecture, is often empty. The spring is dry! Sometimes there is a supposed continuity, with worship being conducted, but it is no longer for the entire academic community; frequently we find a dozen where once there were a thousand. Some reference to Biblical studies is maintained, but without genuine emphasis, because without requirement. The combination of Christian commitment and scholarly achievement, once the standard, has been either neglected or consciously abandoned in hundreds of colleges. One consequence is a general lowering of standards. Now in a frantic effort to maintain a supposedly desirable level of enrollment, entrance standards are being lowered. ... The notion that the college should challenge the world's ways, rather than accept them with acquiescence, seems not to be seriously entertained. By condoning the loss of standards, the college has nothing left except tolerance, which turns out to be the weakest of all the virtues.[25]

Further writings of Trueblood reveal that he is a realist rather than a prophet of doom. He too believes that drifting Christian colleges can be redeemed by a new awareness and therefore recommends concrete action on a programme of disciplined renewal. As an articulate spokesman on the contemporary scene among many others, he is promoting the swing back to the basics in Christian colleges which in the past have offered leadership in promoting ethnic solidarity.

Both the Lutheran Collegiate Bible Institute at Outlook, Saskatchewan, and the Canadian Lutheran Bible Institute at Camrose, Alberta, retain their constitutional heritage and historic expectations of student participation in priority activities. These two institutions remain in the mainstream of supplying workers for the programme of the Church both at home and abroad.

These schools have accepted their uniqueness and have never denied their special role. They have maintained both the principle of student requirement and academic excellence. They have embodied the vision of wholeness and service. They have not permitted a secular worldview to eclipse other basic alternatives. They are unequivocally and unashamedly Christian both in purpose and principle in spite of criticisms and labelling. They stand as heritage institutions of an ethnic group that is part of the western "Bible Belt."

Historically, Norwegian Lutherans accepted the authority of the Bible and its centrality for their lives. Their slogan was "The Word Alone,

Faith Alone and Grace Alone.'' The Bible was placed in the hands of the people, preached from the pulpit and stored in their hearts. Thus brought face to face with God, the individual became responsive and responsible. This resulted in the transformation of life and men of God rose up to have done with lesser things – by choice. So widespread was this experience that whole Norwegian settlements experienced new levels of joy and service in their society. In this society, both personality and property were safe and respected. Their ordered lives confessed the beauty of holiness and of service to their neighbours.

The traditional Lutheran Church in Western Canada with its Norwegian and evangelical Haugean roots has been shocked by several of its new theologians. The battle is on between those who contend for the treasured sources of truth and those who seem preoccupied with speculative thoughtforms deemed foreign to the Gospel. Thus higher criticism, rationalism, secularism, Darwinism and humanism have moved in to make truth relative rather than absolute. In the process many decry that behaviour has become pragmatic, permissive and anchored in pleasure, and that religion has become a civil, respectable adjunct rather than a personal experience, an option rather than a priority.

It was not without considerable conflict that a new American pastor of German descent, serving a congregation of Norwegian background, defended his beer drinking with the boys at the Legion, but also suggested that his council members could have a drink at the parsonage if they so wished. Another new pastor from the United States staged a wine and cheese party in order to get acquainted with the young adults of the congregation. He seemed shocked to learn that so many of the church members were opposed to social drinking. A third American pastor scheduled a ''sock-hop'' in the basement of the church for his large confirmation class. Unfortunately for him, he forget to check this programme out in advance with his Board of Deacons who happened to be strongly opposed to staging dances in the church.

Some Canadian leaders have readily accepted the new emphasis as a means of removing what they conceive to be the shackles of ethnic tradition. For example, the president of Luther Seminary in Saskatoon has criticized the Lutheran church colleges for retaining compulsory chapel over the years and thus, as he hypothesizes, spreading ''the idea of work-righteousness.'' He has recently written: ''One can be thankful that, in recent years, the requirement of compulsory chapel attendance seems to be disappearing from church schools. But the memory lives on and church institutions have other practices that teach the same thing.''[26]

In recent decades many of Norwegian background in common with other Canadians have found themselves alienated from many of the contemporary tendencies of American society and are appalled at the many Canadians ''who are unable to comprehend their own subservience or their own naive stupidity.''[27] All too often Canadians by their own volition have accepted these recent populist patterns and positions. By this process they lose their own unique ideals and historic heritage, usually reflecting some aspect of their European backgrounds. Thereby, those with Norwegian roots are making a final and complete separation from their historic background and melting into a homogenous gob destroying the sparkle of the mosaic.

NORTHERN LIGHTS

Canadians continue to be fascinated by the spectacular movements of *Aurora Borealis* – a phenomenon unique to northern skies in our hemisphere. This atmospheric stream of charged luminous particles is attracted to our North Magnetic Pole. The crackling display, even colourful at times, is there because of the presence of so many charged particles and cannot be attributed to any one particle by itself.

Thus it is with an ethnic grouping in which men have come and men have gone. It is a fascinating passing panorama, a continually changing scene which is difficult for the spectator of the moment to transfix. An ethnic history endeavours to capture and unveil those events and personalities who in interaction accomplished goals or at least commanded attention. The story is usually incomplete when it focuses attention on individual personalities alone for no man accomplishes much apart from others.

Nevertheless, this history has already identified individuals closely and particularly related to the beginnings of the Norwegian presence in Canada from the time of early probing and exploration to the time of major settlements in the Canadian West. Not so much has been written about Norway's legacy to Canada and the relationships between our government and the Government of Norway. Here developments in the vast northern stretches of Canada are of particular interest.

Of the great Norwegian expeditions into the north, Fridtjof Nansen ranks as a pioneer. Otto Sverdrup was also a member of the Greenland expedition, 1888 to 1889. Nansen's brilliant popular description of the expedition in his book *On Skiis Across Greenland* became a best seller in Norway, and has been translated into many languages. Likewise his other book, *The Lives of the Eskimos*, met with a fine response. Nansen's last polar expedition was a trip to the North Pole with his famous ship the *Fram*. He departed from the Oslo harbour in 1893 to return in September, 1896. He and his crew carried out research into the phenomenon of terrestrial magnetism, northern lights, meteorology and many aspects of oceanography. Nansen brought back beautiful sketches and water colours of the *Aurora Borealis*. All this material was duly sifted and published in six large volumes entitled *The Norwegian North Polar Expedition, Scientific Results*. He also published a popular description entitled *With the Fram Across the Arctic Ocean*. This classical polar expedition placed Norway among the forefront of nations in the realm of polar exploration.

207

As noted Otto Sverdrup was a member of the first *Fram* expedition. From 1898 to 1902 Sverdrup was in charge of the second *Fram* expedition. When Sverdrup was prevented from exploring the north coast of Greenland by winter ice conditions, he used the *Fram* as a base for great sled journeys to the northwest and to the south which led to the discovery and exploration of 100,000 square miles of new territory.

In these journeys, undertaken under difficult conditions and often with considerable hardship and danger, Sverdrup and his crew explored the north coast of Devon Island and the south and east coasts of Ellesmere Island and discovered Axel Heiberg, Amund Ringnes, Ellef Ringnes, King Christian and several other smaller islands. These land areas, previously unknown, were all mapped and annexed in the name of the Norwegian king in accordance with formalities which had been traditionally observed for centuries. It was a land area almost as great as all of Norway. Little did Sverdrup realize that his new land claimed for Norway was to initiate a chain of events which were to disturb diplomatic relations between Norway and Canada for the next 30 years. Nor did he or anyone else realize that there were vast reserves of oil and gas in these Arctic islands.[28]

It was not until 1903 that the Canadian government became aware of the particulars of Sverdrup's discoveries and explorations. In April of that year, Sverdrup gave the first detailed account of his journeys to the Royal Geographical Society in London. News of his territorial claim soon reached Ottawa where it caused considerable alarm and embarrassment. In 1880 Britain had entrusted to Canada's safekeeping all of the Arctic islands discovered by British expeditions. But the Canadian government had neglected this Arctic territory to the extent that no government representative had even visited the islands to which Canada had become the heir. Sverdrup had now added to this embarrassing situation by claiming for Norway a large tract of newly discovered territory next to that being looked after by Canada.

The Canadian government decided to remedy the situation immediately and hurriedly organized an Arctic expedition which was dispatched in August of 1903 under the leadership of A.P. Low in the government ship *Neptune*. During the long cruise, Low landed on Ellesmere Island and took formal possession of it in the name of Canada. Subsequently expeditions by Canada under Captain J.E. Bernier claimed all territory discovered and undiscovered which lay in the pie-shaped slice formed by the extension to the north pole of any two lines of longitude which he crossed while in the Arctic. Bernier is thus credited with the introduction of the so-called "sector principle," later officially adopted by the Canadian government and enforced to this day.

Bernier's actions incensed Sverdrup. In 1907, he urged the Norwegian government to send Norwegians to police the lands that he had discovered and to occupy and administer them for Norway. Unfortunately for Norway, the government did not heed his advice.

The situation remained in the balance for many years with neither government making an open move. Between 1913 and 1918 Vilhjalmur Stefansson led sledging expeditions into the Arctic islands on behalf of Canada. During these remarkable journeys Stefansson discovered and claimed for Canada the remaining major islands of the Queen Elizabeth Archipelago.

In 1922, upon the advice of Winston Churchill who was then the Secretary of the Colonial Office in London, Canada decided to occupy and administer all the islands in the Archipelago and thus under international law lay claim to all of the Arctic Islands. The Government of Canada sent new expeditions under Captain Bernier and established RCMP posts on various islands in the north.

In 1928 Sverdrup, now an old man, again urged the Norwegian government to assert its rights to the lands discovered by him. If it would not, he reserved the right to claim from Canada full reimbursement for all the expenses he had incurred during his 1898 to 1902 expedition since then it would really constitute work done by Norway for the Canadian government. Apparently, the Norwegian government did not wish to become embroiled in further dispute with Canada and asked Sverdrup to present the Canadian government with his bill for $67,000.

To avoid any appearance of admission that Norway's claim had any validity, the Canadian government announced in 1930 in separate news releases that it had assumed full sovereignty over the territory discovered by Norway and later that it was making a "grant" to Sverdrup in recognition of his great work in exploration. Canada obtained Sverdrup's original maps and journals from his four-year expedition. In an effort to dissipate any lingering ill feeling towards Canada by the Norwegian people, subsequent Canadian governments returned Sverdrup's diaries to his family and contributed generously to the cost of a statue of Sverdrup erected in Norway in 1957. By 1959 Canada began to realize the real value of the islands discovered by Sverdrup in that the great oil reserves would supply oil and gas for the critical years ahead.

Another great Norwegian polar explorer was Roald Amundsen who claimed most of the glittering prizes which polar exploration had to offer. He forced the North West Passage and reached the South Pole. He was killed when his plane crashed in the Arctic in June, 1928. Nansen spoke these words at the memorial service:

> He found an unknown grave beneath the pure sky of the Arctic where the wings of eternity spread their pinions overhead. But from these vast silent waters, his name will shine with the glory of the Northern Lights as a beacon to Norway's youth throughout the centuries. It is men of courage, of determination and of energy like his, who inspire us with confidence in our race, and give us hope for the future. The world which breeds such sons is still young.[29]

Had Norway pursued a more aggressive foreign policy in the early part of this century, it is quite possible that Norway would have been heir to the vast riches of the Queen Elizabeth Islands. Thus, Canada recognizes Nansen, Sverdrup, her own Stefansson of Icelandic origin and Amundsen for their names all shine "with the glory of the Northern Lights."

When Canada elected to honor Sverdrup in the unveiling of the monument in 1957, the government sent Henry A. Larsen as its special representative. This man had spent most of his life as a RCMP officer on Arctic patrol service. In 1940 he was sent on the ship the *St. Roch* to go from the Pacific to the Atlantic by way of the Arctic and on a second voyage in 1944. This ranks as one of the principal seaborne expeditions of polar exploration.[30] But in July, 1957, Henry Larsen returned to his native land after an absence of 34 years. To him it seemed incredible that he as a Canadian now and an officer in the Royal Canadian Mounted Police should be privileged to represent Canada in Norway at the unveiling of the monument in tribute to Otto Sverdrup. When he arrived at Steinkjaer in Norway, he joined a distinguished group led by the Crown Prince, now King Olav V. Some ten thousand people had turned out to honour their native son, Otto Sverdrup. When Henry A. Larsen spoke his concluding remarks were:

> The names of Sverdrup and Norway will forever be linked with that of Canada through the islands in Canada's Arctic carrying his name and the names of those who assisted him in his work there. This is an additional tie linking our two countries so closely and devotedly together.

Three years later, Henry Larsen was honoured by the award of the Royal Canadian Geographical Society's Massey Medal. As the first recipient of this medal, he received it from His Excellency Governor General Vincent Massey, one of his last official acts in that office. Larsen died in 1964. His only regret and unrealized dream was that he did not live long enough to see his "ugly duckling," the *St. Roch*, properly housed and cared for. However, this famous ship did become a national historic monument and was unveilved in 1966 near the Maritime Museum in Vancouver. His name also lives on in the geography of Arctic Canada where a body of water has been named "Larsen Sound."[31]

Norwegians are not only known for their courage in sailing into unknown waters and charting new lands but also for their humanitarian endeavours on many fronts. Matthew Anderson believed that all Canadians should have some form of protection against the costs of illness, similar to the medical care plans that had operated in Norway since 1890. Thus it was that health insurance in Saskatchewan was pioneered by a "dirt farmer" who forsook a Norwegian fishing schooner to break new land in the Canadian West.

In 1919, he took a trip to Norway to visit his mother. There he had the opportunity to gather more information in regard to health services. In his own mind, he was convinced that a similar plan with some modifications was also needed in Canada. By 1922 he was a municipal councillor in the Rural Municipality of McKillop No. 20. For years he tried to sell the idea to others but it was not until late in the Depression that local support began to swell for his co-operative plan.

In 1938, the rural municipality approved the first programme of complete health insurance in Canada and possibly the first in North America, which became operational June 1, 1939. This "Matt Anderson Plan" operated under the Saskatchewan Municipal Medical and Hospital Services Act. In the beginning fees were modest and services somewhat restricted due to Depression circumstances. By 1944, the idea had spread to at least six other rural municipalities. By 1945 the Saskatchewan government adopted the Saskatchewan Hospital Services Plan. Anderson's persistence paved the way for a first in Saskatchewan from where the idea spread eventually all across Canada. They had been guided by the vision of a Norwegian immigrant.

Anderson was a man of great confidence in Canada. He wrote late in life:

> . . . if the present generation will carry on in the same spirit and determination as the pioneers did, within a reasonable time, Canada will be one of the greatest countries of the world, and its people will live in security and happiness.[32]

Norwegians are noted also for their dedication to egalitarian principles, in common with the other Scandinavian countries. The wellspring of such concepts are anchored in the basics of their religious faith underscoring that they are free men not to be shackled by government or privileged power. Thus it was that Norway appointed the ombudsmand, an official responsible only to Parliament but free to examine the actions of any ministry or department in government if a citizen records a legitimate complaint. So effective were these officials in all of Scandinavia, that today many Canadian provinces have appointed ombudsmen. The word in Norwegian means a civic official to whom one can appeal administrative decisions. The ombudsmand has become in many countries an effective grievance officer subjecting heavy-handed bureaucrats to basic democratic principles and processes.

In the Canadian communities, Norwegians were often leaders in promoting co-operative business, marketing and retailing as exemplified in co-op stores, co-operative fisheries, wheat pools and credit unions. Many of them purchased their insurance from fraternal or mutual groups such as the Lutheran Brotherhood, now Lutheran Life, or the Sons of Norway. To a great extent they were dedicated to the egalitarian principles of co-operation, grassroots management and democratic control of their business affairs – a heritage from Norway.

Norwegians have been ready to offer leadership and active participation in civic, municipal, provincial and federal affairs. For example, Hans Helgeson was an early member of the Legislature of British Columbia as was C.A. Ronning in Alberta. Later Social Credit regimes in these two provinces had such cabinet ministers as Leslie Peterson, A.O. Aalborg, H. Ruste and L.C. Halmrast. For years Robert Thomson was the national leader of the Social Credit Party at the federal level. Space does not permit the long listing of the hundreds of Norwegians who served extended terms on school boards and various municipal positions on hospital boards, rural municipalities and in urban government.

In more recent years, C.A. Ronning has served his country with distinction in the Canadian Foreign Service in China, India, Norway and the Geneva Conferences on Korea and Laos. In 1966 he was Canada's special representative to Hanoi and Saigon where he conducted delicate negotiations with the government of North Vietnam.

In the 1920s Dr. Walter Murray, distinguished former president of the University of Saskatchewan, wrote a paper on the "Continental Europeans in Western Canada." Among his noteworthy comments which fully applied to the Norwegians he wrote:

> The Lutherans are divided into national groups . . . and look beyond Canada for religious leadership. . . . The music of the people is wrought into their religious life. Naturally, the musical and similar organizations usually centre around their churches . . . In every community visited the factor of outstanding importance was their interest in religion. Usually this religion had a national character. Even where personal piety was emphasized, the community relations of these devout persons were impressive.[33]

Among Norwegians, hymnology is a significant part of the musical heritage of the church. The singing of hymns both at church and in the home has been a lively facet of Norwegian expression. From the beginning, their various colleges in Canada became widely known for their excellence and their leadership in sustaining a rich heritage of chorales. In 1942 Ronning reported of his choir:

> The Camrose College a Capella Choir has become one of the most popular activities of the school. It has been gradually developed, over a period of years, and is attempting to make a contribution to the musical life of the community by specializing in the singing of chorales and choruses arranged and composed by Dr. F. Melius Christiansen, familiar to all music lovers as the genius under whose leadership the St. Olaf College Choir has achieved unique success. Last year, in presenting two of these arrangements of old Norwegian songs at the Alberta Music Festival, the Choir received the highest marks given to any chorus and was pronounced by the adjudicator to be one of the most efficient choirs in Canada. The Norwegians in Canada have a heritage in music on the basis of which it is their duty to make a contribution to the life of the country which they have chosen as their home.[34]

212

In more recent times, the Concert Choir of Camrose Lutheran College has maintained a reputation for fine performances of quality music from a choral repertoire that has contributed to the cultural life of the West. The choir has also travelled in many parts of Canada, sung at the New York World's Fair and travelled to Norway for concerts. The choirs and various musical groups from the other colleges engage in annual spring or summer tours and always perform for enthusiastic audiences. For years the male quartet of Camrose Lutheran College was a featured group in concerts all over Alberta.

In 1978, the Concert Choir of the Lutheran Collegiate Bible Institute at Outlook, Saskatchewan, won first prize and national acclaim in a competition sponsored by the CBC and the Canada Council. The choir, in ranking first among high school entrants across Canada, won a $1000 prize and a commemorative plaque. In addition, the choir also received the $500 prize for the best performance of a Canadian choral composition in the competition open to choirs in all categories. This Concert Choir, under the direction of Gerald Langner, travels widely rendering sacred concerts, especially in the western provinces. For example, on March 4, 1979, they sang in the Jubilee Auditorium at Calgary.

Most Norwegian churches have featured choirs and singing groups over the years. The Bardo Male Chorus was a popular group at community functions in previous decades. At Viceroy, Saskatchewan, the Una Orchestra became known far and wide. As early as 1907 and throughout the years, they were featured in Dominion Day celebrations, Regina exhibitions, Grain Grower's conventions and concerts in towns all over southern Saskatchewan.[35] Later on one of the members of this band, Oscar E. Mossing, became the director of the Choral Union for the Young Peoples Luther League in Canada. Through the years this organization has promoted mass choirs of youth who were an important part of national youth conventions held biennially.

The folk music of Norway is being kept alive in Canada by such men as the noted Norwegian accordionist, Olaf Sveen. Since coming to Canada in 1949, Mr. Sveen has had 180 of his compositions published. His folk music delights radio listeners and is available on records and tapes all across the country. As a full-time musician, it is his desire to preserve and cultivate the folk music of the Old World in his new country. His home is at Edmonton, Alberta.[36]

Norwegians have been foremost proponents of education ever since the Reformation. Here Canada has had a host of influential interpreters, teachers at all levels and leaders in education. Many others have distinguished themselves in other professions as parish pastors, doctors, lawyers, psychiatrists, social workers, architects and political roles.

In shaping the Christian uniqueness and spiritual focus of the major institutions of Norwegians in Canada, no one person has had more influence than Dr. J.R. Lavik, who was born in 1881 in a parsonage in Minnesota. He first came in 1910 as a parish pastor to Claresholm,

213

Alberta, but soon moved to Camrose. From the beginning until 1917 he was President of the Alberta Norwegian Lutheran College Association. From 1913-17, he was president of this college. For the next seven years, he was the first president of the Norwegian Lutheran Church of Canada. In both of these key positions, he demonstrated influential leadership and great wisdom in pointing the way for both the Christian colleges and the growing Norwegian Lutheran Church in Canada. Many of his visionary insights were almost prophetic, for it often took many years before the Norwegians got around to implementing his recommendations for sunset homes, Bible schools, a Canadian seminary, incorporation and autonomy for Canada and Christian bookstores. Because of his perceptive insights and spiritual foundations, he served on many key committees and commissions whose recommendations guided the development of Norwegian ethnic institutions in Canada and the United States. Thus he was recognized as the persuasive architect in determining directions and developments in the Norwegian Lutheran Church in Canada during its first 40 years from 1910 to 1954.

After a decade of service as pastor in Minnesota he returned again as district president in 1935 and served until 1937. In 1939 he became the first president of Luther Theological Seminary, a post he held until his retirement in 1954. As president and professor he made a profound impact on the lives of the seminary students.

Over the years his prolific production of articles in church papers, his two books *Power from on High* and *The Christian Church in a Secularized World*, and his many broadcasts over the Evangelical Lutheran Hour reached a wide and responsive audience. He was bold and firm but a man who served in humility and love. His sense of destiny for Canada lives on.

In 1944 a Board of Parish Education under the leadership of Pastor J.B. Stolee inaugurated a Sunday School by Mail service from the school at Outlook. The first director was Ruth McFarlane. This unique service reached out with Christian instruction materials to isolated homes all across Canada and into the far north. In the 1950s "Children's Chapel" became a popular broadcast over a number of radio outlets in Canada. Miss Doris Nelson served as director for some years prior to leaving Canada for missionary service in Africa. In more recent decades this work has been faithfully directed by Miss Edith Vinge and her assistant Miss Helga Svee. In peak years about 1,000 pupils have been reached with regular Christian instruction.

In the area of literary effort, it is well to note Martha Østensø of Winnipeg, who won a literary prize of $13,500 in 1924 for her book entitled *Wild Geese*. This Norwegian girl was born in Bergen, Norway, and later attended the University of Manitoba. Mrs. Magda Hendrickson has received much acclaim for her work in *Pioneer Days in Bardo, Alberta* and *This Land is Our Land*. Dr. Chester A. Ronning has recently published his book *A Memoir of China in Revolution*. The list is incomplete here but further publications are listed in the Bibliography. As a point of special interest, it should be noted that departments at Canadian universities have discovered the great works of the Norwegians both in literature and drama and are offering courses dealing with many of these works in translation. In the area of drama and culture Walter H. Kasa has distinguished himself as both an actor and as Director of Cultural Development in Alberta. In the late 1950s Canadians discovered at their Shakespearean Festival that they had produced an actress of high calibre in Frances Hyland, a Western Canadian of Norwegian parentage.

Norwegians, in common with other Scandinavians, are well known for the beauty of design in their homes, furniture, tableware and clothing. Norwegian sweaters and Hardanger embroidery are prized possessions in many Canadian homes. The Norwegian craftsmanship and design in wood, metal and wool have been well received in Canada. Many specialty stores now feature such items as Norwegian furniture, cutlery and other fine tableware, decorations and lamps of appealing design and unique craftsmanship. Norwegian weaving and rugs as well as feathered comforters have become popular in Canadian homes. Canadians have also adopted the Norwegian *smorgasbord* as a way of serving food, especially to large groups. Thus, Norwegian skills and ideas have contributed to the beauty and individuality of homes in Canada. The Government of Canada has established a Canadian Centre for Folk Culture Studies and the National Museum of Man for carrying out both research and the collection of artifacts related to Norwegian culture and the other ethnic groups that make up Canada.[37]

Canadian painting has also felt the influence of Norwegian artists. In 1912 Lawren Harris and J.E.H. MacDonald of the Group of Seven attended a Scandinavian painting exhibition in the Albright Art Gallery at Buffalo, New York. They were greatly impressed by what they saw in that it caused them to realize what other northern lands had done in their painting. Harris was particularly affected by the decorative compositions of the Norwegian artist Harold Sohlbert, and this inspired him to paint the powerful mountain canvases he did in the early 1930s. MacDonald was more influenced by the Norwegian expressionist Edvard Munch, and some of his paintings approach the mystery and flow of Munch's work which he so greatly admired.[38] Others of the Group of Seven greatly appreciated this bold, colourful and rhythmic pattern as a means of portraying in paint our great and lonely expanses. Until they encountered this Norwegian way of painting, Harris and MacDonald had lacked a meaningful approach or a technique suitable for the Canadian landscape. On being exposed to it they were greatly inspired to the extent that they never forgot what they had seen. It shocked them into recognizing a new way of painting the greatness, the loneliness and the mystery of our land. They returned to work on large canvases, painting *Fine Weather* and *Georgian Bay* on heroic scale and with the reverence due such magnificence in nature. Such was the direct result of the Norwegian painting which enthralled them.[39] The Norwegian influence was here to stay in the work of the Group of Seven and their successors in Canadian art.[40] Harris, who was thus influenced by the Norwegians, was largely instrumental in encouraging Emily Carr to begin painting again after she became discouraged by art critics who did not understand or appreciate her.[41]

Lars Hawkaness, a Norwegian artist, was the first person to give art lessons at the Southern Alberta Institute of Technology and Art in Calgary. He influenced the Canadian artist W.L. Stevenson, who painted in a fluid manner with broad brush strokes and deep earth colours expressing the feel of the land. The early Norwegian influence became a stimulus that was passed from one to the other and we have as a result a richer art treasure here in Canada.[42]

Many Norwegians have painted Canadian subjects. Norwegian-born Minn Sjolseth, who emigrated to Canada in 1953, has travelled to the old Indian villages along the British Columbia coast and painted the landscape and Indian and Eskimo people. Many of her works are in public and private collections in Canada and other lands. But art has many facets, some of them as changing and varied as the Northern Lights. Suffice it to say, the Norwegians have added a facet to Canadian art.

The sport of skiing began in Norway where it can be traced back as far as 4,000 years. A hundred years ago, when the word "ski" was little known in other parts of the world, there were 50,000 Norwegians participating in this outdoor sport. Skiing is still Norway's national sport. In 1965 there were only six golf clubs in all of Norway with 915 members, but there were 1,311 formal ski associations with 99,839 members.[43] The annual *Holmenkollen* ski-jumping competitions attracts the best skiers from all over the world and attracts up to 100,000 spectators. Here in the suburbs of Oslo is also located the world famous museum of skiing.

The acknowledged father of Canadian skiing is Herman (Jackrabbit) Smith-Johannsen, born at Horten, Norway, in 1875. He learned to ski as he learned to walk at the age of two. Eventually he came to Quebec in 1928 where the Laurentians became a special part of his world. He became president of the Montreal ski club in 1931. Johannsen has probably blazed more ski trails than any other living Canadian. Over the years he has organized ski clubs in 23 towns. In 1932, he provided strong support for the pioneer ski lift at Shawbridge – the first real ski lift in North America. The name "Jackrabbit" was given to him by Quebec woodsmen he visited during early cross-country ski trips into the Laurentian wilderness. The Cree Indians, admiring his ability to slalom at high speeds down heavily-wooded slopes, gave him the title *Okumakum Wapoos* – Chief Jackrabbit.

Recognition has come to Johannsen on several occasions. He received Norway's medal of Saint Olav in recognition of his philosophy of man living in fellowship with nature. In 1968 he received an honorary LLD from Sir George Williams University and in 1973 he was awarded membership in the Order of Canada. In 1975, at the ageof 100, he won the veteran's ski race at Sun Valley, Idaho. In 1979, at the age of 104, Johannsen has become a legend in his own time, accepted as the father of cross country skiing in North America. While manufacturers of skiis and related accessories are enjoying the boom of the growing cross country skiing mania, Jackrabbit offers this word of caution: "Keep it simple, for this is one thing Canadian families can do together."[44] Canadians are proud also of Anne Heggtveit, the first Olympic gold medal winner for Canada in championship skiing.

Canadians remember their "northern stars" on the ice, Sonja Henje and Karen Magnusson. These too have brought distinction and honour to our land. There are many more that deserve mention, both of the past and in the present.

Perhaps above all, it was the women whose praises went unsung because in the titanic struggle to conquer the new land, the physically stronger male usually was accorded the dominant role. In her traditional role as wife and mother, the Norwegian woman was often taken for granted. However, the pioneer women more than carried their share of the load both inside and outside of the home. Obviously, the transformation of the gigantic buffalo pasture of the West into myriads of productive communities was accomplished by courageous women working side by side with their strong partners. In fact, the sacrifices and fortitude of pioneer women is an inspiration to any generation. The Norwegian women are part of that record. It seems no wonder that one Englishman blurted out, "What unbelievable women these Norwegians have!"

The most important institution in every Norwegian settlement was the home. Typically, the individual family represented a firmly knit social system where every person, every activity, and every relationship had a rather unshakable place, rhythm and form. Prior to World War II, the typical Norwegian family lived on a farm or in a small urban centre.

The father was the head of the family but mother was often "the neck that turned the head." Children were wanted and loved and usually present in all sizes. Even at an early age they entered into the tasks of the home and the farmyard in a co-operative enterprise where many hands made the work lighter. The many tasks were assigned in a fair and equitable manner according to age and strength. On the farm there were pigs to feed, eggs to gather, cows to milk, weeds to pull, wood to carry, barns to clean and potatoes to hoe. Most of the farm animals had names, were treated almost like pets and usually assigned to individual members of the family for care.

The positive attitude towards work, deeply engrained in Norwegians, was transplanted intact to the environment in Canada. With it there was pride in good workmanship and a desire for beauty, order and cleanliness. The home was a bastion of independence and self-sufficiency – a shelter of security and privacy.

Almost universally, family ties were strong among the Norwegians.

Children respected their parents, often under the firm authority of a loving father. The marriage bond was sacred and permanent. Divorces or separation were exceedingly rare and regarded with moral disapproval when they did occur. There was joy in home ownership but a readiness to share and co-operate with others. The Norwegian family cordially extended hospitality to neighbours with whom they joyfully celebrated the most important events of family life and festivals of both land and church.

Preparations for the festival event of Christmas usually began a month in advance. Animals were slaughtered to provide spiced meats served only during the holiday season. There were special cheeses to make, dried fish to prepare (*lutefisk*) and endless baking of a large assortment of traditional cakes and breads including *flatbrod,* a crisp, very thin unleavened bread. Mothers were exceptionally busy far ahead making clothing, for custom dictated that every member of the family should have at least one new thing to wear for the first time on Christmas Eve.

In the afternoon all chores were finished as early as possible; the animals were all given an extra measure and a sheaf of grain was hoisted on a pole for the birds. Then the entire family bathed, dressed in their best and gathered for the reading of the Christmas story from the Holy Scripture. There followed a special early evening meal over which the mother glowingly presided. Usually rice or cream pudding (*rømmegrot*) was included as an extra special item. Always there would be *lefse*, eaten buttered and rolled. After the meal, the candles were lit on the tree. The youngest members of the family were selected to distribute gifts often lovingly and secretly crafted for one another.

The Christmas tree would be placed in the middle of the living room floor. Young and old joined hands to form a circle and joyfully marched around the lighted tree singing Christmas carols and hymns. For the children this was indeed a climactic evening. On Christmas Day the whole family wended its way to the special church services at the regular hour. Far in advance of reaching the church, the Christmas bells would be ringing out to cheer even the heart of a recent immigrant family now separated from dear ones in Norway.

Christmas Eve was the family's festival, Christmas Day belonged to the church, but from Second Christmas Day onwards, the festivities were sociable. In the pioneer setting for at least 12 days there would be an endless round of visiting from neighbour to neighbour sharing the good fare set forth by busy mothers and their daughters. The long festival renewed and reinforced not only the bonds of family security but also a joyful relationship to God in the true significance of Christmas, while the extensive conviviality bound together all the members of the community. For the Norwegian family, much of this strong Christmas tradition remains.

The baptism or confirmation of a child called for a time of festivity with the godparents present to reinforce the significance of the day. If possible, the pastor would be invited as a special guest.

A common practice in many Norwegian homes is that of daily family devotion after breakfast or the evening meal. A scripture passage would be read followed by commentary and prayer. Often the family would join hands as they sang a song of praise together.

A summer family outing often consisted of a berry-picking expedition, strawberries in June, saskatoons in July, raspberries in August and choke-cherries in September. Of course, there were the school picnics, Sunday School or Church picnics, and community sports days, all of which called for family outings on bright summer days, combined with a sumptuous picnic lunch and new straw hats for the first picnic of the season. In winter seasons, the whole family would often ski or skate together.

The role of pioneer mothers in the closely-knit families should never be minimized. Of the mothers in the Bardo district it is recorded:

> Our pioneer mothers did not have much learning. Most of them had gone to school very little, but they knew how to love and make homes that put many of ours today to shame. They were not rich in worldly goods, indeed most of them were heart-breakingly poor, but never did they turn a cold or hungry traveller from their door. They lived in log huts with sod roofs and wore the same old serviceable clothes year after year. But they had something much finer. They had friendly sympathy for the problems of their neighbors and a deep concern for the welfare of the community. They did not have the smooth complexions and the white hands that indicate a life of ease. But though their faces were tanned and their hands were calloused and work-stained, they had a loving look and a tender touch for all who were in need.[45]

The home was the central institution and hub of all the Norwegian settlements. Here women have always been directors and teachers exercising influence more important than any parliament. Because these early families were usually enduring, they sent forth dependable citizens and leaders into emerging Canadian society, thereby building Canada as a safe and sane country. Solid homes provided a rich legacy to the enduring communities of the West.

RETROSPECT: IN THE FIRST CENTURY

The story of the Norwegians in Canada may be divided into three periods – the Norwegian Period, 1886-1929; the Norwegian-Canadian Period, 1930-1945; and the Canadian Period, 1946 to the present time.

In the Norwegian period, most Norwegians felt most comfortable and possessed a sense of belonging and security when participating in events sponsored by their own ethnic group. They were more Norwegian than Canadian in language, ideas, ideals, worship and ways.

In the transition period, both the Depression and World War II served to break down the walls of separation and to move the Norwegians to think of themselves more as Canadians in common with other groups. By then most Norwegians spoke both languages and participated more generally in Canadian life and community activities.

In the Canadian period, the language issues have been resolved. English has replaced Norwegian in both church and Sunday School. The new generation can no longer speak Norwegian. Ethnic newspapers are struggling or folding. Colleges no longer have a nationalistic emphasis relating to Norway but some have accepted strong new American influences and direction. Norwegians have become Canadians but with some retention of Nordic customs, traditions and attitudes both in the home and selected resilient institutions.

In the first century, the impact of the new land upon the Norwegians has been very marked. Nevertheless, there are both institutions and homes that retain an ethnic identity in spite of great pressures to assimilate and conform. The Norwegians have brought a rich legacy to Canada which continues to contribute to the life and the living of all Canadians.

NOTES

1. *Decorah-Posten,* December 1, 1911.
2. *Let Us Not Forget – A History of Viking and District* (Viking Historical Society, 1968), p. 7.
3. For detailed discussion see W.B. Hurd, pp. 88-96.
4. Memoirs of Mrs. Laura Derdall, Outlook, Saskatchewan (Saskatchewan archives).
5. Ronning thesis, p. 53.
6. *Report of the Norwegian Lutheran Church in America,* in 1940, p. 97.
7. *Ibid.,* 1945, p. 399.
8. W. Burton Hurd, *Ethnic Origin and Nativity of the Canadian People,* 1941 Census, Table LX, p. 127-129.
9. *1971 Census of Canada,* Mother Tongue.
10. See Alan B. Anderson, "Linguistic Trends Among Saskatchewan Ethnic Groups" (Paper presented at National Conference on Ethnic Studies and Research, University of Regina, 1976).
11. *Gjallarhornet,* October 1921 (Paper of the Norsk-Lutherske Ungdomsforening, Calgary, Alberta).
12. See W. Burton Hurd, *Racial Origins and Nativity of the Canadian People,* 1931 Census, pp. 10-13 and p. 257.
13. *Ethnic Origin and Nativity of the Canadian People, 1941 Census,* p. 77.
14. *1961 Census of Canada,* 92-548, Table 57.
15. *The Christian Century,* November 3, 1976.
16. From Augsburg Confession, Article VII.

17. Constitution of the Central Alberta Norwegian Lutheran Inner Mission Society, Articles II and III.
18. Constitition of Camrose Lutheran Church, Section X.
19. Report and Findings of the Camrose College Committee of Inquiry, August 4, 1966. (Members were: H.B. Kildahl, Minot, North Dakota as chairman; O.K. Storaasli, St. Paul, Minn.; and, H. Bangsberg, Bemidji, Minnesota.)
20. Letter to Camrose Board of Regents Members and President, March 16, 1965. This American leader had earlier urged the President of Camrose Lutheran College to read *The Secular City* by Harvey Cox for, in his opinion, this could resolve many problems in the administration of the Christian College.
21. *Christianity Today*, July 2, 1976.
22. Camrose Lutheran College, 1975-76, p. 2. (Calendar)
23. The Edmonton Journal, November 1976.
24. Committee of Inquiry as in footnote 19.
25. *Christianity Today*, November 5, 1976. (From an address delivered at a colloquium on higher education.)
26. William Horden, *Living by Grace* (Philadelphia: The Westminister Press, 1975), p. 19.
27. See Al Purdy, ed., *The New Romans: Candid Canadian Opinions of the U.S.* (Edmonton: Hurtig, 1968), p. iv.
28. *Calgary Herald,* January 29, 1973.
29. Thor Heyerdahl, *Great Norwegian Explorations* (Oslo: Dregers Forlag), pp. 118-119.
30. Henry A. Larsen, *The Big Ship* (Toronto: McClelland and Stewart, 1967).
31. *Ibid.,* p. 217.
32. See Matthew S. Anderson with Harold A. Longman, *Bold Experiment* (Regina, 1969), pp. 1-42.
33. Offprint from Queen's Quarterly in the archives at the University of Regina.
34. Ronning thesis, *op. cit.,* p. 79.
35. Oscar E. Mossing, "We of Excel" (a local history of the Rural Municipality of Excel, 1955), p. 23.
36. *Heritage,* March-April 1973.
37. See Jan Harold Brunvand, *Norwegian Settlers in Alberta* (Ottawa: National Museums, 1974), Paper No. 8.
38. R.H. Hubbard, *The Development of Canadian Art.* Curator of Canadian Art at the National Gallery of Canada, 1947, p. 88.
39. Dennis Reid, *A Concise History of Canadian Painting* (Toronto: Oxford University Press, 1973), pp. 138-139.
40. W.S. Reid, ed., *The Scottish Tradition in Canada*, p. 229.
41. Lorne E. Render, *The Mountains and Sky* (Glenbow-Alberta Institute: McClelland and Stewart, 1974), p. 184.
42. *Ibid.,* p. 143.

221

43. *Statistisk Arbok, 1966*, p. 282.
44. The Calgary Herald, January 25, 1979.
45. Ragna Steen and Magda Hendrickson, "Our Pioneer Mothers" in *Pioneer Days in Bardo, Alberta* (Tofield, Alberta: The Historical Society of Beaver Hills Lake, 1944), p. 165.

SEVEN

Today and Tomorrow

Most of the Norwegian pioneers began the struggle in the new land under harsh circumstances. Often they were first sheltered in humble sod or log shacks, but most of their children were born in frame houses. After decades of hard work, they rose above their early poverty.

Had their aims been low they would have remained in the shacks in which they started. They were not content with mean things. In spite of incredibly persistent hardships, especially during the dark years of the Depression, they proved themselves to be giants upon the earth because their faith and hope was anchored in enduring values beyond themselves and in their readiness to try again. They persisted.

Slowly the frontier receded before them. Eventually they established solid communities clustered around larger meaningful institutions. The Norwegian identity in Canada is still identifiable because of strong homes that perpetuate many of the customs and traditions of the Old Country and because of special social, spiritual and educational institutions that have not completely surrendered that which is treasured and distinctive.

Norwegians in Canada remain a small scattered minority. As citizens of Canada intermarried, became increasingly urbanized and subject to many other levelling influences of North American society, can they hope to survive as an ethnic group? Perhaps the greatest hope for ethnic survival lies in the fact that Norwegian Canadians have discovered modern Norway and hence new pride in their historic roots.

PURVIEW OF THE CONTEMPORARY CONTEXT

Norwegians in Canada as an ethnic-origin category are exceeded by the British, French, German, Italian, Ukrainian, Dutch, Jewish and Polish in that order. The Norwegians are the largest of the Scandinavian group. Norwegians exceed the Hungarian, Greek, Chinese, Yugoslav, Swedes, Danes, Finns, Belgian, Austrian, Japanese, Icelandic, Romanian and

TABLE 12

Norwegians in Canada Born in Norway			
1901	1,256	1941	26,914
1911	20,968	1951	22,969
1921	23,127	1961	22,267
1931	32,679	1971	16,350

Source: Decennial Censuses

Lithuanian groups in that order. In the 1971 Census, Norwegians in Canada constituted 0.83% of the population, representing 179,290 out of 21,568,310 people.[1] In the 1971 Census there were only 16,350 people in Canada who reported Norway as their place of birth.[2] As shown in Table 12 this is the smallest number ever reported in any recent decennial census.

The Norwegian-born immigrants are dying out. With them the knowledge of the Norwegian language is going. Most Norwegian language newspapers have disappeared. Churches are no longer founded on ethnic appeal because mergers with other Lutheran groups place Norwegians in minority positions here also. Colleges and seminaries are beginning to manifest secularistic and populist trends. Concentration on traditional sentimental themes about "old Norway" is fading. Ethnic organizations that rely on participation by immigrants and their children and that require a knowledge of Norwegian are in a losing battle for survival.

In 1971, Norwegians born in Europe were spread unevenly across Canada. Out of 16,350 reported, 7,075 were in the Province of British Columbia alone as shown in Table 13. Of all the provinces of Canada, British Columbia most closely resembles Norway in environmental features.

Yet there were 179,290 people in Canada in 1971 that reported that they were Norwegian by ethnic origin. Because so many Norwegian women in Canada are married to men of other races, and thus by census rules are not counted as having children of this ethnic origin, this tends to reduce the numbers in the Norwegian grouping. Nevertheless, as shown in Table 14, the number of Norwegians by ethnic origin continues to grow.

CURRENT MIGRATION FROM NORWAY

For the period 1896 to 1900, the distribution by ethnic origin of immigrants admitted to Canada was not fully recorded by the Department of Citizenship and Immigration. However, as shown in the table in the Appendix, there were 40,364 immigrants of Norwegian ethnic origin admitted to Canada in the years from 1900 to 1930. The peak year was 1927

TABLE 13

1971 Distribution of Norwegians in Canada Born in Norway

British Columbia	7,075	Nova Scotia	260
Alberta	3,035	New Brunswick	70
Ontario	2,440	Yukon	50
Saskatchewan	2,215	Newfoundland	40
Manitoba	715	North West Territories	30
Quebec	530	Canada Total	16,460

Source: 1971 Census of Canada, 92-727, Table 34.

TABLE 14

Norwegians in Canada by Ethnic Origin

	1921	1931	1941	1951	1961	1971
British Columbia	6,570	8,258	16,690	27,503	39,450	53,245
Alberta	21,323	27,360	29,628	33,766	42,305	51,305
Saskatchewan	31,438	39,755	38,213	35,625	37,204	36,160
Manitoba	4,203	5,263	5,955	6,740	7,811	8,960
Ontario	3,416	5,172	7,123	10,938	15,144	20,590
Quebec	705	1,504	1,512	1,693	2,647	3,820
New Brunswick	588	601	652	1,009	1,225	1,410
Nova Scotia	482	501	687	1,214	1,706	1,980
Prince Edward Island	10	17	16	37	68	90
Newfoundland	—	—	—	333	486	745
Yukon	107	108		252	369	485
North West Territories	14	19	252	156	266	505
Canada Total	68,856	88,558	100,728	119,266	148,681	179,295

Source: Decennial Censuses

when 5,102 were admitted. However, in the 48 years from 1930 to 1978, only 15,431 Norwegians were admitted with none arriving in 1936 or in 1944. In the last eight years from 1970 to 1978 only 1,362 have been admitted. This is an average of 170 per year compared to the overall average of 725 over the past 77 years, or 1,345 in the first 30 years starting in 1900. Since 1930, there has been limited infusion of Norwegians into Canada. See Table 16 in the Appendix.

Immigration statistics from the federal government for the current decade show that those Norwegians who come to Canada now are predominantly in the age grouping from 20 to 34. Their occupational

TABLE 15

Canadian Destination of Recent Immigrants from Norway							
Declared Destination	1970	1971	1972	1973	1974	1975	19
Newfoundland	0	4	3	1	1	1	
Prince Edward Island	0	0	0	0	0	0	
Nova Scotia	11	13	4	7	5	11	
Quebec	25	11	15	37	27	25	
Ontario	85	35	43	47	70	52	3
Manitoba	6	3	2	2	2	8	
Saskatchewan	5	1	1	0	5	13	
Alberta	15	8	21	17	40	15	2
British Columbia	87	48	44	90	77	60	5
North West Territories and Yukon	0	0	0	1	0	1	
Total	234	123	133	202	227	186	14

Source: Immigration Statistics from Manpower and Immigration, Ottawa.

clusters are in the following order: professional, service and recreation, manufacturing, clerical, transportation and communication, construction and commercial or financial.

The professional group continues to be predominant and in 1970 included such categories as: engineers, physicians and surgeons, professors and teachers, scientists, science technicians, dentists, optometrists, architects, economists, interior decorators and statisticians. The service sector included cooks, waiters and domestic help. The third large grouping, manufacturing, included such occupations as machinists, mechanics, tailors, electronic technicians and glass workers. In contrast to earlier migration periods, it is noteworthy that there are few if any labourers and farmers. A considerable number of fishermen and loggers find their way to either the west or east coasts of Canada.

The pattern of Norwegian immigration to Canada varies much from the distributions of previous decades when the provinces that principally attracted immigrants from Norway were Alberta, Saskatchewan, Manitoba and British Columbia. In this decade the order of priority is as follows: British Columbia, Ontario, Quebec, Alberta, Nova Scotia, Manitoba, New Brunswick, Newfoundland and Saskatchewan. The numbers are shown in Table 15.

The current number of immigrants from Norway has been small and largely removed from the historic rural settlements of Norwegians in Western Canada. In fact, the numbers who come to Ontario, Quebec, Nova Scotia, New Brunswick and Newfoundland cannot readily attach themselves to their own ethnic institutions because they never developed on a permanent basis in these provinces. Norwegians who come to Canada today are usually fluent in English before they come and are readily accepted into the urban centres of Canada as professional, service and technical workers. The situation is conducive to early assimilation into the Canadian scene. Of these new Norwegians in Canada it can be said, "They came, they saw, and they were assimilated."

The prospects for growth in Norwegian immigration to Canada are not promising. Norway's economy today is a far cry from that which prevailed from 1850 to 1930. Modern Norway's economy is soundly diversified and balanced. Next to the Soviet Union it is the most planned economy of all. Its growth is regular and consistent. There is practically no unemployment. Of the 25 countries that make up the Organization for Economic Cooperation and Development, Norway ranks third in per capita gross national product. In 1975 this was $7,100, thus exceeding the United States by $50 being only behind Sweden and Switzerland by about $1,300.[3]

The modern Norwegian enjoys a comfortable life, close to a beautiful nature rich in unspoiled forests, splendid fjords and long ski slopes. He belongs to a large middle class in a society where few are very rich and even fewer are very poor. The country's prosperity has produced a model welfare state that is generous, humane and democratic.

Today Norway sits on a continental shelf rich in vast reservoirs of oil and gas. Beginning in 1975, Norway became Europe's first exporter of oil. The new wealth now available to Norway is completely state owned, and is fully integrated from exploring, owning, refining, transporting and selling within the pace of Norwegian planning and economic goals. It appears that Norway is on the way to becoming one of the world's richer nations.

The American oil executives have discovered that the Norwegians cannot be pushed. "They are aggressive and stubborn," says an admiring American oil executive who has wrestled with authorities in Norway over licenses to exploit the underwater shelf. The Norwegians are open only to developments which profit the greatest number of people over the longest possible time. "They think they have a good life now," an American oil executive says. "They don't want the hustle, bustle and pressure we want to put on. They like to leave their offices at 4:30 in the afternoon and go skiing outside of Oslo."[4]

Under the circumstances now prevailing in Norway, it can be safely concluded that there will be no exodus of Norwegians to Canada in this century. In fact, their relatives in Canada find it to be increasingly difficult to dislodge them from their beautiful vacation homes in the mountains or by the sea to come to Canada for a visit. Their life in Norway is rich and full; very few will leave the homeland to live in Canada. In fact, in 1977 only 100 came from Norway to Canada.

THE DISCOVERY OF NORWAY

The early immigrants were so absorbed with keeping alive in the new land that in their struggle with the frontier wilderness few could find time to write of their adventure. And their children, the first generation of Canadians, were often determined to shed their ethnicity and to prove themselves as competitive Canadians free of labels or any second class status. Their children, the grandchildren of the pioneers, could no longer speak Norwegian. However, they did manifest a certain curiosity about customs, foods, traditions, old pictures and in general the family tree. The current generation has had both time and money to investigate ethnic background. The more they discovered, the more they wanted to know. They began to marvel at their heritage. With zeal, many endeavoured to search out the pioneer paths, to comprehend the magnitude of the early struggles and to appreciate the cost of present accomplishments.

It is sad, but true too often, that it is the third and even the fourth generation that really undertakes the sentimental journey into the past to record strategic exploits and trace the paths of the pioneers. They find it a difficult but a rewarding task. They wonder why the task was left so long, for now much is shrouded by uncertain dates and confusing events.

In this situation, travel back to Norway to search out one's ancestors has become increasingly popular. Inexpensive charter flights sponsored by such groups as the Sons of Norway or the Scandinavian Historical Society have spurred such travel. Interest in Norwegian art, values and history is on the upsurge among people of Norwegian heritage as well as among many other nationalities. In short, Canadians have become very interested in their roots. The first generation born in Canada often tended to shy away from the different customs of their forefathers. Succeeding generations were more relaxed and curious about their backgrounds and their history. The media have promoted interest in the land and life of Norway. The charter flight opportunity clinched the decision.

So popular are the Nordic tours that in 1977 it is estimated that about 3,000 people of Norwegian descent participated in sixteen non-stop flights directly to Oslo, Norway, from Vancouver, Calgary and Winnipeg. In addition, there were an equal number of direct flights to Copenhagen from Vancouver, Edmonton, Calgary and Winnipeg. Many who first land at Copenhagen proceed to Norway on the same tour. The average length of stay in Norway on most charter tours is about 30 days. In addition, there are many individuals who make their own arrangements for a trip to Norway.

They thought they might be going to a primitive medieval land. They were surprised to find a cultured, civilized and comfortable society of congenial people. They were welcomed with such warm-hearted courtesy and consideration that suddenly they felt very much at home and began to marvel at these Norwegians who also spoke English.

It was not too difficult to trace the ancestral records. Every parish where there had been no unfortunate fires had excellent records in superb order, although the fact that the pioneer immigrants changed their names when coming to Canada created a few problems. Many solid old homes that were birthplaces of the pioneers still stood. There were paths and places of vital historical interest, old photos of dignified ancestors and family likenesses among the living. Visits to museums, parks, galleries and exhibitions convinced the visitor that here was a land rich in culture and heritage. Travel about the land of Norway proved to the Canadian that here was a country of superb beauty – the thrilling ride up and down a Norwegian fjord nestled in stillness below beautiful mountains, green forests, crashing waterfalls and rustic farms; the long climb over twisting roads to a quiet retreat or *seter* on a mountain plateau or a hike through a forest so farmed and protected that it seemed to be a virgin forest. Even the cities were full of roses and parks and patches of forest for hiking and skiing. The countryside was clustered with well-kept farms and dotted with villages, lakes and spired churches.

Public buildings like Oslo's new city hall are full of picturesque murals, varied sculptures and reliefs of stone and wood commissioned by the many great artists of Norway. The homes are distinctively creative and original featuring various skills of the owners and their families. One senses that the home is the castle – a place of security, enjoyment and gracious sharing and hospitality. Large windows look out upon majestic scenery and restful views.

Norway used to be a harsh land based on small holdings related to agriculture. Now Norwegians have learned to live by skills and wits and thus to overcome. Agricultural land is scarce but they have learned to maintain a high standard of production. Falling waters have been harnessed to produce a superabundance of electrical power to operate the present industrial and manufacturing plants. Because power is available in so many areas of the country, industry is not concentrated in any one area or even in the cities but is distributed all over the land, providing a demand for educated and skilled labour all across the nation. Thus Norway has found that the key to the development and proper utilization of its natural resources has been the priority development of its human resources through a superb educational system.

With this base and through much planning and co-operation, Norway has developed a comprehensive programme of social services, providing medical and hospital treatment for all irrespective of income and a state pension scheme which looks after the aged. Every large school has a dentist and a school nurse. The standard of health is remarkably high and the infant mortality rate the lowest in the world.

The lifestyle is relaxed but efficient. In proportion to her population Norway is easily the world's leading shipping nation and commands about six per cent of the world's total tonnage. Therefore, Norwegians are much aware of the world about them. The study of English is compulsory, beginning in Grade 5 of the elementary school. It is not uncommon to see the Oslo businessman on his way home at about four o'clock with three newspapers tucked under his arm, *Aftenposten, Dagbladet* and *Arbeiderbladet*, representing Conservative, Liberal and Labour points of view, which the city dweller reads in order to be fully informed on current issues. There is no monolithic press in Norway. Television and radio programming focuses on cultural, informative and educational topics rather than heavy doses of entertainment. There is no commercial advertising because all broadcasting is operated by the state company *Norsk Rikskringkasting*.

Norway publishes some 16 million books each year and has the greatest number of published book titles per inhabitant of any country in the world.[5] There are government-subsidized public libraries all over the land. People seem to have time to read. Norwegian design in industry and crafts embodies technical efficiency, creative richness and natural beauty in combination. This is amply illustrated in furniture, glassware, tableware, cutlery, textiles, silver smithing, copper tooling, various textiles and enamelware. The traveller to Norway purchases such items to bring back to Canada.

The above glowing description is typical of what the Norwegian from Canada discovers to his pleasure when he returns to the birthplace of his ancestors. This discovery of Norway is a counter trend to the recently developing signs of declining interest in the culture and loyalty related to this remote land. Norwegian ethnicity, far from dying out, has taken a different shape because of pride in discovery of a rich past and distinctive people. Suddenly, there is new interest in ethnic organizations and even in learning the language of Norway. There is a realization of the fact that there is much from which to learn and benefit in the Nordic setting. There is a desire to recapture and retain a rich heritage. Professor Einar Haugen of Harvard University said at a recent conference on heritage: "Ethnicity isn't automatic in the third and subsequent generations. It has to be nurtured and encouraged."[6] Such contacts with Norway are having significant effects upon Canadians of Norwegian extraction. They are preserving in a new way the self-identity and cultural distinctiveness of Norway in Canada.

IDENTITY ON THE ROAD AHEAD

What makes immigrants into good citizens? Certainly not that overzealous love of birthplace that causes a person to mourn for years at having departed from his native land, nor depth of alienation from the regime in his homeland that causes the new land to be made into a base for intrigue and rebellion abroad, nor such a sense of shame for one's past that one cannot adjust to the opportunities of a new life.

The Norwegians have been fortunate in that they have retained a profound love for the fjords and valleys of Norway while at the same time have remained conscious of the fact that it was northern nature and economic conditions that impelled them to emigrate. It is of prime importance that these impelling forces were primarily impersonal conditions rather than individual persecution or discrimination. Hence, this group of immigrants from Norway never felt called upon to join any rebellious crusaders. They loved their ancestral home in Norway; they took pride in their ancient heritage. Yet they recognized the new land as the chance for a better life and therefore they entered fully into it. Without sorrowing too much, they kept their love for things past with thankfulness for the new land which they tried to shape along with many others to be a land of equal opportunity and privilege.

Canada has in many ways recognized the Norwegian part in discovering and developing Canada. The national park on the northerly tip of Newfoundland attests to the early Viking presence there. The Munk memorial at Hudson's Bay recalls the tragedy of that early expedition. The display of the *St. Roch* in the Marine Museum at Vancouver recalls the brave work and voyages of Henry Larsen. When Crown Prince Harald of Norway came to Toronto September 18, 1976, to unveil a granite monument in commemoration of Little Norway, established during World War II, the friendship between Canada and Norway was again underscored.[7] Saskatoon has a park named "Leif Erikson Park" established in 1930. The mayors of both Winnipeg and Calgary have proclaimed October 9 as Leif Erikson Day. October 9, 1972, was that special day in Calgary for the Scandinavians when Mayor Rod Sykes officially proclaimed "Leif Erikson Day" in a flag raising ceremony in front of city hall. In the United States a resolution was approved by Congress on September 2, 1964, requesting President Johnson to proclaim October 9th in each year as Leif Erikson Day. This was formally done shortly thereafter. It is to be hoped that Canada too will take such a step whereby this day will be recognized on the entire continent, but especially in the land which he first discovered.

Many Norwegian communities have traditionally celebrated Norway's Independence Day on May 17th. The Norwegians in northern Saskatchewan, using Birch Hills as a centre, have revived their Norwegian traditions and celebrate this special day. Magna Boyes has reported:

> . . . the lunch committee went about planning a suitable Scandinavian menu. Of course there would be lefse, Krum Kager, Kronser, goro and much more. Contributions of music and verse to the program were solicited from surrounding districts. Slides from Norway would be shown. The hall took on a certain atmosphere with flag streamers and candlelit tables.
>
> The day and hour arrived. Long before curtain time it was apparent that the Vikings were coming! More than 200 people crowded into the hall. It was an emotional experience of excitement and nostalgia as memories were rekindled. After all, how often does one

hear the Norwegian national anthem sung? Where else might you expect to hear "Per Spellmann" played on the violin? And what happens to you when you see the very meadow where you skipped as a child? Time shrinks, or stands still altogether.[8]

That was the first meeting in 1970. The organization is now known as the Scandia Club. It meets in the largest available auditoriums, for now there are some 500 persons attending. Special talents have been discovered by the programme. Projects have been undertaken by the Scandia Club. Native costumes are a part of the day. There is a display of Norwegian crafts including weaving, wall hangings, silver, carvings and antique items. In connection with the regional library of the area a assortment of books on the literature, history, music fiction and crafts of the Norseman has been established. Also included are song books with music, records, tapes and films. The Department of Youth and Culture at Regina has given a grant for this latter project. Overseas travel to Norway has been encouraged and Norwegian-language classes fostered under the adult education programme in the area. As many as 56 students have been enrolled. Guest speakers have been invited to address annual meetings. The Scandia Club has discovered that "the colorful mosaic is more attractive. When a girl marries she is not required to give up all contacts, customs and memories of her own family. The more intermingling of uncles, cousins, grandparents, the richer the family becomes."[9]

Because the current generation is curious about its ethnic background, more Norwegian settlements can follow the example of northern Saskatchewan in providing a cultural programme on a high plane rising above the mundane social repetition of lubricated banquets, old-time dancing or an evening of Norwegian whist. Nor can Norwegian culture be transmitted by "Scano Bingo" in some Scandinavian centre. The Norwegian communities that build constructive and intellectually satisfying programmes that appeal to young Canadians, can hope to exist beyond the "originals" from Norway. The *bygd* clubs, built solely on clan and language, are now gone in Canada. Likewise, some of the Sons of Norway lodges face an uncertain future unless they build programmes that appeal to the younger generation of Canadians who have Nordic backgrounds. It will have to be something more constructive than the effort of the Norwegian who annually bought a stick of dynamite to explode in a country rock pile on every Norwegian day of independence.

On the road ahead, the Scandinavian Seminar affords a special opportunity for college undergraduates, graduates and others to live and learn abroad. Those of Norwegian beginnings would choose to study in Norway in preference to the other Scandinavian countries. For one academic year the student is immersed in the Norwegian milieu, acquiring fluency in the language and becoming comfortable in the culture. Applications are considered on a first come-first served basis by the Scandinavian

Seminar with offices in New York.[10] By the end of July, those who have been accepted are transplanted overnight into a new country, a new language, a new people and a new way of life. After three weeks of concentrated language-learning, the student lives with a Norwegian family for some time. By the end of the language course, the student is assigned for the full term of a Folk School matched to the needs and interests of the student. The Christmas holidays are spent with the Norwegian family or in travel. Just after the New Year all participants in the Scandinavian Seminar gather for discussion, project planning, language tests, recreation and fellowship. The final term is spent in studies at the Folk School. Folk Schools in Norway are small, residential coeducational colleges for adults. Educational experience is grounded in close relationships between teachers and students. They are "schools for life" designed to develop the whole person. These "People's Colleges" of Norway have functioned for more than a century as symbols of democracy and as schools for leadership training. The seminar is limited to a maximum of 120 men and women each year. It affords an unusual opportunity of living and learning in Norway.

For those who cannot afford a whole year in Norway there is the six week summer session at the University of Oslo which sponsors the International Summer School. All classes are conducted in English but there are ample opportunities to study the language and culture of Norway as well as extensive opportunities for guided weekend tours. St. Olaf College at Northfield, Minnesota, processes all applications from both Canadians and Americans.

Contacts with Norway should work both ways, and to some extent they have. For example, in 1975 to commemorate the beginning of immigration to America from Norway, P.W. Lonning, Bishop of Frederickstad, addressed rallies at Saskatoon, Vancouver, Camrose and Winnipeg.

The survivial of a minority ethnic culture is not possible unless the group wills to resist assimilation by predominant groups. In the case of the Norwegians, this study has demonstrated the important role of the clergy, the church, the college, the club and contact with the homeland in maintaining the cultural heritage and ethnic identity. Where such functional roles are lacking or fleeting, assimilation comes quickly and thoroughly. This has been amply demonstrated in Ontario where ethnic leadership has been largely lacking. In fact, there are more people of Norwegian racial origin in Ontario than in Manitoba, but here Norwegians have been integrated into the urban society of this province.

For Norwegians in Canada, recent church mergers and current Americanization trends have diluted the unique Norwegian identity in terms of clergy, church and college. Most clubs based on the Norwegian language and local clans have folded. Other ethnic associations are surviving as social organizations often under the Scandinavian umbrella, but here many are largely failing to promote programmes that appeal to

233

the new generation in terms of cultural stimulation and creativity. Currently, the numerous contacts with Norway are renewing an awareness of the cultural heritage and ethnic uniqueness of Norwegians.

PROSPECT

Periodically, there are scattered voices that deny our oneness as a people of Canada. The media, often lacking maturity and usually devoted to sensationalism, select these strident voices and amplify them across our vast dominion. Such distortion and lack of perspective betrays our nationhood.

Despite our differing origins, we are one Canadian family by adoption and birthright. Despite our geography, we are further united by rail and history, constitution and destiny. This is not to deny our diversity. Because we are such a young nation, most of us are not far removed from our non-Canadian origins. The peoples of Canada will not be reduced to the lowest common denominator.

In this jet age, we are rediscovering our roots. We treasure anew the richness of our ethnic heritage and would vest it again in Canada. As a group, the Norwegians in Canada and their offspring have been accepted as positive citizens and as "first-cousins" to many. In the early years there were planned efforts to mould all into the Anglo-Saxon model. Here Norwegians lost their language. Then they lost their accent. Currently, Canada does not require denial of the rock from which its various peoples were hewn. Much of the cultural baggage which used to be in the attic is now being examined in the warmth of the family room as the foundations supporting our present Canadianism are under scrutiny and evaluation. Life must be lived forward, but it can only be understood backward.[11]

In new measure, there is awareness of obligation and opportunity to share the treasures from our distinct heritage and to illuminate even the smaller gems in the Canadian tiara. When explained in the language and setting of Canada, this heritage becomes a source of inspiration and treasure in the hearts and minds of a far greater number than just those of the Nordic race.

Ours is the privilege of releasing for Canada values that sustained the spirit and life of our forbears for generations. If we pass on without opening the treasure chest, it may never be done. Like householders of old, we must bring forth from our treasured heritage even that which is old and relate it to that which is new.

Norwegians would join hands and hearts with other Canadians of every background and promote the Canadian vision of national unity through the full recognition of our cultural diversity. If there is mutual respect among Canadians as equals, this continuing national enrichment and sharing of unique diversity will promote regional identity, provincial entity and national solidarity.

NOTES

1. 1971 Census of Canada, 92-723, Table 1.
2. *Ibid,* Table 34.
3. *The Calgary Herald,* September 1, 1976.
4. *Ibid.,* January 10, 1974.
5. *Facts About Norway* (Oslo: Aftenposten, 1966), p. 51.
6. *Minneapolis Tribune,* May 7, 1973.
7. *The Calgary Herald,* September 20, 1976.
8. *The Western Producer,* May 9, 1974.
9. *Ibid.*
10. The full address is: Scandinavian Seminar, 100 East 85 St., New York 10029.
11. Sentence attributed to Soren Kierkegaard.

Appendix

MY FIRST YEARS IN CANADA*
by N.C. Brun

In the year 1859 two brothers, Peter and Ludvig Brandt, had left Norway and settled somewhere near Montreal. Though natives of Trondheim both of them had spent several years in Lofoten and were experienced fishermen.

When therefore the Canadian government conceived a plan to settle the coast of the St. Lawrence Bay with Norwegians these two brothers were among the first to move there in 1860. These two and a third brother, Fredrick, who with his family and his mother came with us, were my cousins on the mother's side.

Our family consisted of my parents and I. We could not in fairness blame anyone that we decided to settle in Gaspe, but naturally did so in the above mentioned circumstances. The same may be said about a number of families from Trondheim who landed in Gaspe in July 1861, though the ship The Brother's (Captain Goa) continued the voyage to Quebec with the greater number of his passengers, about 175 emigrants. Perhaps I should have mentioned that our maid, Ovidia Olsen, travelled with us, paying her own passage. Later she settled in Chicago where she owned a house on West Ohio Street near Center Avenue where she also died.

Gaspe Bay is separated from St. Lawrence Bay by a promontory, Pointe Gaspe. The town made no unfavorable impression, and the ridges around the town and bay, covered by evergreens, are uncommonly beautiful. The same may be said about the whole stretch of land southward which by the fishing village of Perce ca. twenty or thirty miles from Gaspe gradually runs into the Bay of Chaleur which stretches towards New Brunswick in a westerly direction.

About 20 miles south from the town of Gaspe the two brothers mentioned above had taken land about three miles inland from the coast which here is called Corner o' the Beach. My father and three Tronders, coachmaster Johansen, Berg and Taylor Andersen with families took their homesteads – four or five miles from the Brandt families and about three miles into the primeval forest. The other and greater part of Tronders took land between these two settlements but a little farther from the coast. Practically all land along the coast had been taken and settled, in part by Englishmen, but chiefly by French Canadians. The fact that we had no access to the coast contributed more than anything else to our discouragement, for most of us had come for the sake of the fishing at the same time as we hoped to own our farm as we were accustomed to in Norway.

---

*translated by Knute Bergsagel
from *Symra*, Vol. VII, No. 2, 1911.

As far as I can remember there was never any census taken of the Norwegian immigrants in these three small settlements, but it is estimated that we were about thirty families.

Very few if any of them were influenced by Christopher Kloster, but at about this time another larger group of immigrants had landed in Gaspe – about seventy families from Stavanger. We, however, did not have much contact with them, as they settled chiefly in the woods on the west side of Gaspe. Thus a total of about 100 Norwegian families were settled on the Gaspe, not in a colony but scattered over an area of 30 to 40 miles in extent. Still the town of Gaspe was the centre for them all. It is possible that some of those from Stavanger did not arrive until 1862 . . .

In the meantime my father and the other neighbors had picked out their homesteads and it was important to get started to get ready for the winter. But to get the land through the almost impenetrable forest was not easy. Roads had to be build and bridges across small rivers constructed.

In our predicament the government came to our aid, and every able-bodied man got all the work he could handle for a reasonable, daily wage. If I remember correctly my father got $1.25 per day – I got one dollar – boarding ourselves, of course. We were all satisfied; it seemed to us that we were being paid for working for ourselves. Roads were thus cleared to each of the three above mentioned settlements so one could get through with wagons. The worst pest under this construction work was the mosquito. However, we got used to them so that we did not mind their stings so much.

As soon as the road work was somewhat finished the work of clearing and buildings homes began. Most of the homesteads had sufficient timber for all the building necessary. When winter set in our house was not ready and Berg's was not built, so these two families shared a house with Coachman Johansen the first winter. The Andersens lived alone; their house was smaller.

Before we were finished with our building operations late in October it began to rain. And such rain! A bridge we had built had to be rebuilt twice because the current carried it away. Then a heavy snowfall dislodged it. It was rebuilt four times in all that winter. It was a severe winter, many old bridges and mills which had been used for years were washed away. Christmas Eve we had to crawl out through the attic window and found eight feet of loose snow outside. Prospects for Christmas were not good. We had fuel and in our little neighborhood also food, but many were short; a barrel of flour had gone up to $20.00 in Gaspe, and later on that winter it could not be bought for any price.

The main reason for this state of affairs was that all ship traffic ceases as soon as the St. Lawrence River freezes so that nothing can be imported. The native population had that year been increased by several hundred immigrants. The wheat harvest was good if there had been mills to grind it.

But the newcomers – why did they not provide for the winter? Most of them had provided to the extent that they were able. The matter of provisions for the winter had been brought to the attention of the newcomers as early as September. I remember to this day quite clearly the immigrant agent, Christopher Kloster, as he sat and stroked his beautiful beard and tried to convince my father of the necessity to hoard the necessary food supplies for the winter before it was too late. Since he was sailing his smack to Quebec anyway and flour and pork and everything else could be bought there for half the price it would cost in Gaspe, there would be a considerable saving.

My father declined on the ground that his family was so small that the saving to us would be negligible; but most of the settlers were caught and surrendered their savings some to the last dollar. My father became involved in that he for friendship's sake bought a neighbor's interest for $70.00 because he decided to go to the United States.

And now the time of patient waiting began for us as well as for all others. Week after week passed and no word from Kloster, but considerable about him. Rumor had it that the money had been taken from him for debt and he was in jail; that he and his smack and the cargo had been lost at sea; and that he had escaped to the States, etc. There was still some food left among the people, but the future looked dark and the prices rose steeply.

At last one day there came word that Kloster was at Corner O' Beach with boat and cargo. It was towards the end of October. And I remember well that we got the goods and drove home in pouring rain. Unfortunately we did not get all that was ordered and some got nothing.

In Quebec he had gotten so much freight to Gaspe that he had room for only a fraction of the orders he had taken from newcomers. My father got three barrels of flour, some pounds of butter, pork, coffee and sugar, all for a little more than twenty dollars for the $70.00 he had paid in.

The worst was that those who needed it most got least and at Gaspe prices. But in a couple of weeks he would be back but they waited in vain for his return.

It is reasonable to suppose that for some reason he could do no better than he did and his own family was no better off than the rest.

But there was One whose all seeing eye had seen with clarity what was hidden to our eyes. But for His care many a newcomer would that winter have closed his eyes in the agony of hunger.

In November towards the end of the month a large bark sprung a leak in the bay outside Gaspe. It had to dock for repair, but the damage was so great that it could not be fixed on short order. It was therefore necessary to unload most of the cargo which consisted of many

239

thousands bushels of corn (maize). When the government heard about the distress among the newcomers orders were quickly given to use the corn to alleviate the suffering among the new settlers.

Under these circumstances it is not just to blame the Canadian government for neglect. It could not have done more than it did one way or another. It should not be faulted for wanting settlers and the area was not unsuited for settlers as was evidenced by the comparatively large population already settled. That the conditions nevertheless became such that settlers without means had to leave the land is not unique.

To prepare food from maize presented a problem inasmuch as the mills had been destroyed by the flood. The small domestic coffee mills were used. In our neighborhood there was a handmill brought from Norway which was in use day and night. When spring came the millstones were completely worn out. In other places they cooked the corn to get the shell off. All in all the corn was a great boon to all the settlers and without it the winter would have been dark indeed. God rules.

During the winter we struggled with sawing boards from the logs with a hand saw and the lumber piles grew day by day. My father had bought a cow in the autumn and hay for the cow. The hay was five miles away and we had the pleasure of carrying the three tons of hay on our backs. In the spring when we had decided to leave the settlement we got less than half price for the cattle and nothing for the lumber.

When spring came one after the other of the settlers decided to go to the States. Mother and I wanted to join them, but father's answer was always that we had spent all we owned and it was not possible to start anew in another place. But when in the middle of April we still had eight feet of snow father gave up. There seemed to be no hope for spring and summer.

After a month's fishing, this time with Captain Holst, and as soon as steamship traffic to Quebec resumed all in our little neighborhood and many more embarked on the first boat.

Several times I have mentioned the pine forests, but pine and fir were not the only varieties. Hard maple and birch were very common, and the cedar made almost every swamp impenetrable. The soil was good and sufficiently fertile to yield good crops, but the frost did much damage and the summer was short.

In Quebec we were pleased to meet especially two men. One was Pastor Abraham Jacobson who had come as missionary. His services were the first Norwegian service we had attended since we left Norway. The other was Christopher Kloster. I cannot now recall what settlement father and he agreed on, but I know that he arranged for passage to Chicago for us.

We came to Chicago so short of money that we had to borrow some from our former maid to buy our first meals. But we were two to work and only three to eat. Though our sojourn in Canada may have set us back some, it was in the providence of God a blessing.

The last I heard from our old neighbors all Norwegians had left. I am told that Gaspe is now an important city with considerable trade and lumber industry. The forests have been cleared for many miles and the population is progressive and prosperous. It was our misfortune that we came a little too early.

TABLE OF HISTORICAL HIGHLIGHTS

c. 787 Northern Sea Rovers first attack along the English Channel
c. 870 Norwegian Vikings colonize Iceland
c. 985 Eric the Red colonized Greenland
c. 1000 Leif Eriksson lands in North America
c. 1010 The Karlsefni Expedition sails to Vinland
c. 1015 Snorri, first white child born in America
    1066 William the Conqueror wins Battle of Hastings
c. 1075 End of dominant Viking period
    1347 Last recorded voyage to Markland
    1350 Greenland colony fades
    1349 – 1350 Bubonic plague kills half the people of Norway
    1380 Norway united with Denmark
    1477 Columbus visits Iceland
    1492 Columbus reaches West Indies
    1497 Cabot reaches east coast of North America
    1517 Lutheran Reformation begins
    1534 Cartier lands on Gaspe shore
    1536 Lutheranism made Norway's official religion
    1588 Defeat of Spanish Armada
    1608 Quebec founded by Champlain
    1610 Henry Hudson discovers Hudson Bay
    1619 Jens Munk to Hudson Bay
    1620 Pilgrim fathers land at Plymouth Rock
    1670 Hudson's Bay Company founded
    1759 Capture of Quebec by Wolfe
    1763 Canada is ceded to Great Britain
    1776 American declaration of independence
    1811 Red River colony started
    1814 Norway establishes her own constitution
    1819 – 1820 Franklin expeditions
    1821 Merger of HBC and NWC
    1825 First boatload of Norwegian settlers land at New York
    1840 Cunard inaugurates first Atlantic steamship service
    1849 Repeal of Navigation Laws
    1850 Norwegians begin arriving via Quebec to U.S.A.
    1854 Norwegians begin several attempts to settle in Quebec
    1861 – 1865 American Civil War

1867   Confederation. U.S.A. purchases Alaska

1869   Canada takes over Hudson's Bay Company territory

1869   First Red River Rebellion

1870   Manitoba becomes a province

1871   British Columbia admitted to Confederation

1872   Dominion Lands Act

1874   North West Mounted Police organized

1875 – 1876 Icelandic settlements in Manitoba

1878   First railroad in Manitoba connects Winnipeg and St. Paul, Minnesota

1880   Buffalo herds destroyed

1881   CPR starts construction

1882   Provisional districts: Alberta, Athabasca, Assiniboia and Saskatchewan

1883   CPR reaches Calgary

1885   Second Riel Rebellion

1885   Completion of CPR to West Coast

1886   Eau Claire Colony of Norwegians at Calgary

1892   Influx of Norwegian homesteaders really begins

1893   Replica of Viking ship crosses Atlantic in 28 days

1894   Bardo and Bella Coola settlements started

1900 – 1913 Peak of railway expansion and influx of settlers

1905   Norway ends dynastic union with Sweden

1905   Alberta and Saskatchewan created as provinces

1906   First samples of Marquis wheat distributed

1911   Camrose Lutheran College founded

1914   Outbreak of Great War

1915   Outlook College founded

1923   Alberta Wheat Pool organized

1929   Beginning of world's greatest Depression

1930   Canada assumes sovereignty of North and provides grant to Norway's Sverdrup

1939   Canada declares war

1940 – 1944 Polar exploration by Henry Larsen

1945   World War II ends

1947   Canadian Citizenship Act where people of Dominion officially become "Canadian Citizens"

1962   Viking settlement discovered in Newfoundland

1965   Vinland map of 1440 declared genuine

1977   Some 3,000 Canadians take charter flights to Norway

TABLE 16

Number of Norwegian Immigrants Arriving in Canada from Norway, 1900-1975

1900/1	265	1919	176	1938	12	1957	1,337
1901/2	1,015	1920	412	1939	27	1958	471
1902/3	1,746	1921	489	1940	17	1959	354
1903/4	1,239	1922	448	1941	9	1960	341
1904/5	1,397	1923	1,670	1942	27	1961	180
1905/6	1,415	1924	3,216	1943	3	1962	208
1906/7	876	1925	841	1944	0	1963	290
1907/8	1,554	1926	2,607	1945	52	1964	259
1908	654	1927	5,102	1946	269	1965	324
1909	1,285	1928	2,241	1947	178	1966	534
1910	2,019	1929	2,549	1948	355	1967	554
1911	1,829	1930	1,049	1949	355	1968	465
1912	1,798	1931	66	1950	237	1969	341
1913	1,698	1932	54	1951	896	1970	239
1914	967	1933	29	1952	1,209	1971	127
1915	196	1934	34	1953	939	1972	134
1916	359	1935	27	1954	993	1973	203
1917	230	1936	0	1955	709	1974	229
1918	71	1937	22	1956	842	1975	187

Source: Immigration Statistics from Manpower and Immigration, Ottawa.

TABLE 17

Origin of Scandinavian Ethnic Groupings in Canada in 1921, 1931 and 1941

Ethnic Grouping	1921 Number	%	1931 Number	%	1941 Number	%
Norwegian						
Born in Canada	23,568	34.2	39,241	42.1	54,843	54.4
Born in U.S.A.	22,186	32.2	21,451	23.0	18,929	18.8
Born elsewhere	23,102	33.6	32,551	34.9	26,946	26.8
Total	68,856	100	93,243	100	100,718	100
Swedish						
Born in Canada	21,727	35.3	34,632	42.6	47,356	55.4
Born in U.S.A.	11,625	18.9	10,750	13.2	9,274	10.9
Born elsewhere	28,151	45.8	35,924	44.2	28,766	33.7
Total	61,503	100	81,306	100	85,396	100
Danish						
Born in Canada	8,910	42.2	12,776	37.4	19,784	52.8
Born in U.S.A.	4,122	19.5	3,880	11.4	3,482	9.3
Born elsewhere	8,092	38.3	17,462	51.2	14,173	37.9
Total	21,124	100	34,118	100	37,439	100
Icelandic						
Born in Canada	8,741	55.1	12,684	65.5	15,733	74.7
Born in U.S.A.	1,008	6.3	1,011	5.2	927	4.4
Born elsewhere	6,127	38.6	5,687	29.3	4,390	20.9
Total	15,876	100	19,382	100	21,050	100
Grand Total	167,359		228,049		244,603	

Source: Census of Canada, 1921, 1931 and 1941.

EARLY SETTLERS IN CENTRAL ALBERTA

In the nineties and early part of the new century several Norse settlements were founded in districts radiating eastward from Wetaskiwin. Following is a register of the earliest Norse pioneers in each of these settlements:

CROOKED LAKE – 1892

The first settlers at Crooked Lake were O. Didrikson and family in 1892, followed a year later by Edmund Thompson and G. Bronken and family. From then on until 1902 the following came, most of them accompanied by their families: O. Rogn, T. Dahl, T. Waflen, E. Skjel, O. Kjorlien, Marit Jevne (widow with four children), I. Kjøs, A. Lee, E. Kjøs and a Mr. Eriksen.

NEW NORWAY – 1894-1899

To New Norway in 1893 came the Olstad brothers and others, filed on homesteads, and returned to Fosston, Minnesota. The following year they began moving up with their families. 1894 – Even Olstad, Gullik Iverson, Peder Haukedal and family, P. Ausness, Christ Johnson, Mr. Jensen. 1895 – Lars and Ludwig Olstad and parents, Ole M. Olstad, Ole Brandvoid. 1897 – Ole Olstad Jr. and family, Thomas Skattebo, Frank Olsen. 1899 – C. Hermstad.

BARDO – 1894

In 1893 Martin Finseth, Nils Jevning, A. Malmberg and J. Wallerbeck came from Crookston, Minnesota. They were looking for suitable land for the formation of a large colony. In 1894 they returned with a large party, several of whom located at Bardo. (Index of Bardo settlers at end of register.)

SKANDIA – 1894 to 1902

The settlement of Skandia was started in 1894 by the following families: Thore Grue, his parents, Mr. and Mrs. S. Grue Sr., John Moe, Ole Movoid, Andrew Bøe, Edmund Thompson, the Saetres, and A. Larsen. Some of the other settlers were: Tom Roholt, S. Bronken, T. Hanell, John Broen and his mother Ingeborg Broen, M. Steen, H. Mortenson, P. Tyberg, C. Berg, O. Areson, T.E. Nelson. Families up to 1901: S. Kringen, H. Lomnes and son Bert, C. Kjelstad, O. Skaret, C. Broen, Throndsons, Carl Anderson. (Swedes Gust Anderson, Jim Erickson, John Nelson.) G. Hendrickson. 1902 – Elling, John and Ole Olson, H. Hendrickson families. The three Lyseng brothers, Albert, Eric and Knut came land-hunting in 1900. Moved up with families 1902.

ST. JOSEPH – 1899 to 1902

Martin Thompson, Thomas Olson, John Lund, Hans Sandbo, Kristen Solid (1894 to Skandia), Mr. and Mrs. Ole Sware, Simon and Lars Grue (to Skandia in 1894) moved to St. Joseph in 1910-11.

ASKER – 1895 to 1900

The first settlers in Asker were O.C. Ravnsborg in 1895, and Mr. and Mrs. R. Ravnsborg a year later; 1896-1901, the following families arrived: A.

Woyen, A. Void, C. Paulson, T. Wettre, E. Hoybak, G. Draft, E. Krefting, O.O. Craft, C. Thorstad, O. Halvorson, Mrs. Woyen and three sons. The first Post Office was opened in 1900.

Source: "Pioneer Days in Bardo, Alberta."

EDMONTON – 1898 to 1901

Two of the first Norse settlers in Edmonton were Gilbert Berg and a family by the name of Roholt. Hans Simonson and family (to Bardo 1894) moved to Edmonton in 1898. Simon Simonson and family (to Bardo 1894) moved to Edmonton 1901. Later in the new century the J. Stephenson and Roach Olson families were amongst the first to help organize a Norse congregation in 1908.

CAMROSE – 1895 to 1900

Ole Bakken, Mr. Raundal (before 1895). In 1895 the following families settled: Lars Bjaaland, John Spoketi, Peder Skafse and Ole Statlemo. 1899-1900: Andrew Kjorlien, Tosten Hoyme, C. Erickson.

EDBERG – 1895 to 1898

Edberg received its first contingent of settlers with the arrival in 1895 of the N. Hustad family. 1898 – Ole Rasmussen. Halfway between Edberg and New Norway were Jens Ram, H. Djuve and H. Lien with their families.

ROSEBUSH – 1900-01

1900 – Kravik and family. 1901 – the following families: E. Sand, J. Lien, M. Langmo, J. Olson, J. Hanson, B. Benson, A. Lien, also the following single men: A. Anderson, A. Flohr, and K. Knutson. 1902 – P.H. Olufson and family.

FERRY POINT – 1902

N. Duklet and Iver Bjørge families in 1902. About the same time, Mr. Zakariasen and H. Olson. A little later the following families: P. Olson, O. Olson, C. Olson and A. Moland.

MEETING CREEK – 1901

John Anderson, James Anderson and family, M. and Mrs. Ellefson.

BETHANIA – 1901-02 (Donalda)

1901 – G. Olson and son, A. Hegbert and grandson, Anton; 1902 – Oscar and Peter Olsen, B.J. Stolee and family, Haakon Stolee, Mathias Olson, and the following families: T. Vikse, A. Jerstad, P. Johnson, S. Hilde, N. Eikland and Thore Eikland. 1903 – Jacob Vikse, Jacob M. Stolee and family.

MARTINS – 1902-03

P.P. Kjosness and family, Inger Jacobson, ("Besta" Jacobson, mother of Mrs. Kjosness); Fredrick Christianson, Olaus Jacobson, Ole Ronnie, all with families; Mr. and Mrs. A. Anderson, Mr. and Mrs. A. Olson; J. Jacobson, K. Winsness, E. Arneson, A. Grosland, J. Roseth, J. Whol and family, Mr. and Mrs. E. Christianson, John Lund.

247

VIKING – 1902-04
    J. Haagenson, John Kringen, John Lokken, Carl Boraas, Nels Haagenson (families following year), O.B. Nordstrom, G. Boraas, Ed. Benson, Carl Olsen, Oluf Kjetland, Gilbert Sorenson, Tom Berg, S. Hafso, O. Sorenson, O. Haagenson, O. Salveson, O. Benson, Ingvald Thompson.

EARLING – 1902
    1902 – Following families: O. Mosby, A. Smorlie, H.O. Bratrud, H. Stensruds and A. Evenson. 1903 – Helleksons, Ritlands, Gundersons.

TRONDHJEM (Round Hill) – 1901 to 1904
    1901-02. Following families: Andrew and Nils Foss, J. Wade, A. Fergstad, Nils Mathisen, George Bruce, Iver and Albert Bruce, Ludvig Pederson. K.K. Quail and Fergstad families first settled in Crooked Lake in 1901, moving to Round Hill in 1904-05.

BAWLF – 1901-03
    Endre Saby and family. Ed. Stove and Albert Ness. 1902 – Mr. and Mrs. Gulbrand Hanson, Mrs. Marie Sanden and son, Gerald; Lars Jackson and family; 1903 – O.R. Olson, Tom Hagen and G.I. Anderson families, Mr. and Mrs. Bergquist, O. Molstad.

BETHLEHEM – 1898-03
    1898 – J. Waldun and F. Johnson families. 1900-03 – Mr. and Mrs. Albert Kringen, Petro, Pauline and Clara Kringen, Mr. and Mrs. J. Throndson, Mrs. Watland, E. Olson, Sikstroms, O. Skalins, G. Bard, J. Slind and family.

KINGMAN – 1894 to 1902
    The first settlers in the Kingman District were: In 1894 – Thore Ovelson and wife Anne, children, Ovel, Sophie, Clara, Andrew, Julia, Olaus; Knut Ovelson, widower and children William, Hanna, Oscar, S.D. Simonson and wife Lena, children, Henry, Clarence, William, Oscar, Minnie, Daniel, Inger; Hans Simonson and wife Annie, and three children; (above families all from Moorehead, Minn.), Nils Mosland. 1895 – Halvor Nomland and family (first settling near Dinant). 1902 – The P. Scramstad, Berge and Fuglem families, M. Bolseng, C. Lindberg, Mrs. Anne Bjerkeg, and the A. Langbell, T. Sydboe and Eric Hoflin families. 1903 – S. Hele, P. Gunderson.

RYLEY – 1902
    The following settlers located in the Ryley District in 1902, together with their families: Ole Hagen, A. Bugge, P. Oslund, B. Lillemoe, A.O. Lee, C. Asp, M. Jacobson, T. Bendiksen, M. Killian, P. Davick, N. Solberg, B. Lyslo, J. Flotree, P. Gjerde, H.E. Wiklun, J. Thorsley; also C. Reinert, T. Reinert, and K. Helgeland. A little later, O. Nord, Bert Ness, M. Sundlie, J.H. Hill, P. Slind, O. Oslund, and J. Hjelter together with their families.

AMISK CREEK – 1894 to 1902
    The first settlers in the Amisk Creek District were Paul Flaaten and wife Aagodt who arrived in June 1894, followed by Mr. R. Berg and his son

Robert, P.C. Moen with family, A. Erickson; 1895 – Mrs. A. Erickson, daughter Alma, and Peder Aas; 1901 – Pearson and wife, L. Anderson with family, Mrs. Olianna Lillo and two sons. The Iver Annebo, P. Aasmo, I. Olson families and A. Patterson were later arrivals.

1894 –   Settlers coming to Bardo, 1894

Martin Finseth and wife Karen, (d. 1884) from Sør-reisen, Norway, to Red River Valley in 1876. (m. Barbro Anderson 1885.) Came to Canada with children, Peder, Andrew, Iver, Bennie, Alma.

(Following families all from Bardo, Norway to Red River Valley 1876.)

Nels Jevning and wife Maren (d. 1884) m. Olea Stelen 1890 (d. 1895). Came to Canada with children Johan, Olaf, Ingeborg, Magna, Anton, Ragna, Johnnie, and Peder together with wife Magna.

Peder B. Anderson (came to Canada with wife Marit and children, Bennie, Palmer, Inga.)

Bersvend Anderson and wife Marit (d. 1886). (Children, Anders, John, Kristine, Barbro, Olea, Ingrid, Peder, and Ole, all born in Norway). Came to Canada 1894 with son Peder.

(Following families all from Bardo, Norway, to United States 1893.)

John Lerbekmo, to Crookston, Minn.; Wife Dorthen, from Norway to Canada in 1895, with children, Peder, Marie, Jenny. Carl Lerbekmo (brother of John Lerbekmo).

Halvor Haugen and wife Gjertrud, to Crookston, Minn.; to Canada, with children, Peder, Ingrid, Marit, Marie.

Johannes Johnson and wife Ingred, to Neby, Minn.; to Canada with children, Johan, Peder, Hilmar.

Johan Arndt Johnson.

Lars Johnson and wife Maria, to Neby, Minn.; to Canada with children, Amanda, Alma, Sclmer.

1895 –

Olav Brocke and wife Anne, children, Gustava, Gunder, Torval, Torfinn.

1896-97

George Bruce, Emil Gjertsen, Jørgen Quam, Iver Gronberg, Tollef Carlson and Espen Hansen with families. Martin Hansen (Denmark), Ole Bakken, Rock County, Minn.

1900 – 1901

(Following all from Bardo, Norway): Asbjorn Moen and wife Gunhild, to Crookston, Minn.; to Canada with children, Iver, Borghild, Ingolf; Martin Elde and daughter Alma; Edwin Johnson; Andreas Johnson; Jacob Boness. Jacob Boness Sr.; Hans Boness and children, Olaf, Trina, Petra; Mrs. Andreas Johnson and children, Astrid and Harald; Mrs. Martin Eide and children, Lauritz, Johannes, Clara, Joe; Johannes Johnson Sr. and wife Annie, daughter Karen; Ingebrigt and Ane Haugseth and son Ingvart; Sigrid and Emma Viken; Gea Stelen; Johannes and Lars Foshaug.

Following from United States: Lars Pederson, Arnold Steen, Martin and

Oluf Berg, O. Grondahl and family; Hans Jenses, wife Agnethe and children, Clara, Hannah and Agnes; Ole Jensen; Agnethe Jensen and daughter Jennie; Anton Bartnes and wife Bergitte, Ole and Delia. Louis Qualley and wife Tillie and children, George and Florence; Ole Nelson.

1902 – 1903

From Bardo, Norway: M.B. Ness and wife Inga; Halvor Eggen and wife Ingeborg and children, Maria, Karen, Hildur, Peter, Olfrid; Simon and Ane Haaksvold; Johan Olson, wife and children, Helge, Signe and Ole. Following arrived from U.S.A.: Simon Nordhus and wife Maria, and children Raymond, Theresa; Axel Kindley; Carl and Nils Langerud; Albert Christenson; C.J. Rude and wife Marie, children, Clarence, Emil, Nora, Alice. From Sweden: M. Ostman, wife and sons, Willie and Hjalmar.

1904 –

From Minnesota: John B. Anderson (originally from Bardo, Norway) and wife Gjertrud, adopted children, Albin, Martha and Bernhard; Hans Hillerud.

Later arrivals were: Elnar and Olea Haugland; Oliver Fosmoe and family; Ingebrigt Forseth and Family; Ole Forseth and wife; O. Livelten and family; Johan Viken and family; Alfred Stronstad and Anna; Marie and Borghild Kristiansen. From the United States: Simon Hankstad and wife, children Hans and Johanna; T.A. Rorem and family; Anton Horte and family. Direct from China came missionary H.N. Ronning and children in 1907; Mrs. O. Breckan, Ingolf and Carey from Eagle Hill, Alberta; Otto Johansen and wife, and Inge.

NOTE – Other Norse communities, which now have active congregations, were later started east of Bardo, near Bruce, Irma and Sedgewick.

PIONEER PASTOR'S SERMON:
CRUMBS FROM THE FIRESIDE

Old and enfeebled as I am, I feel a strong desire in my heart to pass on a few crumbs, and by means of these to witness as long as I am able, and convey a greeting to friends especially, but also to all our people who lie so close to my heart.

Though we know not our own hour, nor the end of the present age, this we know, our Lord has bidden His Church to labor zealously while yet it is day. To be a light and a salt in the world, to be God's living witness both by teaching and life, this is the true calling and mission of the church.

O God, be gracious to us and our people, both lay and learned. O God, send Thy living Spirit into our midst as a fire that shall consume our slothfulness. A baptism of the Spirit is what our Church needs just now; with Spirit-filled witnesses that shall plead unitedly before the throne of grace.

Listen ye Christians, listen learned brethren, this is a time that calls us to united action. Certainly the Enemy is united in opposing God's cause. If then the church be disunited, how can it escape defeat? Will not the sad result be that all the more become the Enemy's prey.

But the crying need of the day, I venture to say, is this: that lay and learned alike sit at Jesus' feet and learn of Him; that we become as little children, each counting the other greater than himself. Then shall the flood-tide of God's love wipe out all disharmony and strife.

God is a God of love; abide in Him, and we shall love God and love one another. To walk in love is to heed the highest commandment of God. And the world, seeing this, shall wonder at it; and many shall be won who now walk in doubt and ask: "where is the right and the true way?"

God's people are a missionary people. As the bearers and interpreters of the Gospel, they are to bring to every land and nation the glad tidings of salvation in Christ. Yet dare we who are so few and so weak do battle against the hosts of Satan? Dare we hope to overcome so formidable a foe?

Alas, it is true as written, that Satan is strong in the children of unbelief. People of every nation are as carrion for ravening birds. Is this a hopeful mission field for weak souls to labor? Yes, for our Lord has said (and His covenant is sure), "Behold, I am with you always."

When we observe the signs of the times which herald the future, ought we not as christians make common cause against the cherished gods of the age? For they sound forth an evangel of death; they would dethrone our Savior as God, and label the atonement as nonsense.

Countless are the winds of doctrine sweeping in upon us, and great is the carnal strife and confusion. "Lo, here is Christ; or lo, there is Christ." Listen to the answering voice of Jesus: "Do not believe those lies, they are from Satan himself, who in the conflict against Christ and His Word is striving to tear apart and scatter His Church and His children.''

Behold the eager, restless, rushing life of the world. A mad race for power and possessions in which the servant of Mammon alone can find pleasure. A covetous man is an idolatrous slave, having no heart for the welfare of the down-trodden and oppressed.

Observe too, those who love a life of indulgence and ease. The lust of the eye, the lust of the flesh, and the vain-glory of life are all that their hearts desire. Think of the time and the means they consume. Indeed many will even borrow in order to deck themselves out in all the latest modes and finery, while giving not a thought to find their final end.

Yes, the world is diligent in using its time for all that it honors and holds dear. "Keep up with the times" is the hue and the cry, but the demands go far beyond necessities; for the love of display is as a yawning chasm devouring time and means. While, alas, the day of reckoning is quite forgotten.

To curb the pillages of alcoholism takes more than feeble jottings. Against this monopoly of deadly drink we must raise concerted weapons. When wilt thou arise, O Christendom, and denounce this cursed traffic in terms that the country and its law-makers will be obliged to heed?

The storm of protest raised against the saloon traffic has put fear in the hearts of the liquor barons, so now they promise to mend their ways and carry on in a much more respectable way if only the saloon be permitted to flourish. But a saloon is a saloon, and alcoholic drink is still poison; and it will still be the same old story: thousands enslaved by liquor.

Such is the world about us, and sad and dark indeed is the outlook. A world engulfed in an ocean of sin constantly agitated by the power of the Evil One. Truly Satan is at work in the children of disobedience. Who is able to overthrow such a Power?

Be not afraid, little flock of God; the Lion of Judah has conquered. Behold far and near a Light has appeared in the darkness. It illumines us and those about us; for many unto salvation, for others unto judgment who continue in the bondage of unbelief.

The unnumbered hosts whom John saw before the throne with palms of victory in their hands clearly testify what our King is able to accomplish through those whom He sends forth to gather His guests from among all people on the face of the earth, that His wedding table may be filled.

Day by day the conflict being waged between the King and the Dragon grows more bitter. Doomed souls by the thousands of thousands are being delivered out of the hand of the King of Death. Our Leader goes from victory to victory overthrowing the citadel of Satan. Are we christians to be slackers in the fight?

No, we are the army of the Lord. Marshalled under the banner of the cross, we embrace His promise: "Lo, I am with you." At His Word to fare forth to win dearly-bought souls for Him. Next to our own salvation, there is for us no greater joy than to see some brother or sister of whatever race it may be, saved into the family to God.

AMEN

I would voice an Amen to our Immanuel's praise. Let the stammering tongue be loosed, cold and ice melt away. Love shall still be victorious, the bond of peace bind us together; and the storms of Satan shall be stilled at the mighty words of Jesus: "Fear not, for I am on board."

Source: Norwegian Sermon by Bersvend Anderson when he was about 89 years old, November 1, 1910. (Translated by his son Palmer Anderson).

Bibliography

(See footnotes at the end of each chapter for further Bibliography)

Selected Books

Abbott, Edith. *Historical Aspects of the Immigration Problem: Select Documents.* Chicago: The University of Chicago Press, 1926.

Andersen, Per Sveaas. *Vikings of the West: The Expansion of Norway in the Early Middle Ages.* Oslo: Johan Grundt Tanum Forlag, 1971.

Anderson, Arlow W. *The Norwegian-Americans.* Boston: Twayne Publishers, 1975.

Berton, Pierre. *The Last Spike.* Toronto: McClelland & Stewart, 1971.

Bjork, Kenneth O. *West of the Great Divide: Norwegian Migration to the Pacific Coast.* Northfield, Minnesota: Norwegian-American Historical Association, 1958.

Blegen, Theodore C. *Norwegian Migration to America 1825-1860.* New York: Arno Press, 1969.

____. *Grass Roots History.* Minneapolis: University of Minnesota Press, 1947.

____. *Norwegian Migration to America: The American Transition.* Northfield: Norwegian-American Historical Association, 1940.

Broadfoot, Barry. *Ten Lost Years, 1929-1939: Memoirs of Canadians Who Survived the Depression.* Toronto: Doubleday, 1973.

Brun, N.C., ed. *Fra Ungdomsaar (Den Forenide Kirkes Historie i Femogtyve Aar).* Minneapolis: Augsburg Publishing House, 1915.

Brunvand, Jan Harold. *Norwegian Settlers in Alberta.* Ottawa: National Museum of Man, 1974.

Burnet, Jean. *Next-Year Country: A Study of Rural Social Organization in Alberta.* Toronto: University of Toronto Press, 1951.

Cagner, Ewert, et al. *The Viking.* New York: Crescent Books, 1972, by arrangement with Tre Trychare, Cagner & Co.

Canada. *Canada Year Book, 1905-.* Second Series. Ottawa: Government Printer, 1905-.

254

Canada. *Census of Canada* (Decennial). Ottawa: Statistics Canada.

Canada. *Census of the Prairie Provinces. 1916-.* Ottawa: Statistics Canada.

Canada. Royal Commission on Bilingualism and Biculturism. *Book IV. The Cultural Contribution of Other Ethnic Groups.* Ottawa: 1970.

Canada. *Sessional Papers.* Ottawa: Public Archives of Canada.

Canada. *The Canadian Family Tree.* Ottawa: Queen's Printer, 1967.

Cherland, C.M. *The Lutheran Legacy.* Calgary: Century Calgary Publications, 1975.

Citroen, H.A. *European Emigration Overseas Past and Future.* Hague: Martinus Nijhoff, 1951.

Corbett, David C. *Canada's Immigration Policy: A Critique.* Toronto: The University of Toronto Press, 1957.

Cultural Contribution of Newcomers to Canada. Ottawa: Citizenship Branch, Department of Citizenship and Immigration, 1965.

Dawson, C.A. "Group Settlement: Ethnic Communities in Western Canada," in *Canadian Frontiers of Settlement,* eds. W.A. Mackintosh and W.L.G. Joerg. Vol. VII. Toronto: Macmillan, 1936.

Dawson, C.A. and R.W. Murchie. "The Settlement of the Peace River Country," in *Canadian Frontiers of Settlement,* eds. W.A. Mackintosh and W.L.G. Joerg. Toronto: Macmillan, 1934.

Dawson, C.A. and Eva R. Younge. "Pioneering in the Prairie Provinces," in *Canadian Frontiers of Settlement,* eds. W.A. Mackintosh and W.L.G. Joerg. Vol. VIII. Toronto: Macmillan, 1940.

Department of the Secretary of State. *Our History.* Ottawa: Information Canada, 1970.

Drake, Michael. *Population and Society in Norway 1735-1865.* Cambridge University Press, 1969.

Dybvig, Philip S. and Randolph E. Haugan. *The Forward March of Faith.* Minneapolis: Augsburg Publishing House, 1943.

Enterline, James Robert. *Viking America: The Norse Crossings and Their Legacy.* New York: Doubleday, 1972.

Erasmus, Peter as told to Henry Thompson. *Buffalo Days and Nights.* Calgary: Glenbow-Alberta Institute, 1976.

Eskrick, Muriel. *The Norwegian Settlers Eagle Hill and Bergen.* Calgary: Glenbow-Alberta Institute, 1971.

Evenson, George O. *Adventuring for Christ: The Story of The Evangelical Lutheran Church of Canada.* Calgary: Foothills Lutheran Press, 1974.

Gibbon, John Murray. *Canadian Mosaic.* Toronto: McClelland and Stewart, 1938.

Gjerset, Knut. *History of the Norwegian People* (2 Vols). New York: MacMillan, 1915.

Gray, Edward F. *Leif Eriksson Discoverer of America A.D. 1003.* London: Oxford University Press, 1930 (including translations of the Vinland sagas).

Gray, James H. *Men Against the Desert*. Saskatoon: The Modern Press, 1967.

———. *The Winter Years*. Toronto: Macmillan, 1966.

———. *Booze: The Impact of Whisky on the Prairie West*. Toronto: Macmillan, 1972.

Guillet, Edwin C. *The Great Migration: The Atlantic Crossing by Sailing-Ship Since 1770*. Toronto: Thomas Nelson & Sons, 1937.

Hagen, Andres. *The Viking Ship Finds*. Oslo: Universitetets Oldsaksamling, 1966.

Hansen, Marcus Lee. *The Atlantic Migration 1607-1870*. Cambridge: Harvard University Press, 1940.

Hedges, J.B. *Building the Canadian West: The Land and Colonization Policies of the Canadian Pacific Railway*. New York: 1939.

Hendrickson, Magda. *This Land Is Our Land*. Calgary: Foothills Lutheran Press, 1972.

Heyerdahl, Thor et al. *Great Norwegian Expeditions*. Oslo: Dreyers Forlag.

Holand, Hjalmar R. *Explorations in America Before Columbus*. New York: Twayne Publishers, 1956.

Hurd, W. Burton. *Origin, Birthplace, Nationality and Language of the Canadian People*. Ottawa: Dominion Bureau of Statistics, 1929.

———. *Racial Origins and Nativity of the Canadian People*. Ottawa: Dominion Bureau of Statistics, 1937.

———. *Ethnic Origins and Nativity of the Canadian People*. Ottawa: Queen's Printer, 1941.

Immigration Statistics – Canada (1950-). Ottawa: Manpower and Immigration, 1950-

Ingstad, Anne Stine. *The Discovery of a Norse Settlement in America: Excavations at L'Anse aux Meadows, Newfoundland, 1961-1968*. Oslo: Universitetsforlaget, 1977.

Ingstad, Helge Marcus. *Westward to Vinland*. Toronto: Macmillan, 1969.

Kopas, Clifford R. *Bella Coola: A Story of Effort and Achievement*. Vancouver: Mitchell Press, 1970.

Larsen, Henry A. *The Big Ship*. Toronto: McClelland and Stewart Ltd., 1967.

Larsen, Karen. *A History of Norway*. Princeton, 1948.

Lavik, J.R. *The Christian Church in a Secularized World*. Minnesota: Augsburg, 1952.

LIFE. World Library. *Scandinavia* (Chapter 5, Children of the Midnight Sun). New York: Time Incorporated, 1963.

Lindal, W.J. *The Icelanders in Canada*. Winnipeg: Viking Printers, 1967.

Little Norway in Pictures: Royal Norwegian Air Force in Canada. Toronto: Reginald Saunders.

Loken, G., *A History of Hastings Lake Lutheran Bible Camp Association, 1937-1977*. Camrose: Gospel Contact Press, 1977.

———. *A History of Trinity Lutheran Church*. Calgary: University Printing, 1975.

Lovall, Odd Sverre. *A Folk Epic: The Bygdelag in America*. Boston: Twayne, 1975.

_____. *Cultural Pluralism versus Assimilation.* Northfield, Minnesota: The Norwegian-American Historical Association, 1977.

Macdonald, Norman. *Canada: Immigration and Colonization 1841-1903.* Toronto: Macmillan, 1966.

MacEwan, J.W. Grant. *West to the Sea.* Toronto: McGraw-Hill, 1968.

McClung, Nellie L. *Clearing in the West.* Toronto: Thomas Allen, 1935.

McGowan, Don C. *Grassland Settlers.* Regina: Canadian Plains Research Center, 1975.

MacGregor, James G. *A History of Alberta.* Edmonton: Hurtig, 1972.

Malmin, Rasmus, O.M. Norlie and O.A. Tinglestad. *Who's Who Among Pastors in All of the Norwegian Lutheran Synods of America, 1843-1927.* Minneapolis: Augsburg, 1928.

Mann, William Edward. *Sect, Cult and Church in Alberta.* Toronto: University of Toronto Press, 1955.

Martin, A.J., and F. Wulfsberg. *Across the North Sea.* Oslo: Aschehoug & Co., 1955.

Mowat, Farley, *Westviking.* Toronto: McClelland and Stewart, 1965.

Nelson, E. Clifford and Eugene L. Fevold. *The Lutheran Church Among Norwegian-Americans: A History of the Evangelical Lutheran Church* (2 vols.). Minneapolis: Augsburg, 1960.

Njus, Joel M., trans. *Autobiographical Writings of Hans Nielsen Hauge.* Minneapolis: Augsburg Publishing House, 1954.

Norborg, Sverre. *An American Saga: A History of the Sons of Norway in the United States and Canada.* Minneapolis, 1969.

Norlie, O.M. *History of the Norwegian People in America.* Minneapolis: Augsburg, 1925.

Norris, John, ed. *Strangers Entertained: A History of the Ethnic Groups of British Columbia.* Vancouver: Evergreen Press, 1971.

Norwegian-American Studies and Records (Norwegian-American Studies). Vols. 1-27. Northfield, Minnesota: Norwegian-American Historical Association, 1926-1977.

Oleson, Trggvi. *Early Voyages and Northern Approaches, 1000-1632.* Toronto: 1963.

Ostenso, Martha. *Wild Geese.* Toronto: McClelland and Stewart, 1961.

Palmer, Howard. *Land of the Second Chance: A History of Ethnic Groups in Southern Alberta.* Lethbridge: The Lethbridge Herald, 1972.

Peel, Bruce B. *A Bibliography of the Prairie Provinces to 1953.* Toronto: University of Toronto Press, 1956 (also supplement 1963).

Pohl, Frederick J. *The Viking Explorers.* New York: Thomas Y. Crowell Company, 1966.

_____. *The Viking Settlements of North America.* New York: Clarkson and Potter, 1972.

Qualey, Carlton C. *Norwegian Settlement in the United States.* New York: Arno Press, 1970.

Robertson, Heather. *Salt of the Earth: The Story of the Homesteaders in Western Canada.* Toronto: James Lorimer & Co., 1974.

Rohne, J. Magnus. *Norwegian American Lutheranism Up to 1872.* New York: Macmillan, 1926.

Rolvaag, Ole E. *Giants in the Earth: A Saga of the Prairie.* (Translated by L. Concord and the author). Oslo, 1925 and New York, 1927.

Ronning, N.N. and H.N. Ronning. *The Gospel at Work.* Minneapolis, 1943.

Semmingsen, Ingrid. *Veien Mot Vest.* (Annel Del – Utvandringen fra Norge 1865-1915). Oslo: Aschehoug, 1950.

Skardal, Dorothy Burton. *The Divided Heart.* Lincoln: University of Nebraska Press, 1974.

Steen, Ragna and Magda Hendrickson, *Pioneer Days in Bardo, Alberta.* Tofield, Alberta: Historical Society of Beaver Hills Lake, 1944.

Stolee, Amalia. *Diary for 1907.* Edmonton: Provincial Archives of Alberta.

Stolee, Haakon J. *Faith is the Substance: A History of the Stolee Family.* Edmonton: Provincial Archives of Alberta.

The Flatey Book and Recently Discovered Vatican Manuscripts Concerning America as Early as the Tenth Century. London, New York: 1906.

The Hauge Movement in America. Minneapolis: Lutheran Free Church Publishing Co., 1941.

The Lur. Camrose: The Scandinavian Historical Society publication.

Ulvestad, Martin. *Nordmaendene i Amerika: Deres historie og rekord* (2 vols.). Minneapolis: History Book Co., 1907 and 1913.

Wyllie, M.A. *Norway and Its Fjords.* London: Methuen & Co., 1907.

Selected Articles

Bersagel, Knute. "Bydelagsbevaegelsen i Canada" in *Nordmands-Forbundet,* 23:184-185 (June, 1930).

Bersagel, Knute and G.O. Evenson, trans. "My First Year in Canada by N.C. Brun" in *The Lur,* 1975 and in *Symra,* Vol. VII, No. 2, 1911.

Blegen, Theodore C. "An Early Norwegian Settlement in Canada." *Canadian Historical Association, Annual Report,* 1930, pp. 83-86.

Bjork, Kenneth O. "Scandinavian Migration to the Canadian Prairie Provinces, 1893-1914" in *Norwegian-American Studies,* Vol. 26, 1974.

————. "The Founding of Quatsino Colony" in *Norwegian-American Studies,* Vol. 25, 1972.

Boe, Eugene. "Pioneers to Eternity: Norwegians on the Prairie" in *The Immigrant Experience: The Anguish of Becoming American.* Baltimore: Pelican Books, 1971.

Brekken, Thea. "A Trek to Grande Prairie in 1910" in *The Lur,* Issue 2, 1976.

Froyen, Kaja. "Early Alberta Congregations and Settlement Memories 1904-1913." Edmonton: Provincial Archives of Alberta.

Haugen, Einar. "Norwegian Migration to America" in *Norwegian-American Studies and Records,* Vol. 18, 1954.

Hassing, Arne. "Norway's Organized Response to Emigration" in *Norwegian-American Studies,* Vol. 25, 1972.

"He Blazed a Trail on Skiis" in *Readers' Digest,* March 1972, pp. 44-50.

Holand, Hjalmar R. "An Early Norwegian Fur Trader of the Canadian Northwest" in *Norwegian-American Studies,* Vol. 5, 1930.

Ingstad, Helge. "Vinland Ruins Prove Vikings Found the New World" in *National Geographic.* Washington: National Geographic, 1964.

Knaplund, Paul. "Norwegians in the Selkirk Settlement 1815-1870" in *Norwegian-American Studies and Records,* Vol. 6, 1931.

Kolden, Agnes. "Recollections of Pioneer Days" in Saskatchewan Archives, Saskatoon.

La Fay, Howard. "The Vikings" in *National Geographic.* Washington: National Geographic, 1970.

Lindal, Walter J. "The Contribution Made by the Scandinavian Ethnic Groups to the Cultural Enrichment of Canada." Essay Royal Commission in Bilingualism and Biculturism, 1967.

Lovall, Odd Sverre. "The Bygdelag Movement" in *Norwegian-American Studies,* Vol. 25, 1972.

"Norwegians in Canada" in *Citizen,* Vol. 13, No. 4, Oct. 1967, pp. 12-22.

Olsen, Ingvar. "Nordmand i Canada" in *Nordmands-Forbundet,* 24: 87-91 (March, 1931).

Semmingsen, Ingrid. "Norwegian Emigration to America During the Nineteenth Century" in *Norwegian-American Studies and Records,* Vol. II, 1940.

Strom, Theodore. "A Few Memories of When Calgary and I Were Young" in Glenbow-Alberta Institute Archives, Calgary, Alberta.

Unpublished Theses

Engen, Harold. "A History of the Evangelical Lutheran Church of Canada." B.D. Thesis, Luther Theological Seminary, Saskatoon, 1955.

Loken, G. "An Analysis of the Junior College in Alberta: Progress, Program and Prospect." Master's Thesis, University of Alberta, 1965.

———. "A Study of the Government of The Folk High Schools of Norway." Doctoral dissertation, University of Alberta, 1968.

Ronning, Chester A. "A Study of an Alberta Protestant Private School, The Camrose Lutheran College." Master's Thesis, University of Alberta, 1942.

Sartinson, Telmor. "Dr. J.R. Lavik – Canada Too, Lord." B.D. Thesis, Luther Theological Seminary, Saskatoon, 1968.

Stolee, Peter B. "The Norwegian Lutheran Church in Canada." Master's Thesis, Luther Seminary, St. Paul, 1936.

Tysseland, Harold. "Present-day Expressions of Haugeanism in America." B.D. Thesis, Luther Theological Seminary, Saskatoon, 1954.

Selected Norwegian Newspapers

Decorah-Posten (Decorah, Iowa), 1874-1972. Files in the St. Olaf College Library, Luther College Library, Decorah, and in the Minnesota Historical Society, St. Paul.

Fram (Fargo, North Dakota), 1898-1917. File in the University of North Dakota Library, Grand Forks.

Fremad (Sioux Falls, South Dakota), 1894-1935. File in the St. Olaf College Library.

Hyrden (Saskatoon, Saskatchewan), 1924-1949. File in Luther Theological Seminary, Saskatoon.

Minneapolis Tidende (Minneapolis), 1887-1935. Files in the St. Olaf College Library and in the Minnesota Historical Society.

Nordvesten (St. Paul), 1881-1907. Files in the St. Olaf College Library, Luther College Library, and in the Minnesota Historical Society.

Normanden (Grand Forks and Fargo, North Dakota), 1887-1954. File in the University of North Dakota Library.

Noranna (Winnipeg and Vancouver), 1910-   . File in Vancouver office.

Scandia (Chicago), 1899-1939. File in the St. Olaf College Library.

Skandinavian (Chicago), 1866-1940. Files in the Minnesota Historical Society and in the St. Olaf College Library.

Visergutten (Story City, Iowa, Canton, South Dakota, and Fargo), 1893-1955. File in the St. Olaf College Library.

Washington Posten (Seattle), 1889-1961. File in the St. Olaf College Library.

Archives

Evangelical Lutheran Church of Canada Archives at Luther Theological Seminary, Saskatoon (including annual reports and yearbooks of the church, congregations and auxiliaries).

Glenbow-Alberta Institute Archives, Calgary, Alberta (including local community histories).

Norwegian-American Historical Association Archives, Northfield, Minnesota.

Provincial Archives in capital cities across Canada.

Public Archives of Canada, National Ethnic Archives, Ottawa.

Royal Norwegian Embassy Archives, Ottawa.

University Library Archives across Canada.

Taped Interviews with Norwegian Pioneers

Author: Dr. G. Loken, The University of Calgary, Alberta.

National Ethnic Archives, Ottawa.

Provincial Archives of Alberta.

Saskatchewan Archives Office, University of Regina, Saskatchewan.

Index

Lutheran College, Outlook College, Lutheran Collegiate Bible Institute, Luther Theological Seminary
Eielsen, Elling: 46, 131
Emigration: 27-36, 224-226
Engen, Fred: 158
Engen, Harold: 25n, 125n, 182n, 183n
Eric the Red: 5, 231
Eskrick, Muriel: 74, 100n
Ethnic Organizations: 172-180, 232, 233
Ethnic Press: 167-172
Evangelical Lutheran Hour: 214
Evenson, G.O.: 101n, 105, 125n, 151, 158-159, 166, 182n, 183n

Family: 217-218
Fatland, H.G.: 150

Gaspe: 17-23, 45
Glen, Mary: 82
Granskou, C.M.: 134, 160, 182n
Great Depression: 97, 102-120, 123-124, 178, 199
Greenland: 4-5, 8, 11, 24
Grimley, O.B.: 155, 157, 174
Gronlid, H.O.: 154, 157
Grosse Isle: 17
Grue, Thore S.: 67
Grundahl, K.C.: 160
Gunderson, Sten: 105, 106
Gusdal, L.B.: 94-96

Hagen: 86
Hagen, A.B.H.: 163
Hagen, Hans: 86
Halmrast, L.C.: 212
Hauge, Hans Neilsen: 29, 32, 38-130, 201, 206
Haugen, Fred: 160
Haugen, O.H.: 180
Hawkness, Lyle: 216
HBC: 48-49, 54, 177
Hedlin, Ed: 160

Helgeson, Hans: 76, 211
Hendrickson, Magda: 42, 47n, 99n, 136, 182n, 183n, 214, 222n
Henje, Sonja: 217
Henricks, P.M.: 85
Hoeflicher, Gordon: 160
Holfeld, Karl: 146, 152
Homesteads: 35, 37-40, 54
Horden, William: 167, 206, 221n
Houg, Carl M.: 106-108, 125n
Hoveland, L.J.: 72
Hyland, Frances: 215

Iceland: 8, 24, 26n
Indians: 4, 48-50, 54-55, 48, 99n, 102
Ingstad, Helge: 9-10
Intermarriage: 197
Internal Migration: 113-115
Iversen, Iver: 166

Jacobson, Abraham: 21, 135
Jacobson, Charlotte: 26n
Jacobson, S.T.: 125n, 146
Jensen, Rasmus: 12
Joel, Mildred: 159, 182n
Johannsen, Herman (Jack Rabbit): 216
Johnson, Horace: 110
Jorgensen, A.: 33, 46n

Kaiser, David: 160
Kasa, Ole: 73
Kensington Rune Stone: 11-12
Koppan, Cliff: 100n

Langley, T.J.: 97
Language: 145, 192-196, 224. Also see Ethnic press
Language Issues: 194-196
L'Anse aux Meadows: 9-10
Larsen, Henry: 210, 221n, 231
Lavik, J.R.: 139, 141, 147-8, 150, 152, 162, 166, 183n, 213-214
Lefsrud, John: 74, 100n
Lewis, A.G.: 162

264